The European Convention on International Commercial Arbitration

The European Convention on International Commercial Arbitration

A Commentary

Edited by
Gerold Zeiler
Alfred Siwy

Wolters Kluwer

Published by:
Kluwer Law International B.V.
PO Box 316
2400 AH Alphen aan den Rijn
The Netherlands
E-mail: international-sales@wolterskluwer.com
Website: lrus.wolterskluwer.com

Sold and distributed in North, Central and South America by:
Wolters Kluwer Legal & Regulatory U.S.
7201 McKinney Circle
Frederick, MD 21704
United States of America
Email: customer.service@wolterskluwer.com

Sold and distributed in all other countries by:
Air Business Subscriptions
Rockwood House
Haywards Heath
West Sussex
RH16 3DH
United Kingdom
Email: international-customerservice@wolterskluwer.com

ISBN 978-90-411-8590-7

e-Book: ISBN 978-90-411-8591-4
web-PDF: ISBN 978-90-411-8592-1

Editors

Gerold Zeiler is a partner at *zeiler.partners* and an expert in national and international dispute resolution, with a strong focus on international commercial arbitration and complex litigation. He has represented clients and served as arbitrator in domestic and international arbitration proceedings—more than 200 at the last count and is a seasoned litigator before Austrian courts. In 2018, the ICC World Council appointed Gerold as the Austrian member of the ICC Court.

Alfred Siwy is a partner at *zeiler.partners* and an expert in national and international dispute resolution, with a strong focus on international arbitration and litigation. Alfred advises clients in commercial and investment arbitration under various sets of rules, including the ICC, VIAC, UNCITRAL and ICSID rules.

Contributors

Lisa Beisteiner is a partner at *zeiler.partners* and an expert in national and international dispute resolution, with a strong focus on international arbitration and litigation. Lisa has extensive experience advising clients in all aspects of commercial and investment arbitration under various sets of rules, including the ICC, VIAC, UNCITRAL and ICSID rules.

Andrea de la Brena is counsel at *zeiler.partners* and an expert in international commercial and investment arbitration. She is a Mexican attorney and provides advice to Mexican companies regarding disputes and corporate matters.

Markus Schifferl is a partner at *zeiler.partners*. He is a specialist in international and domestic arbitration, contentious proceedings before the national courts and company law. Markus regularly represents clients before ICC, VIAC, UNCITRAL, DIS and ad hoc arbitral tribunals as well as before Austrian Courts.

Summary of Contents

Table of Contents

Preface

1. This commentary provides a comprehensive overview of the provisions of the European Convention on International Commercial Arbitration ("ECICA" or the "Convention") concluded on 21 April 1961, in Geneva, and certain related topics of international commercial arbitration for a better understanding of the relevance of some of these provisions. The Convention came into force on 7 January 1964 (the ninetieth day following the fifth deposit of the instrument of ratification), with the exception of paragraphs 3 and 7 of Article IV, which entered into force on 18 October 1965. The ECICA came into force shortly after the Convention on the Recognition and Enforcement of Foreign Arbitral Awards of 10 June 1958, New York ("New York Convention (NYC)"). These two conventions were the first modern body of rules concerning international commercial arbitration. While the NYC focuses on the enforcement and recognition of international awards, the ECICA addresses a broader range of procedural aspects.

2. Initially, the ECICA had sixteen signatories; today it has thirty-one parties, including certain non-European States ("Contracting States"). Thus, the ECICA is applicable to a large geographical region with a high number of international trade transactions. The ECICA remains one of the few international legal instruments in which rules and principles not only regarding the enforcement of awards or arbitral agreements but also regarding certain aspects of the conduct and procedure of international commercial arbitration have been codified. Although the ECICA's drafters originally conceived it as an instrument to remove obstacles arising from differences between the domestic legal systems of Eastern and Western European countries, its application now exceeds its historical purpose. The novelty introduced by some of the ECICA's provisions remains the key foundation for international commercial arbitration still today.

3. Commentators have pointed out that the ECICA's potential has sometimes been undermined and not fully exploited.[1] For this reason, the Committee for Trade,

1. Emmanuel Gaillard and John Savage eds., *Fouchard, Gaillard and Goldman on International Commercial Arbitration*, p. 143 (Kluwer Law International, 1999); Christian Konrad, *Buried in Oblivion? The Significance and Limitations of the European Convention on International*

Industry and Enterprise Development of the United Nations Economic Commission for Europe ("UNECE") established an Arbitration Advisory Group in order to evaluate the ECICA's current status and review its provisions in order to determine whether any amendments could be made to keep the convention in step with current arbitration practice. After its analysis, the Advisory Group concluded that the ECICA "*provides a utility beyond that of other, existing conventions, in particular as a common set of minimum standards to be observed in international arbitration.*"[2] At its second meeting, in November 2000, the Advisory Group recommended, nonetheless, some amendments in order to update the Convention. Although these recommendations have not been adopted yet, the conclusions of the Advisory Group demonstrate that today, almost fifty-six years after its conclusion, the ECICA continues to be of great practical relevance. Therefore, a thorough analysis of the functionality, advantages, and disadvantages of each of its provisions and their influence on contemporary arbitration rules is fundamental for its future application.

4. The materials reviewed for this Commentary include the Final Act for the Special Meeting of Plenipotentiaries for the purpose of negotiating and signing the ECICA ("Final Act"), the ECICA's provisions and its Annexes, and the relevant accessible case law of domestic courts of the Contracting States, subsequent agreements concluded between some Contracting States, i.e., the 1962 Paris Agreement[3] and the 1972 Moscow Convention,[4] and a wide variety of scholarly writings on the matter.

Commercial Arbitration (2 November 2010) available http://kluwerarbitrationblog.com/2010/11/02/buried-in-oblivion-the-significance-and-limitations-of-the-european-convention-on-international-commercial-arbitration/; Stefan Kröll, *The European Convention on International Commercial Arbitration: The Tale of a Sleeping Beauty*, in Austrian Yearbook on International Arbitration, 61–74, pp. 3 and 4 (Klausegger and others eds., 2013).

2. Committee for Trade, Industry and Enterprise Development of the Economic Commission for Europe, *Revision of the 1961 European Convention on International Commercial Arbitration*, Note by the Secretariat on the fifth session (30 March 2001), TRADE/2001/16, p. 3.
3. The Agreement Relating to Application of the European Convention on International Commercial Arbitration, Paris, 17 December 1962.
4. Convention on the Settlement by Arbitration of Civil Law Disputes Resulting from Relations of Economic and Scientific-Technical Cooperation, Moscow, 26 May 1972.

PART I Introduction

Alfred Siwy & Andrea de la Brena

1. The European Convention on International Commercial Arbitration (ECICA) is a rather unique convention in the area of international commercial arbitration as it governs a number of somewhat unrelated topics. It governs procedural issues of the arbitration itself, such as the establishment of the arbitral tribunal, the relationship between tribunals and national courts, conflict of laws issues, the impact of the setting aside of an award on its enforceability. All these various topics shall be addressed in this commentary. However, some of the provisions of the Convention require some background comments against which the commentary is to be read. In the following chapters the issue of subjective arbitrability, the applicable law in commercial arbitration, and the relevance of *ordre public* in setting aside proceedings shall be examined.

CHAPTER 1

Subjective Arbitrability in International Commercial Arbitration

INTRODUCTION

2. The ECICA touches upon a number of basic aspects of international commercial arbitration which are still relevant and widely discussed. However, to fully appreciate the impact of the first steps taken by the Convention to regulate these matters at an international level it is worthy to place them into a broader context.

3. The first topic will be the question of subjective arbitrability which was dealt with by the drafters of the ECICA, particularly in Article II. This provision will be examined in detail in the Commentary to Article II herein. It suffices to mention that the ECICA is one of the few, if not the only, international instrument on international commercial arbitration expressly regulating the matter of subjective arbitrability.

4. First, the notion of subjective arbitrability will be described to delimit its scope (§1.01). Second, the type of existing restrictions on subjective arbitrability at a domestic stage will be put forward (§1.02). Third, the relevance of subjective arbitrability in the context of domestic legislation will be reviewed to conclude whether subjective arbitrability is still a relevant matter in the current setting of international commercial arbitration (§1.03). Fourth, the debates on the applicable law to the matter of subjective arbitrability will be analyzed (§1.04). Finally, the consequences of failing to comply with the requirements on subjective arbitrability will be set out (§1.05).

§1.01 THE NOTION OF "SUBJECTIVE ARBITRABILITY"

5. The word "arbitrability" was developed in the context of arbitration to identify the controversies that may be submitted to arbitration proceedings.[1] The term is new and "*[o]nly by the end of the 20th century did the doctrine begin to use the term 'arbitrability' in a more frequent and reliable manner*" and, thus, the domestic law in many jurisdictions does not refer to the term expressly.[2]

6. There are two types of arbitrability. The first one is where a specific dispute or subject matter cannot be solved through arbitration in view of national mandatory law and public policy restrictions.[3] The second is where certain persons are considered unable to submit their disputes to arbitration because of their status or function. The latter type is commonly referred to as "subjective arbitrability" or "arbitrability *ratione personae*" which may be defined as the ability of certain individuals to submit their disputes to arbitration proceedings.[4] Some commentators have broadened the term by referring to the "capacity" of the parties to the arbitration. In the Commentary to the Vienna Rules on International Commercial Arbitration the authors of Article 1 maintained that "*[s]ubjective arbitrability can be missing where a party lacks the required legal capacity but also where a party [...] is not properly represented in the conclusion of the arbitration agreement.*"[5] Also, this group of commentators has maintained that, for instance, the State's prohibition to submit a dispute to arbitration "*falls fairly clearly within classic definitions of legal capacity.*"[6]

7. Other commentators have posited that the terms "subjective arbitrability" and "capacity" are distinguishable.[7] According to them, capacity refers to the ability of natural or legal persons to conclude legal acts which generally is a matter of consent;

---

1. Philippe Fouchard and Emmanuel Gaillard have traced back the origin of the term to the arbitrator Berthold Goldman. Emmanuel Gaillard and John Savage eds., *Fouchard, Gaillard and Goldman on International Commercial Arbitration*, p. 312, mn 533, fn. 304 (Kluwer Law International, 1999).
2. Carlos Alberto Carmona, *Subjective Arbitrability-A Brazilian Perspective*, in Jurisdictional Choices in Times of Trouble, Dossiers of the ICC Institute of World Business Law, Volume 12, pp. 180–190 (Bachir Georges Affaki and Horacio A. Grigera Naón eds., Kluwer Law International; International Chamber of Commerce (ICC), 2015).
3. Emmanuel Gaillard and John Savage eds., *Fouchard, Gaillard and Goldman on International Commercial Arbitration*, p. 312, mn 533 (Kluwer Law International, 1999).
4. Carlos Alberto Carmona, *Subjective Arbitrability-A Brazilian Perspective*, in Jurisdictional Choices in Times of Trouble, Dossiers of the ICC Institute of World Business Law, Volume 12, pp. 180–190 (Bachir Georges Affaki and Horacio A. Grigera Naón eds., Kluwer Law International; International Chamber of Commerce (ICC), 2015).
5. Franz T. Schwarz and Christian W. Konrad, *Article 1: The Institution*, in The Vienna Rules: A Commentary on International Arbitration in Austria (Kluwer Law International, 2009).
6. *Formation, Validity and Legality of International Arbitration Agreements,* in International Commercial Arbitration, pp. 636–942, pp. 729–230 (2nd ed., Gary B. Born ed., Kluwer Law International, 2014).
7. Jan Paulsson, *May a State Invoke Its Internal Law to Repudiate Consent to International Arbitration?*, 2 Arbitration International 90 (1986); Emmanuel Gaillard and John Savage eds., *Fouchard, Gaillard and Goldman on International Commercial Arbitration*, mn 533–534 (Kluwer Law International, 1999); A. Steingruber, *Consent in International Arbitration*, mn 3.19–3.21 (1st ed., 2012).

e.g., a mental disability.[8] States often use different separate entities for their activities and, therefore, a question of capacity might arise when a person who agreed on arbitration did not have the power to bind the State.[9] Subjective arbitrability, in contrast, is more a matter of restrictions in view of a State's interest to restrict the capacity of a type of persons from submitting a dispute to arbitration. However, these restrictions are self-imposed and, therefore, could be waived by the State.[10] Limitations to capacity cannot be waived.[11] This second view seems to be the prevailing view.[12] As discussed below, this distinction is relevant for determining the applicable law and the consequences of a failure.

8. The paradigmatic example of subjective arbitrability is the restriction of certain States and State-owned entities to participate in a commercial arbitration.

§1.02 THE RESTRICTION OF STATE AND PUBLIC ENTITIES TO SUBMIT THEIR DISPUTES TO ARBITRATION

9. States and public entities are one of the major participants in national and international trade; particularly in the case of socialist and former socialist countries, such as Russia.[13] Disputes involving States present certain difficulties in national courts because of traditional doctrines of sovereign immunity, the Act of the State doctrine,[14] and other related obstacles.

10. It has not been uncommon that States or their related organs and entities, in a commercial relationship, conclude arbitration agreements. However, it has also been common that, when a dispute arises, the States or its related entities attempt to disavow the arbitration commitment by alleging the tribunal has no jurisdiction as they are restricted to arbitrate under their applicable law. Hence, the invocation of this argument might lead to undesirable consequences.

---

8. Nigel Blackaby et al., *Redfern and Hunter on International Arbitration*, p. 84, mn 2.40 (5th ed., 2009).
9. *Arbitration with Government and State Owned Entities*, in Comparative International Commercial Arbitration, pp. 733–759, mn 27-16 (Julian D. M. Lew, Loukas A. Mistelis and Stefan Kroll eds., Kluwer Law International, 2003).
10. Nigel Blackaby et al., *Redfern and Hunter on International Arbitration*, p. 84, mn 2.40 (5th ed., 2009).
11. *Ibid.*
12. *Arbitration with Government and State Owned Entities*, in Comparative International Commercial Arbitration, pp. 733–759, mn 27-15 (Julian D. M. Lew, Loukas A. Mistelis and Stefan Kroll, Kluwer Law International, 2003).
13. Carlos Alberto Carmona, *Subjective Arbitrability: A Brazilian Perspective*, in Jurisdictional Choices in Times of Trouble, Dossiers of the ICC Institute of World Business Law, Volume 12, pp. 180–190 (Bachir Georges Affaki and Horacio A. Grigera Naón eds., Kluwer Law International; International Chamber of Commerce (ICC) 2015).
14. This doctrine has been described as being "*a common law principle [...] which prevents the [forum] court from examining the legality of certain acts performed in the exercise of sovereign authority within a foreign country*" *R v. Bow Street Metropolitan Stipendiary Magistrate; Ex Parte Pinochet Ugarte* (2000) 1 AC 61, p. 106 (Lord Nicholls) quoted in Matthew Alderton, *The Act of State Doctrine: Questions of Validity and Abstention from* Underhill *to* Habib, 12(2) MELBOURNE JOURNAL OF INTERNATIONAL LAW 2–26 (2011).

§1.03 THE RELEVANCE OF "SUBJECTIVE ARBITRABILITY" REGULATORY PROVISIONS

11. At the time the ECICA was drafted, the notion of "subjective arbitrability" was still undeveloped and unknown to many States. The ECICA is the first instrument on international commercial arbitration which "praiseworthily"[15] attempts to expressly deal with the matter of subjective arbitrability of the State and its related organs and entities.[16]

12. At the time when the ECICA was concluded, certain domestic arbitration laws contained prohibitions concerning arbitration of controversies when the State, local authorities, and other public entities were involved. This was the case in Belgium.[17] Other laws still request legal or government authorization for these to submit a potential or existent dispute to arbitration proceedings as it is in the case of Venezuela,[18] Saudi Arabia,[19] Iran,[20] and Syria.[21]

13. Most domestic legal systems, however, have deleted these restrictions; this is the case, *inter alia*, in England,[22] Algeria,[23] Morocco, and Greece.[24] Others have limited the restrictions to domestic arbitration proceedings. This is the case of French courts which have set forth a substantive rule providing that a lack of subjective arbitrability may not be invoked to invalidate a contract concluded for the purpose of international trade.[25] Therefore, currently the vast majority of legal systems do not contain this type of restrictions.

14. In fact, some domestic arbitration Acts have expressly incorporated a provision pursuant to which a State or a State-owned entity involved in arbitral proceedings may not invoke its own domestic law to determine the question of subjective arbitrability.[26]

---

15. Nigel Blackaby et al., *Redfern and Hunter on International Arbitration*, p. 84, mn 2.39 (5th ed., 2009).
16. *See* below Commentary to Article II of the ECICA.
17. In Belgium, this prohibition has been abolished, even though some restrictions remain. *See* Code Judiciaire, Article 1676(3).
18. Article 4 of the Commercial Arbitration Act.
19. Law of Arbitration, Royal Decree M/46 (25 April 1983), Article 3: "*Government bodies may not resort to arbitration for the settlement of their disputes with third parties except after approval of the President of the Council of Ministers. This provision may be amended by a Resolution of the Council of Ministers.*"
20. 1997 Iranian International Commercial Arbitration Act. *See* Hamid G. Gharavi, *The 1997 Iranian International Commercial Arbitration Law: The UNCITRAL Model Law á L'Iranienne*, 15 ARBITRATION INTERNATIONAL 85 (1999).
21. Sami Sarkis, *L' autorisation d'arbitrage, obstacles au recours á l'arbitrage des entreprises du secteur public en Syrie*, REVUE DE L'ARBITRAGE (1998), p. 97.
22. English Arbitration Act, 1996, §106; R. Merkin, Arbitration Law, para. 1.41 (1991 and Update August 2013).
23. Algerian Code of Civil and Administrative Procedure, Article 1006.
24. *Judgment No. 3894 of 1976*, XIV Y.B. Comm. Arb. 634 (Athens Ct. App.) (1989). *See also*, *Formation, Validity and Legality of International Arbitration Agreements*, in International Commercial Arbitration, pp. 636–942 (2nd ed., Gary B. Born ed., Kluwer Law International, 2014).
25. *See* Commentary to Article I.
26. Article 177(2) of the Swiss Private International Law Act 1987.

This prohibition is based on the principle that States acting as a party to the arbitration agreement may not evade their obligations by benefiting from their own legislation.[27]

15. Courts and arbitral tribunals, based on the principles of good faith or *pacta sunt servanda*, have accordingly declined to recognize a State or a State-owned company's allegation on a lack of subjective arbitrability due to a domestic law restriction.[28] Furthermore and even though the matter of sovereign immunity is not discussed in this commentary, courts may find that by entering the agreement to arbitrate a State or a related entity that claims sovereign immunity will have waived any immunity it might have had.[29]

16. In 1988, the Institute of International Law adopted a resolution according to which a State, a State enterprise, or a State entity may not invoke its incapacity to enter into an arbitration agreement to refuse to participate in an arbitration to which it has previously consented.[30]

17. The ECICA was, therefore, the precursor of a "*growing international consensus to the effect that where a state entity has agreed to resolve disputes by international arbitration, it cannot rely on its own domestic laws in order to avoid submitting to the arbitral process.*"[31]

18. For this reason, today Article II of the ECICA no longer has substantial practical effects as it is widely accepted that a State and its related organs and entities cannot invoke a domestic prohibition to circumvent its obligations arising from an arbitration agreement.

§1.04 THE APPLICABLE LAW TO THE QUESTION OF "SUBJECTIVE ARBITRABILITY"

19. Under the Geneva Convention for the Execution of Foreign Arbitral Awards of 1927, in order for the award to be recognized, the submission to arbitration must be valid under the law applicable thereto and the subject matter must be capable of settlement by arbitration under the law of the enforcement State.[32] Therefore, both laws were relevant to the matter of arbitrability.

27. International Law Commission, *Draft Articles on Responsibility of States for Internationally Wrongful Acts*, November 2001, Supplement No. 10 (A/56/10), chp.IV.E.1, Adopted by the International Law Commission at its fifty-third session (2001). Article 32 of these articles provides: "*The responsible State may not rely on the provisions of its internal law as justification for failure to comply with its obligations under this part.*"
28. Patricia Nacimiento, *Article V(1)(a)*, in Recognition and Enforcement of Foreign Arbitral Awards: A Global Commentary on the New York Convention (Herbert Kronke, Patricia Nacimiento et al. eds., Kluwer Law International, 2010).
29. *Arbitration with Government and State Owned Entities*, in Comparative International Commercial Arbitration, pp. 733–759, mn 27-50 (Julian D. M. Lew, Loukas A. Mistelis and Stefan Kroll, Kluwer Law International, 2003).
30. Rev. arb. 1990, p. 931, 933; Article 5: YCA 1991, p. 233, 238.
31. Nigel Blackaby et al., *Redfern and Hunter on International Arbitration*, p. 84, mn 2.39 (5th ed., 2009).
32. Article 1(2) of the 1927 Geneva Convention.

20. Thereafter, the New York Convention (NYC), in Article V(1)(a), provides that the validity of the arbitration agreement is governed by "*the law to which the parties have subjected it or, failing any indication thereon, under the law of the country where the award was made.*" Furthermore, at the enforcement stage, Article V(2)(a) and V(2)(b) permit refusal of recognition and enforcement if the subject matter of the differences is not capable of settlement by arbitration or is against public policy under the law of the enforcement State.

21. Finally, the ECICA, in Article VI(2), contained an applicable law provision to determine the validity of the arbitration agreement which distinguishes between the law applicable to the capacity of the parties and to the remaining issues.[33] Therefore, the determination of which is the applicable law to the matter of subjective arbitrability is a question closely related to the debate on whether this matter is one of the capacities of the parties or rather one of the public policy's concerns.

22. If the matter is qualified as one of capacity, in civil law countries the applicable law would very likely be the national law of the individual or legal person and, in common law systems, the law of the domicile.[34]

23. However, some commentators have criticized that the latter view is incorrect:

> The prohibition to enter into an arbitration agreement or the submission of the latter to previous authorizations are foreign to concerns of protection of a person who is presumed incapable of defending its interests. Rather, they should be treated as provisions of nonarbitrability motivated by public policy concerns.[35]

24. Therefore, a second view is that the arbitral tribunal should resolve the question on the applicable law as it would in any other case where it is confronted with public policy rules.[36]

25. Under this second view, according to the ECICA, the applicable law would be, in the first place, the law to which the parties have subjected their arbitration agreement; second, failing any indication thereon, the law of the country in which the award is to be made; third, failing any indication on the first and second points, the competent law by virtue of the rules of conflict of the court seized of the dispute.

26. It may also be the case that the seized court decides to apply the same laws to all aspects of the validity of the arbitration agreement, including capacity and arbitrability. Therefore, in such cases the debate on whether subjective arbitrability should be

33. *See* Commentary to Article VI.
34. Emmanuel Gaillard and John Savage eds., *Fouchard Gaillard Goldman on International Commercial Arbitration*, pp. 241–380, mn 538 (Kluwer Law International, 1999).
35. Bernard Hanotiau, *The Law Applicable to Arbitrability*, in Improving the Efficiency of Arbitration Agreements and Awards: 40 Years of Application of the New York Convention, Vol. 9, ICCA Congress Series, pp. 146–167 (Albert Jan van den Berg ed., Kluwer Law International, 1999).
36. *Ibid.*

considered a question of capacity or one of public policy's concerns is reduced to a matter of terminology.[37]

§1.05 FAILURE TO COMPLY WITH THE "SUBJECTIVE ARBITRABILITY" REQUIREMENT

27. Failure to comply with the "subjective arbitrability" requirement might lead to the annulment or refusal to enforce or recognize the arbitral award by the seized domestic court. The grounds according to which the court could base its decision could vary depending on whether the requesting party alleged the failure as a matter of capacity or arbitrability.

28. On the one hand, Article V(1)(a) of the NYC provides that the incapacity of either party constitutes a ground for denying the recognition and enforcement of an arbitral award. On the other hand, under Article V(2)(b) of the NYC, the recognition and enforcement of the award may also be refused when such actions would be contrary to the *ordre public* of the country where the enforcement is sought. As these grounds are not exclusive, the requesting party may base its request for annulment or denial of recognition and enforcement on both grounds.

29. As lack of subjective arbitrability to enter into an arbitration agreement might affect the enforcement and recognition of the arbitration agreement and award, private parties should verify that no such restrictions exist when they enter into an arbitration agreement with a State party or even "*include an express reference in the arbitration agreement that the state party has complied with all necessary procedures.*"[38]

37. Emmanuel Gaillard and John Savage eds., *Fouchard Gaillard Goldman on International Commercial Arbitration*, p. 313, mn 533 (Kluwer Law International, 1999).
38. *Arbitration with Government and State Owned Entities*, in Comparative International Commercial Arbitration, pp. 733–759, mn 27-8 (Julian D. M. Lew, Loukas A. Mistelis and Stefan Kroll eds., Kluwer Law International, 2003).

Chapter 2
The Applicable Law in International Commercial Arbitration

§2.01 THE RELEVANT RULES DETERMINING THE APPLICABLE LAW

1. The first step to determining the law applicable to the substance of the dispute is to determine the conflict of laws rule which designates such a law. Arbitration is often considered to be, first and foremost, a result of party autonomy and, consequently, the law applicable is often considered to be subject to the will of the parties (if they have made such choice). However, the choice of law by the parties is relevant only if a conflict of laws rule declares it relevant. Hence, regardless of whether the parties have chosen the law applicable or whether the tribunal is to determine it itself, the first step will always have to be the determination of the applicable choice of law rule.

2. The conflict of laws rule determining the law applicable will be found in the *lex arbitri* or, following the choice of institutional rules, in arbitration rules. The latter, however, is essentially also a result of party autonomy, as arbitral institutions' rules only apply by choice of the parties. Additionally, international treaties on arbitration may include conflict of laws rule which the arbitrators need to adhere to. Lastly, as will be addressed later in this section, European legislation may also play a role.

3. The role of conflict of laws rules applicable in domestic proceedings before courts is, therefore, reduced in arbitration. The arbitrator will apply the rudimentary conflict of laws rules he finds in the abovementioned instruments. These, however, commonly consist only of provisions granting the parties to choose the law applicable to their dispute and providing the tribunal with a little guidance in the absence of such choice.

4. Modern arbitration laws and institutional rules all follow one of three approaches. The tribunal will apply the law designated by the conflict of laws rule it determines to be applicable, the law of the State with the closest connection to the dispute, or the law the tribunal considers appropriate.

5. The first of these approaches is the one taken by the Convention, various national *leges arbitri*, and some arbitration rules.[1] This approach will be addressed in greater detail in the Commentary to Article VII below.[2]

6. The second approach is taken, in particular, in the German Code of Civil Procedure[3] and the Swiss Private International Law Act[4] as well as various institution rules.[5] It represents the most basic enunciation of a conflict of laws rule. The application of the law of the State with the closest connection to the facts of the case is the very basis of all conflict of laws systems going back to *von Savigny*, hence the conflict of laws systems of the civil law countries.[6] The arbitrator is, therefore, bound to apply the law designated by this rudimentary conflict of laws rule. There is some discussion on whether this provision indicates that an arbitrator is bound by the national conflict of laws system (which are essentially nothing but a collection of more refined rules designating which State has the closest connection in various cases provided for in individual conflict of laws rules) or whether he is free to determine the applicable law without recourse to national law.[7] In practice, however, this point is mostly irrelevant. As the national conflict of laws rules are nothing but more refined manifestations of the closest connection rule, the arbitrator will arrive at the same result in most cases.[8] However, the legal certainty provided by hard and fast conflict of laws rules is reduced as the arbitrator may determine that the closest connection in a specific case lies with a State other than that designated by the conflict of laws rules of the *lex fori*. Factors that may influence his decision are, in particular, the expectations of the parties; hence, if the parties may have considered other conflict of laws rules than those of the *lex fori*

1. Article 33(1) of the 1976 UNCITRAL Arbitration Rules (note the different approach taken in the 2013 version of the Rules).
2. Cf, below commentary to Article VII of the ECICA.
3. Article 1051(2) German Code of Civil Procedure.
4. Article 187(1) Swiss Private International Law Act.
5. Article 33(1) Swiss Rules of International Arbitration and Article 39(2) Law No. 27-1994 Promulgating the Law Concerning Arbitration in Civil and Commercial Matters in Egypt.
6. Kegel, *The Crisis of Conflict of Laws*, in RdC 112 (1964-II) p. 91.
7. The German legislator had the former solution in mind, Comments on the Governmental Bill to § 1051 ZPO reprinted in Berger, *Das neue Recht der Internationalen Schiedsgerichtsbarkeit (The New German Arbitration Law)*, p. 260 (1998); *see also* Sandrock, *Die objektive Anknüpfung von Verträgen nach § 1051 Abs. 2 ZPO*, 46 RIW 321, p. 323 (dfv Mediengruppe, 2000); Junker, *Neuere Entwicklungen im internationalen Privatrecht*, RIW, 741, p. 745 (dfv Mediengruppe, 1998); scholarship overwhelmingly and rightly could not find any indication of such a reference in Section 1051 *see* Schlosser in Stein and Jonas, *Kommentar zur Zivilprozessordnung*, mn 8 to Section 1051 (22nd ed., Mohr Siebeck, 2013); Martiny, *Die Bestimmung des anwendbaren Sachrechts durch das Schiedsgericht*, in FS Schütze, 529, p. 540 (Geimer ed., C.H. Beck, 1999); Kronke, *Internationale Schiedsverfahren nach der Reform*, 44 RIW, 257, p. 262 (dfv Mediengruppe, 1998); Schlosser, *Bald neues Recht der Schiedsgerichtsbarkeit in Deutschland?*, 40 RIW, 723, p. 727 (dfv Mediengruppe, 1994); Blase, *Die Grundregeln des Europäischen Vertragsrechts als Recht grenzüberschreitender Verträge* (Quadis, 2001), pp. 161ss; Junker, *Deutsche Schiedsgerichte und Internationales Privatrecht (§ 1051 ZPO)*, in Berger et al. (ed.), FS Sandrock, p. 443 (Recht und Wirtschaft, 2000); Solomon, *Das vom Schiedsgericht in der Sache anzuwendende Recht nach dem Entwurf eines Gesetzes zur Neuregelung des Schiedsverfahrensrechts*, RIW pp. 981ss (dfv Mediengruppe, 1997).
8. Schlosser in Stein & Jonas, *Kommentar zur Zivilprozessordnung*, mn 8 to Section 1051 (22nd ed., Mohr Siebeck, 2013).

when concluding a contract, the arbitrator may apply the reasoning used in those rules. The approach, therefore, has the benefit of allowing the tribunal some flexibility while maintaining a high standard of predictability.

7. The third approach provides the arbitrator with the greatest margin of flexibility and the parties with the least predictability. Examples include various arbitration laws, such as that of Austria,[9] France,[10] or the Netherlands,[11] and arbitration rules,[12] most prominently the ICC Rules.[13] The approach does not require the arbitrators to apply any conflict of laws rules or to use them as guidance.[14] The arbitrator does not even need to take the closest connection of the facts of the case with a certain State into account.[15] In practice, however, arbitrators will commonly reason their conflict of laws decision and will apply, or at least be guided by, some conflict of laws rule, be it that of the *lex fori*, that of the country with the closest connection to the case, or another appropriate rule.

§2.02 THE RELEVANCE OF EUROPEAN UNION REGULATIONS

8. The conflict of laws rules for contractual and noncontractual obligations have been harmonized within the European Union (EU) by two regulations, the Rome-I[16] and the Rome-II[17] Regulation. These instruments supersede national law and are to be applied by all national courts and do not require any implementation by national legislators. They both contain numerous detailed conflict of laws rules. There is some uncertainty in legal literature, which has not been solved by either European or national courts, as to whether these Regulations also apply in arbitration proceedings and thereby supersede the conflict of laws rules applicable in arbitration.

9. The discussion focuses mainly on whether the two Regulations are intended to apply to arbitration proceedings taking place within the EU or whether the conflict of laws rules in the *leges arbitri* still apply. The Regulations as EU law would supersede any national arbitration laws if their scope of application were identical to the national law,[18] i.e., if the Regulations are to be interpreted to govern also the determination of the applicable law in arbitration. This is the point on which the opinions differ.

10. The predominant approach is that the Regulations by their wording and legislative history clearly never were intended to apply to arbitration proceedings.

9. Article 603(2) Austrian Code of Civil Procedure.
10. Article 1511(1) French Code of Civil Procedure.
11. Article 1054(2) Dutch Code of Civil Procedure.
12. *See*, e.g., Article 35(1) of the UNCITRAL Arbitration Rules 2013; Article 27(2) Vienna Rules; Article 24(2) DIS Rules; Article 27(1) SCC Rules.
13. Article 21(1) ICC Rules.
14. Hausmaninger in Fasching, *Kommentar zu den Zivilprozeßgesetzen*, mn 70 to Section 603 (2nd ed., Manz, 2007).
15. Mankowski in Czernich, Deixler-Hübner & Schauer eds., *Handbuch Schiedsrecht*, mn 6.138 (Manz, 2018).
16. Regulation (EC) No. 593/2008.
17. Regulation (EC) No. 864/2007.
18. Costa / ENEL, Case No. 6/64.

11. A large number of authors, however, consider that the Regulations must be applied by arbitrators seated within the EU for various reasons. First, they believe that because the Regulations explicitly state that they do not designate the law applicable to arbitration agreements, one can conclude that they do apply to the contracts forming the substance matter of the arbitration. The Brussels Regulation excludes "arbitration" as such from its scope,[19] so the difference in wording must have a difference in meaning.[20] Second, the *effet utile*, as a fundamental maxim of interpretation of EU law, would dictate the application in arbitration as the majority of disputes between enterprises would be excluded from the scope of the Regulations as they are decided in arbitration. Third, there is no reason to believe that EU law applies to the substance of the dispute, as has been held by the European Court of Justice (ECJ) in a number of cases, but would not apply to issues of conflict of laws.[21]

12. The applicability of the Regulations to arbitrations conducted within the EU is, as per today, unclear and will likely be subject to a clarification by domestic or European courts in the future.

13. However, if the Regulations are found applicable and, therefore, supersede the conflict of laws rules in the *lex arbitri* of the Member States, they may still be overridden by Article VII of the Convention in most cases. According to Article 351 of the Treaty on the Functioning of the European Union (TFEU), treaties in force for EU Member States before their accession remain in force. If they are incompatible, Member States are required by Article 351(2) to "*take all appropriate steps to eliminate the incompatibilities established.*" This rule applies to Member States' obligations deriving from the treaties as well as secondary legislation.[22] While the provision does not prevent the EU from enacting legislation contrary to the treaty obligations of its Member States,[23] it permits them to adhere to their treaty obligations.[24] The European Convention, therefore, overrules the Rome Regulations in all Member States of the Convention which are also members of the EU.[25]

19. Article 1(2)(d) of Regulation 1215/2012.
20. Pfeiffer, *Kollisionsrecht im Schiedsverfahren*, in ÖJZ, pp. 343–344 (Manz, 2015).
21. Mankowski, in Czernich, Deixler-Hübner & Schauer eds., *Handbuch Schiedsrecht*, mn 6.100 (Manz, 2018).
22. Nikos Lavranos, in Groeben, Schwarze & Hatje, *Europäisches Unionsrecht*, Article 351 Rz 4 (7th ed., Nomos, 2015).
23. GA Lagrange Schlussanträge zu EuGH 27.02.1962—C-10/61 (Kommission/Italien); EuGH 20.03.1990—C-62/89; EuGH 04.07.2000—C-84/98; Pache/Bielitz, *Das Verhältnis der EG zu den völkerrechtlichen Verträgen ihrer Mitgliedstaaten*, in EuR, 316 p. 329 (Nomos, 2006).
24. Nikos Lavranos, in Groeben/Schwarze/Hatje, *Europäisches Unionsrecht*, Article 351 Rz 12 (7th ed., Nomos, 2015).
25. The Rome-I Regulation came into force on 17 December 2009, the Rome-II Regulation as of 11 January 2009. As all states which are party to the Convention and the EU became parties to the Convention before these dates, Article 251 TFEU applies to all of them.

§2.03 MANDATORY RULES

14. Neither Article VII of the Convention nor the rudimentary conflict of laws rules provided in national arbitration laws contain any guidance for arbitrators on the possible application of mandatory rules. Article 9 of the Rome-I Regulation, however, does.

15. There is a margin of uncertainty about which rules qualify as mandatory rules. The distinguishing feature of mandatory rules which separates them from rules aimed at balancing the interests of the parties is the interests served by such mandatory rules: Mandatory rules serve over individual public purposes or national or economic policies. This approach is also reflected in Article 9(3) of the Rome-I Regulation which determines that mandatory rules are rules "*the respect for which is regarded as crucial by a country for safeguarding its public interests, such as its political, social or economic organization, to such an extent that they are applicable to any situation falling within their scope, irrespective of the law otherwise applicable to the contract under this Regulation.*"

16. The definition contains two elements. First, the Regulation distinguishes mandatory rules from other rules by reference to the interests they protect. Mandatory rules must protect the political, social, or economic organization of a State but not weaker parties in cases where commercial reality distorts equal bargaining power and contractual equilibrium, e.g., rules of consumer protection and labor law.[26] This criterion, however, is broad and has been considered to include rules enacted, e.g., for the right of the commercial agent for his compensation payment.[27]

17. Second, the Regulation requires that the rule be enacted with the legislative intent for it to be applied irrespective of the otherwise applicable law. This requirement will in most cases not be spelled out by the legislator but will have to be determined by interpretation of the rule.[28]

18. The rules on the application of mandatory rules is a matter of considerable dispute. While Article 9(3) of the Rome-I Regulation limits the applicable mandatory rules to those of the *lex loci solutionis*, there is no inherent reason to follow this limited approach in international commercial arbitration (unless one were to consider the Rome Regulation directly applicable in arbitration, as discussed above).

---

26. H. J. Sonnenberger in Säcker et al. eds., *Münchener Kommentar zum BGB*, Vol. 10, No. 44 (5th ed., C.H. Beck, 2010) to Einl IPRG; Helmut Heiss, *Die Vergemeinschaftung des internationalen Vertragsrechts durch "Rom I" und ihre Auswirkungen auf das österreichische internationale Privatrecht*, in JBl, pp. 750ss (Springer, 2006).
27. *Ingmar v. United Kingdom*, Judgment of 9 November 2000, Case No. C-381/98, paras 23ss.
28. Dieter Martiny in Säcker et al. eds., *Münchener Kommentar zum BGB*, Vol. 10, No. 115 (5th ed., C.H. Beck, 2010) to Article 9 Rome-I Verordnung; Wengler, *Die Anknüpfung des zwingenden Schuldrechts im internationalen Privatrecht*, 54 ZVglRWiss, 168, p. 183) (dfv Mediengruppe, 1941); Zweigert, *Nichterfüllung auf Grund ausländischer Leistungsverbote*, 14 RabelsZ, p. 283 (Mohr, 1942); Neumeyer, *Die Notgesetzgebung des Wirtschaftsrechts im IPR*, 2 BerGesVR, p. 35 (1958), p. 35; *see*, generally, Coester, *Die Berücksichtigung fremden zwingenden Rechts neben dem Vertragsstatut*, ZVglRWiss 82, p. 1 (8ss) (dfv Mediengruppe, 1983).

19. The traditional civil law approach would allow for the application of the mandatory rules of a State with a close connection to the facts of the case if the legislative intent of that State that the rules apply to a certain case can be determined by the judge.[29] This theory respects the prerogative of a State to enact rules on certain areas of public interest that will apply in cases in which the close connection of a case to that State justifies their application. In the area of competition law, to name an example, the impact on the market of a State may justify the application of its competition law rules on an anticompetitive contract governed by foreign law.

20. United Kingdom (UK) and US law take a wholly different approach to the matter. As neither State is a party to the Convention, they are of little interest in the present context.[30]

21. An arbitrator is not directly bound by any conflict of laws rules that would mandate the application of mandatory rules. However, for two reasons the arbitrator will have to consider the application of mandatory rules regardless of the choice of law of the parties. First, the rules protect the fundamental values of the States enacting them. As the ECJ, in the *EcoSwiss* case, made clear, Article 101 of the TFEU (then Article 85 of the European Community Treaty) is to be considered of such fundamental importance that any violation of it would require the setting aside of an award by national courts. Hence, as the arbitrator is obliged to deliver an award that can be enforced, he is obliged to apply such rules. Further, the legitimacy of arbitration as a form of dispute resolution would suffer greatly if the parties could opt out of the application of mandatory rules. For both reasons, arbitrators are under an obligation to consider the application of mandatory rules.

22. From a legal point of view, the choice of law of the parties does not extend to mandatory rules; they apply regardless of such a choice of law. Hence, even if the applicable conflict of laws rule in arbitration requires the arbitrator to apply the chosen law, mandatory rules of a third legal order may be applied nevertheless. The arbitrator could choose to follow Article 9 of the Rome-I Regulation, which is narrow and would only permit the application of the rules of the *lex loci solutionis*, or another conflict of laws rule which would permit the application of other rules, the application of which is reasonable in a given case. In any case, the rules of the place of possible enforcement may for practical purposes be of more significant relevance.[31] However, from a legal

29. Siehr, *Ausländische Eingriffsnormen im inländischen Wirtschaftskollisionsrecht*, 52 RabelsZ, 41, p. 92 (1988); Wengler, *Die Anknüpfung des zwingenden Schuldrechts im internationalen Privatrecht*, 54 ZVglRWiss, 168 p. 183 (dfv Mediengruppe, 1941); Zweigert, *Nichterfüllung auf Grund ausländischer Leistungsverbote*, 14 RabelsZ, p. 283 (1942); Neumeyer, *Die Notgesetzgebung des Wirtschaftsrechts im IPR*, 2 BerGesVR, p. 35 (1958); *see*, generally, Coester, *Die Berücksichtigung fremden zwingenden Rechts neben dem Vertragsstatut*, 82 ZVglRWiss, p. 1 (8ss) (dfv Mediengruppe, 1983).
30. *See* on this matter, Siwy, *Mandatory Rules in International Commercial Arbitration*, in Austrian Yearbook on International Arbitration, pp. 165ss (Klausegger et al. eds., 2012).
31. Mankowski, in Czernich, Deixler-Hübner & Schauer eds., *Handbuch Schiedsrecht*, mn 6.170 (Manz, 2018).

perspective, it is the close connection between the enacting State and the facts of the case that justify their application, not the place of possible enforcement, so that this criterion has not prevalence if the State of enforcement has no other connection with the case.

CHAPTER 3

The Role of *Ordre Public* in Enforcement Proceedings

INTRODUCTION

1. One of the distinctive features of the Convention is its Article IX, which allows for the enforcement of foreign awards which have been set aside in their State of origin due to a violation of the *ordre public*. This, however, does not prevent the State in which enforcement is applied for from reviewing whether the award is in conformity with its own notion of public order under Article V(1)(e) of the NYC.

2. The effect of Article IX is, therefore, to shift the review of the award for its conformity with public order from the State in which the award was rendered to the State in which enforcement is sought, thereby avoiding the possibility that an award set aside for parochial reasons ceases to have legal effect outside its State of origin. This, however, comes at the price of multiplying proceedings as the underlying party may have to resist enforcement in a multitude of countries.

§3.01 THE NOTION OF *ORDRE PUBLIC*

3. While Article IX of the Convention will be discussed further on in greater detail in the commentary to this provision, it is purposeful to put this provision into context, discussing the notion of public order in greater detail at this point.

4. Already, the notion of public order as such is subject to some dispute. There seems to be consensus that the public order of a State includes the "*state's most basic notions of morality and justice*"[1] or, as the ECJ put it, the public order of a State would be

1. *Parsons & Whittemore Overseas Co., Inc. v. Société Générale de l'Industrie du Papier RAKTA and Bank of America* 508 F. 2d 969 (2nd Cir., 1974).

violated by the enforcement of a judgment which would be "*a manifest breach of a rule of law regarded as essential in the legal order of the State in which enforcement is sought or of a right recognised as being fundamental within that legal order.*"[2]

5. In most States this will include the most obvious and basic rules which an arbitrator cannot ignore. Examples include the prohibition of money laundering, bribery or fraud, the combatting of trafficking in drugs, or the prohibition of expropriation without compensation.[3] It is hard to assume that any legal order would allow an award to be enforced which violates these most basic values.

6. Beyond these very basic values there may be a less uniform approach as to which rules are considered to pertain to the *ordre public* and opinions will vary from State to State. While rules on the economic organization of a State, such as restrictions of import and export, foreign currency exchange rules or competition law are partially considered to pertain to the *ordre public*; this is by no means a universally shared view.

7. The issue is further blurred by the fact that the notion of public order applicable in proceedings regarding the enforcement of foreign awards is often distinguished from that applicable in domestic proceedings or setting aside proceedings and is referred to as the "*international public policy.*"[4] The international public policy is supposed to be the standard that is applied when reviewing foreign arbitral awards. Hence, the scrutiny of an award would be made according to different rules depending on where it was rendered.

8. The entire matter, however, can be somewhat clarified if no distinction is made between the public policy applicable in setting aside and enforcement proceedings. The modern (and correct) approach recognizes that the notion of public policy is not an absolute but a relative standard.[5] There is no necessity to divide public policy into an internal public policy for domestic awards and an international one for foreign awards.

9. Public policy of a State protects that State's most fundamental legal values. It is a consequence that the closer an award (actually the facts the underlying dispute decided in the award) is connected to a country, the more likely a violation of a fundamental rule of law of that country will lead to a violation of its *ordre public*.[6] Conversely, an

---

2. ECJ Case No. C.7/98, *Krombach v. Bamberski*, para. 19.
3. International Law Association: Final Report on Public Policy as a Bar to Enforcement of International Arbitral Awards, para. 28.
4. Cf. Stefan Kröll and Peter Kraft, in Karl-Heinz Böckstiegel, Stefan Kröll and Patricia Nacimiento eds., *Arbitration in Germany, The Model Law in Practice*, mn 79 to Section 1059 (Kluwer Law International, 2007); Schlosser in Stein and Jonas, *Kommentar zur Zivilprozessordnung*, mn 135 to Anh 1059 (22nd ed., Mohr Siebeck, 2013); Bucher, *Die neue internationale Schiedsgerichtsbarkeit in der Schweiz*, p. 131 (Helbing Lichtenhahn Verlag, 1989) differing between the *ordre public* international that the arbitrator is to apply and that is relevant in setting aside proceedings and the *ordre public* atténué that applies in enforcement proceedings.
5. *See* Austrian Supreme Court, Judgment 12 October 2011, docket no. 3 Ob 186/11s on the *ordre public* standard in the system of conflict of laws.
6. Stefan Kröll and Peter Kraft, in Karl-Heinz Böckstiegel, Stefan Kröll and Patricia Nacimiento eds., *Arbitration in Germany, The Model Law in Practice*, mn 79 to Section 1059 (Kluwer Law International, 2007).

award that has no connection to a State but to the location of the assets of a party against which enforcement is sought will less likely be considered to violate that State's *ordre public*. In such a case, often only the violation of the most basic rules of justice, such as those shown above, would lead to the refusal to enforce the award.[7] Hence, different standards of *ordre public* may apply depending on the facts of the underlying case. However, the standard does not differ depending on where the award was rendered.

§3.02 THE RELEVANCE OF FOREIGN LAW AS A PART OF THE *ORDRE PUBLIC*

10. The approach requiring a close connection between a State and the facts of a case for that State's *ordre public* to apply is accepted for the application of foreign law. The application of foreign law can result in a violation of a State's *ordre public* if the facts of the case have a sufficiently close connection to that State.[8] This is a measure of respect afforded to foreign legal systems upon which domestic system of values should not be imposed without a sufficiently close connection justifying the repudiation of the foreign legal rule.[9] The mere fact that a domestic court has jurisdiction over a case will not justify the repudiation of foreign law but for in the most extreme cases.[10]

11. The same rule as to the application of foreign law applies to the enforcement of arbitral awards. Also with regard to arbitral awards, the standard of *ordre public* is higher if the facts of the case underlying the dispute and the State in which enforcement is sought are closely connected.[11]

12. The point can be illustrated with regard to the following example. State B considers that interest to be paid in the amount of 100% per year is a violation of the *ordre public*,[12] while it is perfectly legal in State A to award such interest. Assuming an award on such interest is rendered by a tribunal in State A and that both parties have their seat there and the only connection of the case to State B is that one of the parties has assets in that country, the award would likely be enforceable in State B regardless of the fact that the interest rate would violate its *ordre public*. If, on the other hand, one of the parties has its seat in B or the case has any other closer connection to State B, the courts of B would more likely be justified in applying their concept of *ordre public*.

---

7. *Ibid*.
8. Gerhard Kegel & Klaus Schurig, *Internationales Privatrecht*, pp. 521ss (9th ed., C.H. Beck, 2004).
9. S. Lorenz in Bamberger/Roth eds., *BeckOK BGB*, Article 6 EGBGB Rz 16 (C.H. Beck, 2007); Austrian Supreme Court, Judgment 12 October 2011, docket no. 3 Ob 186/11s.
10. Sonnenberger in Säcker et al. eds., *Münchener Kommentar zum BGB*, Vol. 11, Article 6 EGBGB Rz 82 (5th ed., C.H. Beck, 2010).
11. Stefan Kröll and Peter Kraft, in Karl-Heinz Böckstiegel, Stefan Kröll and Patricia Nacimiento eds., *Arbitration in Germany, The Model Law in Practice*, mn 79 to Section 1059 (Kluwer Law International, 2007); Schlosser in Stein and Jonas, *Kommentar zur Zivilprozessordnung*, mn 135 to Anhang 1059 (22nd ed., Mohr Siebeck, 2013).
12. *See*, e.g., Austrian Supreme Court, Judgment 26 January 2005, docket no. 3 Ob 221/04b; *see* on the point, also, Lovrek and Musger, in Czernich, Deixler-Hübner and Schauer eds., *Handbuch Schiedsrecht*, mn 16.78 (Manz, 2018).

§3.03 FOREIGN MANDATORY RULES

13. A related question is whether the enforcement of an award can be rejected for a violation of the *ordre public* if the award violates a rule pertaining to the *ordre public* of a third country. This question is of particular relevance in the context of Article IX of the Convention which permits the enforcement of awards set aside in the State of origin. If an award fails to apply the competition law of the State of origin this may be a violation of the *ordre public* of that State. If State A is in the EU, such violation would be confirmed by the ECJ in its decision in *EcoSwiss* case. However, if enforcement is sought in another State, either because it was not challenged or because the Convention is applicable, the question arises whether the latter State can refuse the enforcement and on which grounds.

14. The State in which enforcement is sought certainly cannot simply ignore all violations of the basic rules of a foreign legal system. Arbitral tribunals in certain situations cannot turn a blind eye on mandatory rules.[13] Some, though not all, of these rules pertain to the *ordre public* of the State enacting them. If a foreign award ignores or misapplies such rules, this can lead to a violation of the *ordre public* of a State in which enforcement is sought. The reason for refusing enforcement can only be a violation of the *ordre public* of the State in which enforcement is sought, not a violation of a foreign *ordre public.*[14]

15. The State in which enforcement is sought can, therefore, when assessing whether to refuse enforcement due to a violation of the *ordre public*, determine whether the tribunal should have applied foreign mandatory rules but failed to do so. The *ordre public* of the State in which enforcement is sought can be violated in such a case under certain circumstances as a complete disregard of such rules would run counter to comity among States[15] and would jeopardize the framework of international trade, which itself is part of the *ordre public.*[16]

16. The State in which enforcement is sought, however, must first determine that the result of the award is contrary to its *ordre public*. This excludes a *révision au fonds* of the award and will limit the review to clear-cut cases in which a foreign mandatory rule was clearly misapplied or violated. It is up to the forum State to decide which test to apply regarding the applicability of the foreign mandatory rule to the dispute decided in the award. Second, the forum State must have enacted a rule similar to the foreign

13. *See* on this above, Chapter 2.
14. Berger, *Devisenrecht in der internationalen Wirtschaftsschiedsgerichtsbarkeit*, ZVglRWiss, 316, p. 326 (dfv Mediengruppe, 1997).
15. Remiro Brotóns, *La Reconnaissance et l'exécution des Sentences arbitrales étrangères*, RdC169, p. 247 (Les Petites Affiches, 1984-I).
16. Schlosser in Stein and Jonas, *Kommentar zur Zivilprozessordnung*, mn 145 to Anhang 1061 (22nd ed., Mohr Siebeck, 2013); Schlosser, *Das Recht der internationalen privaten Schiedsgerichtsbarkeit*, pp. 634ss (2nd ed., Mohr Siebeck, 1989); Jermini, *Die Anfechtung von Schiedssprüchen im internationalen Privatrecht, NAch dem schweizerischen Bundesgesetz über das Internationale Privatrecht, rechtsvergleichende Ausblicke*, mn 580ss (Schulthess Juristische Medien, 1997).

mandatory rule or the latter must be compatible with the system of values of the State in which enforcement is sought.[17]

17. This Swiss Supreme Court has had the opportunity to assess whether an award which allegedly misapplied EU competition law could be set aside due to a violation of the Swiss *ordre public*. It held that there are fundamental legal and moral rules which are common to all States and, therefore, are also part of the Swiss *ordre public*. Rules on the protection of competition, however, vary and, as the Supreme Court pointed out, some socialist systems have not implemented such rules at all. Hence, foreign rules of competition law could not be considered part of the Swiss *ordre public*.

18. This approach, however, if followed stringently, will essentially exclude a violation of the Swiss *ordre public* in most cases. Also, the combat of money laundering, to name an example, is implemented to a varying extent in the States of the world and there are various approaches on how to prevent such laundering. This, however, would not exclude that enforcement of an award which ignores such rules could be refused. A comparison of the foreign rule and that rules and values of the forum is sufficient without a review of all the legal systems of the world. After all, it is the *ordre public* of the forum, which encompasses the legal values of that one State, that is relevant for deciding on whether an award can be set aside or refused recognition.

19. Under the Convention the possibility to refuse recognition due to a violation of a foreign mandatory rule could potentially be of significant relevance. As an award can be enforced even if it has been set aside in its State of origin for a violation of the *ordre public*, the *ordre public* of the State of enforcement will be of greater relevance than in situations in which enforcement is sought under the NYC. The judge deciding on the enforcement will, therefore, have to review whether the award, which misapplies mandatory rules pertaining to the *ordre public* of the State of origin, violates the forum's *ordre public*. In the latter case, the enforcement of the award will be refused. This would conform to the purpose of the Convention to exclude the effects of setting aside awards for parochial reasons in the State of origin while ensuring the integrity of the international legal system.

17. Lörcher, *Wie zwingend sind in der internationalen Handelsschiedsgerichtsbarkeit zwingende Normen einer "dritten" Rechtsordnung?*, 17 BB Beilage, 3, p. 7 (Beck, 1993); who requires that the forum has enacted a similar rule; Berger, *Devisenrecht in der internationalen Wirtschaftsschiedsgerichtsbarkeit*, in ZVglRWiss, pp. 316, 326, 327 (dfv Mediengruppe, 1997); Bucher, *Die neue internationale Schiedsgerichtsbarkeit in der Schweiz*, p. 131 (Helbing Lichtenhahn Verlag, 1989); with a similar approach Broggini, *Le contrôle des sentences arbitrales internationales par le juge des siège et par le juge de l'exécution* in FS Siehr, 95, p. 110 (Basedow ed., 2000).

PART II Preamble of the Convention

Andrea de la Brena

INTRODUCTION

1. Article 31 of the Vienna Convention on the Law of Treaties ("VCLT") expressly refers to the preamble of a treaty as one element to identify the object and purpose of a treaty. The preamble usually reflects *"motivations, aims, and considerations which are stated as having played a part in drawing up the treaty."*[1] Hence, it is a material part of any convention, which should be taken into consideration in most cases.

2. The preamble of the Convention reads as follows:

> THE UNDERSIGNED, DULY AUTHORIZED,
>
> Convened under the auspices of the Economic Commission for Europe of the United Nations.
>
> Having noted that on 10th June 1958 at the United Nations Conference on International Commercial Arbitration has been signed in New York a Convention on the Recognition and Enforcement of Foreign Arbitral Awards,
>
> Desirous of promoting the development of European trade by, as far as possible, removing certain difficulties that may impede the organization and operation of international commercial arbitration in relations between physical or legal persons of different European countries,
>
> Have agreed on the following provisions:

I ROLE OF THE ECONOMIC COMMISSION FOR EUROPE OF THE UNITED NATIONS

3. UNECE was established on 28 March 1947, by the United Nations Economic and Social Council ("ECOSOC"), first on a provisional basis and, following resolution 414

1. Richard Gardiner, *Treaty Interpretation*, p. 186 (first publication, Oxford University Press, 2008).

C(XIII) of 1951, on a permanent basis. UNECE is a regional commission established to promote economic integration and cooperation among European countries.[2] Originally, UNECE was focused on providing effective aid to countries devastated by World War II. In general terms, it was aimed at promoting economic integration and cooperation among European countries.[3] UNECE's objective has evolved and nowadays it covers a broader range of tasks.[4]

4. During the Cold War, UNECE functioned as a bridge of dialogue and negotiation between Eastern and Western countries. Arbitration was of key relevance for promoting international trade and enhancing economic development. For this reason, simultaneously with the initiative of ECOSOC for the NYC, in the early 1950s, Frederic Eisemann, the ICC Secretary—General at that time, seized UNECE in Geneva to begin working on the Convention to overcome the virtual speechlessness throughout a sharply divided Europe.[5] The idea was to prepare a legal instrument setting neutral grounds for international commercial arbitrations between the two radical Eastern and Western Blocs.

5. The first draft of the ECICA was prepared by the Ad Hoc Working Group on Arbitration under the auspices of the Committee on the Development of Trade of UNECE at its seventh session. Following this session, certain disagreements arose concerning the text of Article IV. Thus, on 5 May 1960, UNECE adopted resolution 7 (XV) requesting a Special Meeting to solve the disagreements and agree on a final text of the Convention. The disagreements were solved during the meetings held from 8 to 12 August 1960 and from 5 to 10 April 1961. Finally, the Executive Secretary of UNECE, Mr. Vladimir Velebit, convened a Special Meeting of Plenipotentiaries from 10 to 21 April 1961 whereby the final draft was presented to the representatives of twenty-two States[6] and two nongovernmental organizations.[7] On the last day, the ECICA was opened for signature.[8]

2. UNECE official website, *History*, http://www.unece.org/mission.html, accessed 6 November 2016.
3. UNECE official website, *Mission*, http://www.unece.org/mission.html, accessed 6 November *2016*.
4. *Ibid*.
5. UN, *Enforcing Arbitration Awards under the New York Convention: Experience and Prospects*, New York 1999, p. 7, available at https://www.uncitral.org/pdf/english/texts/arbitration/NY-conv/NYCDay-e.pdf (last visited 16 December 2016).
6. Austria, Belgium, Bulgaria, Byelorussian Soviet Socialist Republic, Czechoslovakia, Denmark, Federal Republic of Germany, Finland, France, Hungary, Italy, Luxembourg, Netherlands, Poland, Romania, Spain, Sweden, Switzerland, Turkey, Ukrainian Soviet Socialist Republic, Union of Soviet Socialist Republics, and Yugoslavia.
7. International Chamber of Commerce and International Bar Association.
8. Committee on the Development of Trade of UNECE, *Final Act for the Special Meeting of Plenipotentiaries for the purpose of negotiating and signing a European Convention on International Commercial Arbitration*, 350 UNTS 1963-1964, No. 7041.

II RELEVANCE OF THE NYC IN THE DRAFTING OF THE CONVENTION

6. The second sentence of the preamble reflects the relation between ECICA and the NYC. Three years before the conclusion of the ECICA, the NYC was enacted. Both conventions were adopted following World War II with the aim of providing a neutral forum for settling disputes between parties coming from widely different legal backgrounds, particularly between Eastern and Western countries. In the drafting and birth of both conventions, ECOSOC played an important role.

7. In 1919, a group of businessmen, determined to enhance economic prosperity after World War I, founded the International Chamber of Commerce ("ICC"). A few years later, in 1923, due to the relevance of arbitration for international trade, the ICC International Court of Arbitration was established to promote an international convention with the purpose of removing obstacles concerned to the enforceability of the arbitration clause. The initiative of this international convention was taken over by the League of Nations and crystallized in the 1923 Geneva Protocol on Arbitration Clauses.[9] Once the international enforceability of arbitration clauses was addressed by this instrument, a similar instrument, the Geneva Convention on the Execution of Foreign Awards was concluded concerning the enforceability of awards (jointly, the "Geneva Conventions"). However, the Geneva Conventions were subject to certain conditions that restricted their scope of application. For instance, the Geneva Convention on the Execution of Foreign Awards was applicable only in cases where the award was made in a Contracting State and sought to be enforced in another Contracting State.[10] Another restriction was that, under the Geneva Conventions, the arbitration proceedings, including the constitution of the tribunal, must have taken place in accordance to the law where the arbitration took place; hence, they were strongly linked to national legislation.[11]

8. The origins of the NYC can be traced back to 1953, when the ICC issued a new draft of a convention on international commercial arbitration for the purpose of overcoming the limitations of the Geneva Conventions. The NYC, therefore, has a broader scope of application. *Inter alia* it no longer requires that the award sought to be enforced has been made in another Contracting State. The ICC draft was presented to ECOSOC which, later on, proposed an alternate draft and sent it to a number of governments as well as inter-governmental and nongovernmental organizations for comments and observations.[12] In order to agree on a final text, ECOSOC held a conference on 20 June 1958 in New York, at which the NYC was finally adopted by 56 States. Today, it has 156 Contracting Parties.[13]

9. Albert Jan van den Berg, *The New York Arbitration Convention of 1958*, p. 6 (Kluwer International Arbitration 1981).
10. *Ibid.*, p. 7.
11. *Ibid.*
12. *Ibid.*, p. 8.
13. UNCITRAL, Convention on the Recognition and Enforcement of Foreign Arbitral Awards (New York, 1958), last visited 6 February 2017.

9. The scope of the NYC covers two aspects: enforcement of the arbitration agreement and enforcement of the arbitration award. It does not provide a codification of rules on all other stages of international commercial arbitration proceedings. Conversely, the ECICA only indirectly refers to the enforcement of arbitration agreements and awards.[14] Thus, the relationship between the two conventions is complementary.[15] Notably, Article IX of the ECICA indirectly limits the effects of the grounds for setting aside an arbitral award contained in Article V(1)(e) of the NYC.[16]

10. For these reasons, a comprehensive understanding of the ECICA's provisions goes hand in hand with an analysis of the effects and provisions of the NYC.

III OBJECTIVE OF THE CONVENTION

11. The preamble also reflects the main purpose of the ECICA, i.e., to promote the development of European trade by removing obstacles to arbitration proceedings.[17] Following the devastating consequences of the World Wars, economic development was critical and trade between European countries needed to be promoted. However, the differences between the political, economic, and legal systems of the Eastern and Western Blocs generated a general sense of mistrust, which obstructed the development of European trade. Even though arbitration was perceived as a more suitable option for settling international commercial disputes than domestic courts, States were still skeptical about the different approaches and attitude of foreign domestic courts towards arbitration.[18] Thus, harmonization of arbitration rules was essential if international arbitration was to function as an effective dispute resolution mechanism.

12. The ECICA's provisions reflected common ground between the different European legal systems and, in this way, functioned as a means to overcome not only legal but also psychological barriers affecting international commercial arbitration during the Cold War.

---

14. Emmanuel Gaillard and John Savage eds., *Fouchard, Gaillard and Goldman on International Commercial Arbitration*, p. 142 (Kluwer Law International, 1999).
15. Nikolaus Pitkowitz, *Is There Still a Scope of Application of the European Convention on International Commercial Arbitration?*, in Austrian Yearbook on International Arbitration, 93–108, p. 95 (Klausegger and others eds., 2013); Emmanuel Gaillard and John Savage eds., *Fouchard, Gaillard and Goldman on International Commercial Arbitration*, p. 143 (Kluwer Law International, 1999); Christian Konrad, *Buried in Oblivion? The Significance and Limitations of the European Convention on International Commercial Arbitration* (2 November 2010) available http://kluwerarbitrationblog.com/2010/11/02/buried-in-oblivion-the-significance-and-limitations-of-the-european-convention-on-international-commercial-arbitration/ (last visited 15 December 2016).
16. Nikolaus Pitkowitz, *Is There Still a Scope of Application of the European Convention on International Commercial Arbitration?*, in Austrian Yearbook on International Arbitration, 93–108, p. 95 (Klausegger and others eds., 2013).
17. Stefan Kröll, *The European Convention on International Commercial Arbitration: The Tale of a Sleeping Beauty*, in Austrian Yearbook on International Arbitration, 4, p. 4 (Klausegger and others eds., Manz, 2013).
18. *Ibid.*

IV REGIONAL SCOPE OF THE CONVENTION

13. Originally, the ECICA was concluded by sixteen States, including nearly all countries from the former Eastern Bloc, the main economic powers from the Western Bloc, and Turkey.[19] Although the ECICA's background is strongly related to the East–West conflict, according to its preamble the Convention was intended to apply to arbitrations between physical or legal persons of different European States, even in those cases where the parties to the arbitration came from States of the same Bloc.[20]

14. Even if the title of the Convention and its preamble refer to the term "European," in reality, its scope of application is not limited to States located in Europe. In fact, Turkey, Russia, Azerbaijan, Burkina Faso, Cuba, and Kazakhstan are parties to the Convention; conversely, Portugal, the U.K., the Netherlands, and Switzerland are not.[21]

19. Stefan Kröll, *The European Convention on International Commercial Arbitration: The Tale of a Sleeping Beauty,* in Austrian Yearbook on International Arbitration, 4, pp. 4–5 (Klausegger and others eds., Manz, 2013).
20. Dominique Hascher, *European Convention on International Commercial Arbitration of 1961: Commentary,* in Vol. XXXVI, Yearbook Commercial Arbitration, 509, p. 507 (Albert Jan van den Berg ed., Kluwer Law International 2011).
21. Nikolaus Pitkowitz, *Is There Still a Scope of Application of the European Convention on International Commercial Arbitration?,* in Austrian Yearbook on International Arbitration, 93–108, p. 93 (Klausegger and others eds., Manz, 2013).

ARTICLE I

Scope of the Convention

Andrea de la Brena

INTRODUCTION

> *'Article I—Scope of the Convention*
> 1. *This Convention shall apply:*
>   (a) *to arbitration agreements concluded for the purpose of settling disputes arising from international trade between physical or legal persons having, when concluding the agreement, their habitual place of residence or their seat in different Contracting States;*
>   (b) *to arbitral procedures and awards based on agreements referred to in paragraph 1(a) above.*
> 2. *For the purpose of this Convention,*
>   (a) *the term: "arbitration agreement" shall mean either an arbitral clause in a contract or an arbitration agreement, the contract or arbitration agreement being signed by the parties, or contained in an exchange of letters, telegrams, or in a communication by teleprinter and, in relations between States whose laws do not require that an arbitration agreement be made in writing, any arbitration agreement concluded in the form authorized by these laws;*
>   (b) *the term "arbitration" shall mean not only settlement by arbitrators appointed for each case (*ad hoc *arbitration) but also by permanent arbitral institutions;*
>   (c) *the term "seat" shall mean the place of the situation of the establishment that has made the arbitration agreement.*

1. Article I delimits the scope of application of the Convention. According to its title and preamble, the Convention was originally intended to remove obstacles of trade between European countries. Therefore, unlike the NYC, the drafters of the ECICA did not originally consider that this instrument would have a full international scope of application but a regional one,[1] such as the 1975 Inter-American Convention on International Commercial Arbitration (the "Panama Convention"). Hence, the intended territorial scope of the ECICA was, in theory, to be narrower than that of the NYC.[2] However, its scope has been broadened by the accession of various non-European States to the Convention.[3]

2. The substantive scope of the Convention unlike the NYC is restricted to international trade disputes. However, the ECICA covers a broader range of matters than the scope of the NYC, as it not only contains provisions on the enforcement of arbitration agreements and awards but also contains provisions on additional stages of the procedure such as the constitution of the arbitral tribunal, the organization of the proceedings, the jurisdiction of domestic courts, or the applicable law.[4]

3. The Convention is binding upon all Contracting States. Therefore, domestic courts of those States are obliged to apply the Convention's provisions in all cases which meet the conditions of Article I. Hence, in the following both the subjective and objective conditions of its application, as well as the types of arbitration agreements covered by the Convention, will be examined (I). Further, certain procedural aspects, not expressly covered by Article I, will be analyzed (II). Finally, the relationship of the Convention with domestic laws and other treaties, in particular the NYC, will be discussed (III).

I CONDITIONS TO BE MET

4. The ECICA was the first convention that included a definition of the term "international," with respect to arbitration.[5] According to Article I(1), the Convention shall apply to disputes relating to arbitration agreements, awards, and procedures "*arising from international trade between physical or legal persons having (...) their habitual place of residence or their seat in different Contracting States.*" Accordingly, the internationality test has two prongs: the subjective and the objective condition. First,

1. Dominique Hascher, *European Convention on International Commercial Arbitration of 1961: Commentary*, in Vol. XXXVI, Yearbook Commercial Arbitration, 509, p. 507 (Albert Jan van den Berg ed., Kluwer Law International 2011). Emmanuel Gaillard and John Savage eds., *Fouchard, Gaillard and Goldman on International Commercial Arbitration*, p. 141 (Kluwer Law International, 1999).
2. Francisco J. Garcimartín Alférez and Sara Sánchez Fernández, *Recognition and Enforcement of Foreign Arbitral Awards Set Aside or Suspended in the State of Origin*, 8(1) Cuadernos de Derecho Transnacional, 111–124, pp. 113 and 114 (March 2016).
3. For instance, Cuba, Burkina Faso, Azerbaijan and Kazakhstan are also Contracting States.
4. Stefan Kröll, *The European Convention on International Commercial Arbitration: The Tale of a Sleeping Beauty*, in Austrian Yearbook on International Arbitration, 4, p. 7 (Klausegger and others eds., Manz, 2013); Christian Konrad, *Buried in Oblivion? The Significance and Limitations of the European Convention on International Commercial Arbitration* (2 November 2010) available at http://kluwerarbitrationblog.com/2010/11/02/buried-in-oblivion-the-significance-and-limitations-of-the-european-convention-on-international-commercial-arbitration/ (last visited 10 January 2017).
5. Julian D. M. Lew, Loukas A. Mistelis and Stefan Kröll, *Comparative International Commercial Arbitration*, p. 62 (Wolters Kluwer, 2003).

for the subjective condition, the parties to the dispute must reside or have their seat in different Contracting States [A]. Second, as an objective condition, the dispute must arise from international trade between those parties [B]. Article I(2) defines the form requirements of the arbitration agreements falling within the scope of the Convention [C].

[A] Subjective Condition: *Ratione Personae*

[1] Habitual Place of Residence and Seat of Business

5. The Convention applies to the parties of an arbitration agreement who have their habitual place of residence or their seat of business in different Contracting States when concluding the arbitration agreement.[6] To determine the location of the parties, the drafters of the Convention chose two alternative criteria: (i) the habitual place of residence, in cases involving natural persons or (ii) the seat of business, in cases involving legal persons.[7]

6. The Convention will only apply if both parties fulfill one of the two criteria. In this regard, the Convention "*is not applicable in cases where only one party is connected to a Contracting State or both parties are from the same Contracting State.*"[8] However, as will be detailed in Section A 4, in practice, some arbitral tribunals have applied the Convention, even in cases where none of the subjective conditions were met.

7. The habitual place of residence and seat of business exclude nationality as a subjective condition. These conditions ensure that the parties will be seated in a Contracting State while the use of the criteria of nationality could have the effect that the courts of the seat will not implement the Convention if this seat is outside a Contracting State.

8. The term "habitual place of residence" is used in several international instruments, such as the United Nations Convention on Contracts for the International Sale of

6. *Austria No. 13 / E4, Buyer (Austria) v. Seller (*Oberster Gerichtshof), Supreme Court, 3Ob221/04b, 26 January 2005, in Vol. 30, Yearbook Commercial Arbitration, pp. 421–436 (Albert Jan van den Berg ed., 2005); *France No. E4, French Seller v. German Buyer, (Oberlandesgericht)* Court of Appeal, Cologne, Not Indicated, 18 May 1992, in Vol. 19, Yearbook Commercial Arbitration, pp. 856–859 (Albert Jan van den Berg ed., 1994); Italy No. E19, *G & C, S.p.A. (Italy) v. Gersan Elektrik Tic. ve San. A.Ş. (Turkey),* Court of First Instance, Turin, 4 December 2007 in Vol. 34, Yearbook Commercial Arbitration, pp. 1216–1218 (Albert Jan van den Berg ed., 2009).
7. Nikolaus Pitkowitz, *Is There Still a Scope of Application of the European Convention on International Commercial Arbitration?,* in Austrian Yearbook on International Arbitration, 93–108, p. 99 (Klausegger and others eds., Manz, 2013).
8. Dominique Hascher, *European Convention on International Commercial Arbitration of 1961: Commentary,* in Vol. XXXVI, Yearbook Commercial Arbitration, 509, p. 509 (Albert Jan van den Berg ed. Kluwer Law International 2011); Nikolaus Pitkowitz, *Is There Still a Scope of Application of the European Convention on International Commercial Arbitration?,* in Austrian Yearbook on International Arbitration, 93–108, p. 100 (Klausegger and others eds., Manz, 2013); Florian Haugeneder, *The New Austrian Arbitration Act and the European Convention on International Commercial Arbitration,* 23(4) Arbitration International 646, p. 646 (2007).

Goods[9] ("CISG"), the Hague Convention on Child Abduction[10] and the Rome Convention on Choice of Law in Contracts.[11] It has been deliberately undefined in these instruments, in order to prevent rigidity.[12] Similarly, the drafters of the ECICA abandoned all attempts to provide a definition "*when it became apparent that there might be difficulty in arriving at an acceptable definition (...) in view of the multitude of interpretations that may be given to the above term even within a single system of law.*"[13]

9. In an English case, *Re J. (A Minor) (Abduction: Custody Rights),*[14] Lord Brandon held (though on a case not involving the Convention) that the term "habitually resident" shall be understood according to the ordinary and natural meaning of the two words and that it is a matter of fact to be decided taking into account the circumstances of the case.[15] Commentators to the ECICA have also considered the term "habitual residence" as a matter of fact, rather than a matter of law; however, this has not provided much clarification.[16]

10. According to the Black's Law Dictionary, although closely related, there is a difference between the terms "residence" and "domicile," the former "*simply requires bodily presence as an inhabitant in a given place, while domicile requires bodily presence in that place and also an intention to make it one's domicile.*"[17] Certain delegations at the Special Meeting of Plenipotentiaries suggested the term "domicile" instead of "habitual residence," however, this suggestion was strongly opposed "*in view of the confusion that the term 'domicile' is likely to engender in an international instrument.*"[18]

11. The aforementioned dictionary defines "habitual" as "*customary, usual, of the nature of a habit.*"[19] This definition adds to the physical presence an element of

---

9. United Nations Convention on Contracts for the International Sale of Goods, Vienna, 11 April 1980, S. Treaty Document Number 98-9 (1984), UN Document Number A/CONF 97/19, 1489 UNTS 3.
10. Convention on the Civil Aspects of International Child Abduction, The Hague, 25 October 1980, 1 December 1983, T.I.A.S No. 11,670, 1343 UNTS 89.
11. Convention on the Law Applicable to Contractual Obligations (Rome Convention), Act 80/934/ECC, Rome, 19 June 1980, 1 April 1991, OJL 266 9.10.1980.
12. Pippa Rogerson, *Habitual Residence: The New Domicile?*, 49(1) The International and Comparative Law Quarterly, 86–107, p. 87 (January 2000).
13. P. I. Benjamin, *The European Convention on International Commercial Arbitration*, 37 British Yearbook International Law 478, p. 480 (1961).
14. *C v. S (A Minor: Abduction)*, [1990] 2 A.C. 562, cited in Pippa Rogerson, *Habitual Residence: The New Domicile?*, 49(1) The International and Comparative Law Quarterly, 86-107, p. 89 (January 2000).
15. *C v. S (A Minor: Abduction)*, [1990] 2 A.C. 562, pp. 578–579, cited in Pippa Rogerson, *Habitual Residence: The New Domicile?*, 49(1) The International and Comparative Law Quarterly, 86–107, p. 89 (January 2000).
16. Nikolaus Pitkowitz, *Is There Still a Scope of Application of the European Convention on International Commercial Arbitration?*, in Austrian Yearbook on International Arbitration, 93–108, p. 100 (Klausegger and others eds., Manz, 2013).
17. Henry Campbell Black M.A., *Black's Law Dictionary*, p. 1177 (5th ed., 1979).
18. P. I. Benjamin, *The European Convention on International Commercial Arbitration*, 37 British Yearbook International Law 478, p. 480 (1961).
19. Henry Campbell Black M.A., *Black's Law Dictionary*, p. 640 (5th ed., 1979).

consistency and permanency.[20] However, the open question remains how to determine the length of time a person must stay in a place to be considered a habitual resident. A commentator on the general notion of habitual residence, suggests that "*if a residence has lasted longer than a year (...) then notwithstanding that the residence is for limited purpose, it is considered a habitual residence (...)*"[21] Accordingly, the threshold for determining the required time could also vary depending on subjective elements, such as the party's intention to reside in a place.[22] The ECICA does not provide an express answer to the question nor does the related accessible case law. Hence, it seems, in practice, this has not often been a contentious issue.

12. The notion of "seat of business," referred to as *siège social* in French, is defined in Article I(2) of the ECICA as "*the place of the situation of the establishment that has made the arbitration agreement.*" In a case under the CISG, the Provincial Court of Appeal of Stuttgart held that a place of business exists if a party "*uses it openly to participate in trade*" and if the "*requirements of permanence, stability and principally an independent ability to act*" are met.[23]

13. The term "seat of business" was intentionally left without qualification by any additional adjectives, such as "main" or "principal," in order "*to cover the case of an arbitration agreement concluded by a branch office of a firm.*"[24] Therefore, it is not necessary to determine whether the establishment that concluded the arbitration agreement was the "*nerve center*" of the company or the one that generated the highest revenues.[25] In fact, a party may have several places of business but the relevant place would be the one by which the arbitration agreement was concluded.

14. This criterion is different from Article 10 of the CISG and Article I(4) of the UNCITRAL Model Law, which stipulates that if a party has more than one place of business, reference should be made to the place of business with the "*closest relationship to the arbitration agreement,*" which most likely, but not necessarily, will be the one where the arbitration agreement was concluded.[26]

15. The drafters of the ECICA chose the criterion of the "seat of business" instead of the "place of incorporation" in order "*to avoid endless controversy over the respective*

20. Pippa Rogerson, *Habitual Residence: The New Domicile?*, 49(1) The International and Comparative Law Quarterly, 86–107, pp. 96–98 (January 2000).
21. *Ibid.*, pp. 94-95.
22. *Ibid.*, p. 91.
23. *X(Germany) v. Y(Spain)*, *Oberlandesgericht Stuttgart*, 28 February 2000, Internationales Handelsrecht (IHR) 2001, English unofficial translation available at http://cisgw3.law.pace.edu/cases/000228g1.html, last accessed 7 February 2017.
24. P. I. Benjamin, *The European Convention on International Commercial Arbitration*, 37 British Yearbook International Law 478, p. 480 (1961).
25. The "nerve center" and the "business activity" approaches were explained by the US Supreme Court in the case *Hertz Corp. v. Friend*: "*[t]he former relates to place where a corporation's officers direct, control, and coordinate the corporation's activities, while the latter refers to the corporation's revenue stream*". *Hertz Corp. v. Friend*, United States Supreme Court, 559 U.S. (2010).
26. UNCITRAL, Model Law on International Commercial Arbitration (1985), with amendments as adopted in 2006, General Assembly resolution 61/33 Article I(4).

merits of the place of incorporation or the registered office."[27] Therefore, the place of incorporation is irrelevant to the application of the Convention.[28]

16. Unlike Article 1(3) of the UNCITRAL Model Law,[29] the seat of arbitration is not a factor for applicability of the Convention. The difference could be explained by looking at the intention of the ECICA drafters, which was to create an instrument as independent as possible from national systems. Hence, the courts of Member States of the ECICA are to apply the terms regardless of where the place of arbitration is. Undoubtedly, if the place of arbitration is outside a Member State, the Convention will not be relevant for the arbitral proceedings and possible setting aside proceedings but may be for the enforcement of an arbitral agreement or arbitral award.

[2] Parties' Nationality Is Excluded

17. Sometimes, the applicability of an international treaty is determined by the nationality of the parties involved. This is the case, e.g., with regard to the Convention on the Settlement of Investment Disputes between States and Nationals of other States ("ICSID Convention"), the field of investment arbitration, which, requires the investor to be a national of a Contracting State.[30] Unlike the ICSID Convention, the application of the ECICA, however, does not depend on the nationality of the parties.

18. This exclusion avoids potential practical complexities (e.g., cases of double nationality or a genuine link). It also avoids problems with the applications by domestic courts because if one party, national of one Contracting State, is located in a non-Contracting State the domestic courts of the latter State are not obligated to apply the Convention. Therefore, for the application of the Convention, the nationality of the parties is not a relevant factor.[31]

[3] Relevant Date for Evaluating the Location of the Parties

19. The relevant date for evaluating this subjective condition is the date of the conclusion of the arbitration agreement. Consequently, if one or both parties

---

27. P. I. Benjamin, *The European Convention on International Commercial Arbitration*, 37 British Yearbook International Law 478, p. 480 (1961).
28. Florian Haugeneder, *The New Austrian Arbitration Act and the European Convention on International Commercial Arbitration*, 23(4) Arbitration International 646, p. 646 (2007).
29. UNCITRAL, Model Law on International Commercial Arbitration (1985), with amendments as adopted in 2006, General Assembly resolution 61/33, Article I(3).
30. 1965 Convention on the Settlement of Investment Disputes between States and Nationals of other States (ICSID Convention), 575 UNTS 159, 4 ILM 524 (1965), Article 25(1).
31. Nikolaus Pitkowitz, *Is There Still a Scope of Application of the European Convention on International Commercial Arbitration?*, in Austrian Yearbook on International Arbitration, 93–108, p. 99 (Klausegger and others eds., Manz, 2013); Dominique Hascher, *European Convention on International Commercial Arbitration of 1961: Commentary*, in Vol. XXXVI, Yearbook Commercial Arbitration, 509, p. 509 (Albert Jan van den Berg ed., Kluwer Law International 2011).

subsequently decided to change their habitual residence or seat of business, the situation would not prevent the application of the Convention in any way.[32]

[4] Misapplication by Domestic Courts of the Subjective Condition

20. The wording of the Convention indicates that it is not applicable in cases in which only one party is located in a Contracting State, both parties are located in the same Contracting State at the time of the conclusion of the arbitration agreement,[33] or the parties are nationals of different Contracting States but their place of business or habitual residence is not located therein.[34] Despite the wording, certain arbitral tribunals have applied the Convention even in cases in which the subjective condition expressly provided for in Article I was not met.[35]

21. In a case regarding the payment of damages, arising from the noncompliance of the enforcement of an award, the Spanish Supreme Court applied the Convention despite the fact that one of the parties was located in Geneva, Switzerland, which is not a Contracting State.[36] Similarly, a few years later, in a case in which one of the parties was located in the Netherlands, the Spanish Supreme Court applied the Convention.[37]

22. Also, the Italian Supreme Court (*Corte di Cassazione*), applied the Convention, in a case in which both parties were located in the same Contracting State at the time of the conclusion of the arbitration agreement.[38]

32. Stefan Kröll, *The European Convention on International Commercial Arbitration: The Tale of a Sleeping Beauty*, in Austrian Yearbook on International Arbitration, 4, p. 5 (Klausegger and others eds. Manz, 2013).
33. Dominique Hascher, *European Convention on International Commercial Arbitration of 1961: Commentary*, in Vol. XXXVI, Yearbook Commercial Arbitration, 509, p. 509 (Albert Jan van den Berg ed., Kluwer Law International 2011).
34. Nikolaus Pitkowitz, *Is There Still a Scope of Application of the European Convention on International Commercial Arbitration?*, in Austrian Yearbook on International Arbitration, 93–108, p. 100 (Klausegger and others eds., Manz, 2013).
35. Emmanuel Gaillard and John Savage eds., *Fouchard, Gaillard and Goldman on International Commercial Arbitration*, p. 141 (Kluwer Law International, 1999).
36. *X, S.A. v. Y*, Spanish Supreme Tribunal (*Tribunal Supremo*) Civil Chamber, 8 October 1981, ATS 457/1981.
37. *T.H. Van Huystee B.V v. José Enrique Domínguez*, Spanish Supreme Tribunal (*Tribunal Supremo*) Civil Chamber, STS 5279/1986; *see also S.A. Tradax Exportv. S.p.a. Carapelli*, Court of Appeal of Florence (*Corte di Appello di Firenze*), Parties Not Indicated, 22 October 1976, Italy No. 18/ E3, in Vol. III, Yearbook Commercial Arbitration, pp. 279–280 (Pieter Sanders ed., 1978); *SpA Cifuindus v. OFAG: Ofenbau und Feuerungstechnik AG*, Italian Supreme Court (*Corte di Cassazione*), 16 October 1985, no. 5071, Yearbook XIII (1988) pp. 504–509; *Company from Italy v. Firm from FR Germany, Oberlandesgericht*, Hamburg, 22 September 1978, Yearbook V (1980) pp. 262–264; *Wünsche Handelsgesellschaft v. S. Maria srl*, Bundesgerichtshof, 2 December 1982, Yearbook XV (1990) pp. 660–666; *Kern Electrónica, S.A. v. Goldstar Company Limited*, Spanish Supreme Tribunal (*Tribunal Supremo*), 23 July 2001, Yearbook XXXI (2006) pp. 825–833; *Scandlines, AB, et al. v. Ferrys del Mediterráneo, S.L.*, Spanish Supreme Tribunal (*Tribunal Supremo*), 8 October 2002, Yearbook XXXII (2007) pp. 555–566.
38. *Società Atlas General Timbers, S.p.A. v. Agenzia Concordia Line, S.p.A.*, Italian Supreme Court (*Corte di Cassazione*), 18 May 1978, in Yearbook of Commercial Arbitration 267 (1980); *see also Il Nuovo Castoro v. Ministry of Foreign Affairs (Italy)*, Italian Supreme Court (*Corte di Cassazione*), 13 October 2000, no. 13648, Yearbook XXVI (2001) pp. 1141–1148; *Delta Cereales España*

23. Despite these (rather isolated) cases, the prevailing approach is to apply the Convention in accordance with its wording; hence, solely in cases where both parties are located in different Contracting States.[39]

24. The relevance of the Convention goes beyond its direct application. In some cases, in which the conditions for the applicability of the Conventions were not met, courts have applied its provisions as part of the so-called *lex mercatoria* or used it as interpretative guidance when applying other treaties or laws.[40]

[B] Objective Condition: *Ratione Materiae*

[1] Definition of "Dispute"

25. The application of the Convention requires the existence of a "dispute." Unlike other conventions, such as the ICSID Convention, ECICA does not qualify the term by the term "legal."[41]

26. The International Court of Justice ("ICJ") has attempted to provide a definition on several occasions. In the case the *Mavrommatis Palestine Concessions*, the Permanent Court of Justice provided a wide definition: "*a dispute is a disagreement on a point of law or fact, a conflict of legal views or of interests between two persons.*"[42] In an advisory opinion, the ICJ indicated that a legal dispute is "*a situation in which the two sides held clearly opposite views concerning the question of the performance or non-performance of*

SL v. Barredo Hermanos SA, Spanish Supreme Tribunal (*Tribunal Supremo*), 6 October 1998, Yearbook XXVI (2001) pp. 854–857.

39. Emmanuel Gaillard and John Savage eds., *Fouchard, Gaillard and Goldman on International Commercial Arbitration*, p. 141 (Kluwer Law International, 1999). Dominique Hascher, *European Convention on International Commercial Arbitration of 1961: Commentary*, in Vol. XXXVI, Yearbook Commercial Arbitration, 509, p. 509 (Albert Jan van den Berg ed., Kluwer Law International 2011); *see also Société Nationale pour la Recherche, le Transport et la Commercialisation des Hydrocarbures (SONATRACH) v. Ford, Bacon and Davis Incorporated*, Court of First Instance (*Tribunal de Première Instance*), Brussels, 6 December 1988, Yearbook XV (1990) pp. 370–377; *Pabalk Ticaret Ltd. Sirketi (Turkey) v. Norsolor SA (France)*, Supreme Court (*Cour de Cassation*), 9 October 1984 and Court of Appeal (*Cour d'Appel*), 19 November 1982, in Vol. XI, Yearbook Commercial Arbitration, pp. 484–491 (Albert Jan van den Berg ed., 1986); *Dutch seller v. German (F.R.) buyer*, Court of Appeal of Düsseldorf (*Oberlandesgericht*), 8 November 1971, in Vol. II, Yearbook Commercial Arbitration, (Pieter Sanders ed., 1977), pp. 237–238; *SA Pando Compañia Naviera v. sas FILMO*, Court of Appeal of Venice (*Corte di Appello*), 21 May 1976, Yearbook III (1978) pp. 277–278. *Jassica SA v. Ditta Polojaz*, Trieste Court of Appeal (*Corte di Appello*), 2 July 1982, Yearbook X, (1985) pp. 462–464.
40. Stefan Kröll, *The European Convention on International Commercial Arbitration: The Tale of a Sleeping Beauty*, in Austrian Yearbook on International Arbitration, 4, p. 10 (Klausegger and others eds., Manz, 2013); *see also Cie de Constructions Internationales v. DSI*, Supreme Court of Turkey, 10 March 1976, in Rassegna dell'arb. 1980, p. 187; *Il Nuovo Castoro v. Ministry of Foreign Affairs (Italy)*, Italian Supreme Court (*Corte di Cassazione*), 13 October 2000, no. 13648, Yearbook XXVI (2001) pp. 1141–1148.
41. ICSID Convention, 575 UNTS 159, 4 ILM 524 (1965), Article 25(1).
42. *Mavrommatis Palestine Concessions (Greece v. Great Britain)*, Judgment 30 August 1924, 1924 PCIJ (Ser. A) No. 2, 11.

certain treaty obligations."[43] However, in a particular case, these definitions could be too broad, therefore, additional elements must be considered to find a solution.

27. Schreuer has identified some objective elements to determine the existence of a dispute for jurisdictional purposes. First, the level of intensity of prior communications between the parties does not have to be too intense; the formulation of opposing positions by the parties is sufficient.[44] Second, the absence of an opposition to the existence of a disagreement between the parties will not negate the dispute, if the pertaining party does not provide a proper remedy.[45] Finally, silence and failure to accede to the demands of the other party could also prove the existence of a dispute.[46] Consequently, in a particular case, if the application of the Convention is challenged on this ground, these objective elements could be helpful in analyzing whether there is an existence of a dispute.

[2] Notion of "International Trade"

28. The Convention does not apply to any dispute, but only to those which arise from "international trade" between the parties. Despite the fact the NYC was concluded only a few years before the ECICA, the drafters of the ECICA decided to use the term "international trade," instead of the term "commercial relationships" used in Article I(3) of the NYC.

29. Article I(3) of the NYC contains a reservation, which allows the Contracting States to limit the application of the NYC only to those disputes arising out of legal relationships which are considered "commercial" under the law of the State making such declaration. Due to the wording of the reservation, the term "commercial" is more closely linked to a national definition and, therefore, does not offer the possibility of uniform interpretation.[47] For this reason, the drafters chose to use the term "international trade" in Article I to avoid a stumbling block for the uniform application of the Convention, due to diverging interpretations among domestic legal systems.[48] In some countries, a commercial dispute involves commercial persons, while in others, a dispute may be deemed "commercial," irrespective of the nature of the persons involved.[49]

43. *Interpretation of the Peace Treaties with Bulgaria, Hungary and Romania*, Advisory Opinion, 30 March 1950 (first phase), 1950 ICJ Rep. 65, 74.
44. Christoph Schreuer, *What Is a Legal Dispute?*, in International Law Between Universalism and Fragmentation. Festschrift in Honour of Gerhard Hafner, 959–980, pp. 961–963 (I. Buffard, J. Crawford, A. Pellet and S. Wittich eds., Koninklijke Brill NV, 2008).
45. *Ibid.*, pp. 963–964.
46. *Ibid.*, pp. 964–965.
47. Albert Jan van den Berg, *The New York Arbitration Convention of 1958*, p. 54 (Kluwer Law and Taxation, 1981).
48. Dominique Hascher, *European Convention on International Commercial Arbitration of 1961: Commentary*, in Vol. XXXVI, Yearbook Commercial Arbitration, 509, p. 510 (Albert Jan van den Berg ed., Kluwer Law International, 2011).
49. Julian D. M. Lew, Loukas A. Mistelis and Stefan M. Kröll, *Comparative International Commercial Arbitration*, p. 51, mn 4-5 (Kluwer Law International, 2003).

30. Nevertheless, as the ECICA does not provide guidance with regard to the terms of "international trade," it is difficult to reach a uniform consensus on the point. Some commentators have posited that the term should only cover those disputes considered to be of a commercial nature under *lex fori*.[50] However, on account of the drafters' intention to create a uniform system, the "*most convincing view seems that the term needs to be interpreted* ***autonomously*** *rather than referring to national laws.*"[51]

31. An autonomous interpretation would also be more in line with the modern approach to international commercial arbitration under the UNCITRAL Model Law.[52] Unlike the ECICA, the UNCITRAL Model Law contains an illustrative list of international commercial cases, which may function as a guide for this modern approach.[53]

32. For the application of the ECICA, not only an autonomous interpretation is desirable but also a wide one. Indeed, the majority view is that "international trade" should be interpreted broadly.[54] Such broad interpretation would be supported by the fact that, originally, the ECICA "*was to be applied in the East-West trade which at the time of its drafting (...) a restrictive interpretation of the requirement would largely make the Convention void of any scope of application.*"[55]

---

50. Hans Moller, *Schiedsverfahrensnovelle und Europäisches Übereinkommen über die internationale Handelsschiedsgerichtsbarkeit*, NZG 57 (2000).
51. Nikolaus Pitkowitz, *Is There Still a Scope of Application of the European Convention on International Commercial Arbitration?*, in Austrian Yearbook on International Arbitration, 93–108, p. 104 (Klausegger and others eds., Manz, 2013) (emphasis in original).
52. Dominique Hascher, *European Convention on International Commercial Arbitration of 1961: Commentary*, in Vol. XXXVI, Yearbook Commercial Arbitration, 509, p. 510 (Albert Jan van den Berg ed., Kluwer Law International, 2011).
53. Footnote 2 of Article I of the UNCITRAL Model Law provides the following:

> "*The term 'commercial' should be given a wide interpretation so as to cover matters arising from all relationships of a commercial nature, whether contractual or not. Relationships of a commercial nature include, but are not limited to, the following transactions: any trade transaction for the supply or exchange of goods or services; distribution agreement; commercial representation or agency; factoring; leasing; construction of works; consulting; engineering; licensing; investment; financing; banking; insurance; exploitation agreement or concession; joint venture and other forms of industrial or business cooperation; carriage of goods or passengers by air, sea, rail or road.*" UNCITRAL, Model Law on International Commercial Arbitration (1985), with amendments as adopted in 2006, General Assembly resolution 61/33 Article I(1), fn. 2.

54. Emmanuel Gaillard and John Savage eds., *Fouchard, Gaillard and Goldman on International Commercial Arbitration*, p. 140 (Kluwer Law International, 1999); Stefan Kröll, *The European Convention on International Commercial Arbitration: The Tale of a Sleeping Beauty*, in Austrian Yearbook on International Arbitration, 4, p. 5 (Klausegger and others eds., Manz, 2013); Nikolaus Pitkowitz, *Is There Still a Scope of Application of the European Convention on International Commercial Arbitration?*, in Austrian Yearbook on International Arbitration, 93–108, p. 105 (Klausegger and others eds., Manz, 2013).
55. Stefan Kröll, *The European Convention on International Commercial Arbitration: The Tale of a Sleeping Beauty*, in Austrian Yearbook on International Arbitration, 4, p. 5 (Klausegger and others eds., Manz, 2013).

33. In practice, courts and tribunals have endorsed the above view by applying the Convention in a wide variety of cases, including those relating to joint ventures and shareholder disputes.[56]

34. The Court of Appeal of Lyon, in *France-Embryon v. Renato Argonautathe*, interpreted the terms "international trade" broadly. It held that it applies to "*all cross-border economic exchanges and does not, in any case, refer to the national definition, which is strict and technical, of commercial act or trader (commerçant). Any international arbitration between enterprises regarding an economic dispute should be considered as 'commercial'.*"[57]

35. In *Benteler v. Belgium*[58] the parties concluded a joint venture agreement, which contained an arbitration clause. When a dispute arose between the parties, Benteler commenced arbitration proceedings. Belgium, *inter alia*, objected that the matter was not commercial within the meaning of Belgian domestic law and, thus, was not governed by the ECICA. The ad hoc arbitral tribunal held that the contract, which could broadly be characterized as a joint venture agreement, was indisputably within the meaning of "international trade":

> (...) this contract presents various aspects characterised by the movement of goods, services or money across frontiers: transfers of funds between Benteler and ABC, participation by Benteler in the capital of ABC, the relinquishment of shares to Benteler by the State, the making available to the Belgian company ABC of the commercial and technical know-how of German companies, etc. Taken as whole, the protocol unquestionably invokes international commercial interests in the sense of Art. I, para 1(a) of the Geneva Convention.[59]

36. Even a lease contract of office premises granted in France to an international organization has been held to fall within the scope of application of the Convention.[60]

37. Finally, to fulfill this objective criterion, the parties to the dispute are not required to be considered as commercial persons or merchants under their country's domestic law systems.[61]

---

56. Nikolaus Pitkowitz, *Is There Still a Scope of Application of the European Convention on International Commercial Arbitration?*, in Austrian Yearbook on International Arbitration, 93–108, p. 105 (Klausegger and others eds., Manz, 2013); *see also UNI-KOD sarl v. Ouralkali*, Court of Appeal (*Cour d' Appel*), 31 May 2001, in Vol. XXVI, Yearbook Commercial Arbitration, pp. 1136–1140 (Albert Jan van den Berg ed., 2001).
57. *France-Embryon v. Renato Argonauta*, Court of Appeal of Lyon (*Cour d'Appel*), 4 July 1991 in Vol. XIX, Yearbook Commercial Arbitration, pp. 859–862 (Albert Jan van den Berg ed., 1994).
58. *Dipl. Ing. Erick Benteler KG, Helmut Benteler KG v. Belgian State, S.A. ABC*, Interim Award, 18 November 1983 in Vol. X, Yearbook Commercial Arbitration, pp. 37–38 (Pieter Sanders ed., 1985).
59. *Dipl. Ing. Erick Benteler KG, Helmut Benteler KG v. Belgian State, S.A. ABC*, Interim Award, 18 November 1983 in Vol. X, Yearbook Commercial Arbitration, pp. 37–38 (Pieter Sanders ed., 1985) (Unofficial translation from Kluwer Arbitration Law, original in French).
60. *International organization A v. Company B*, ICC Award No. 2091, 14 May 1972, 1975 Rev. Arb. 252.
61. *France-Embryon v. Renato Argonauta*, Court of Appeal of Lyon (*Cour d'Appel*), 4 July 1991, in Vol. XIX, Yearbook Commercial Arbitration, pp. 859–862 (Albert Jan van den Berg ed., 1994);

[C] Basis of Consent for Arbitration

[1] Types of Arbitration Proceedings

38. Article I(2) of the ECICA defines the term "arbitration" as "*not only settlement by arbitrators appointed for each case (*ad hoc *arbitration) but also by permanent arbitral institutions.*" This definition makes clear that this term covers both: ad hoc and institutional arbitration proceedings. Article IV(1) contains the procedure to be followed, depending on whether the parties chose to submit their disputes to an ad hoc procedure or to a permanent institution.

39. On the one hand, where the parties agreed to submit their disputes to an ad hoc arbitration procedure, such parties are free to lay down the procedure to be followed. If the arbitration agreement does not contain an indication of the procedural rules, Article IV(3) provides some rudimentary provisions.

40. On the other hand, if the parties agreed to submit their disputes to a permanent institution, the arbitration proceedings will be subject to the arbitration rules of such an institution.[62] If the parties fail to determine the institution and also fail to agree on a solution, Article IV(3) contemplates the steps to be taken in order to remedy this default.

41. One of the most important features of the ECICA is that Article IV contains a mechanism to remedy the following scenarios: (i) where the parties agree to submit their disputes to an ad hoc arbitration but fail to indicate the procedural rules to be followed; (ii) where the parties agreed to submit their disputes to a permanent institution but fail to determine the institution; and (iii) where the arbitration agreement fails to indicate the type of arbitration to be followed.

42. Therefore, the broad definition of "arbitration" helps to rectify the vagueness or ineffectiveness of an arbitration clause when one of the abovementioned scenarios is present.

[2] Types of Arbitration Agreements

43. Article I(2)(a) of the ECICA defines the term "arbitration agreement" as "*either an arbitral clause in a contract or an arbitration agreement being signed by the parties.*" Pursuant to the wording of this definition, two types of arbitration agreements can be identified: (i) an arbitration clause contained in a contract which generally deals with the settlement of future disputes; or (ii) a separate arbitration agreement concluded for the settlement of existing disputes or future disputes. Article I(2)(a) treats both kinds of agreements to arbitrate equally.

---

see also, Dominique Hascher, *European Convention on International Commercial Arbitration of 1961: Commentary*, in Vol. XXXVI, Yearbook Commercial Arbitration, 509, p. 511 (Albert Jan van den Berg ed., Kluwer Law International, 2011).

62. Article IV of the ECICA.

44. The most common type is an arbitration clause contained in a contract. It is usually a short clause, in most cases, a model clause, because it is agreed between the parties, at an early stage of the relationship, when no disputes have arisen and the particularities of the potential disputes are unknown.[63]

45. An agreement to arbitrate can be either for present or future disputes.[64] The latter is also known as "arbitration by reference" and has characteristics similar to an arbitration clause contained in a contract. In contrast, the former is also known as a "submission agreement" and deals with disputes that have already come up between the parties.[65] One feature of the submission agreement is that it can be tailored in light of the circumstances of the particular case.

46. The ECICA also contemplates the possibility that the arbitration agreement is contained in an "*exchange of letters, telegrams, or in a communication by teleprinter.*" Some of the issues regarding the formal requirements, which shall be present in all the aforementioned types of arbitration agreements, will be discussed in detail in the section below.

[3] Formal Requirements

47. As indicated above, Article I(2)(a) provides the types of arbitration agreements, covered by the Convention. Additionally, it sets down the formal requirements which must be met for the courts and tribunals to recognize the validity of the arbitration agreements under the ECICA. The reason the formal requirements are relevant is to make sure the parties actually consented to arbitration.[66] The ECICA provides the written form as the primary form [a]; nonetheless, it also provides an alternative form, in cases where both Contracting States demand less stringent requirements [b].

[a] Written Form Requirement

48. The definition provided in Article I(2)(a) is similar to the definition contained in Article II(2) of the NYC, which in the relevant part reads as follows: "*the term 'agreement in writing' shall include an arbitral clause in a contract or an arbitration agreement signed by the parties or contained in an exchange of letters or telegrams.*"[67] In addition to the means expressly provided in Article II(2) of the NYC, the ECICA recognizes communications by teleprinter.

49. To avoid the obsolescence of these provisions, the interpretation of the written form should be dynamic and in line with modern means of communication, which

63. Nigel Blackaby et al., *Redfern and Hunter on International Arbitration*, p. 72, mn 2.03 (6th ed., 2015).
64. *Ibid.*
65. *Ibid.*
66. Julian D. M. Lew, Loukas A. Mistelis and Stefan M. Kröll, *Comparative International Commercial Arbitration*, p. 130, mn 7-5 (Kluwer Law International, 2003).
67. New York Convention (NYC), Article II(2).

were unknown when the convention was drafted.[68] Article 7(2) option 1 of the UNCITRAL Model Law suggests a contemporary definition of the written form by acknowledging the existence of modern means of communication which can be easily adapted to future developments.[69]

50. Commentators have noted that the parties who include an arbitration clause in a contract do not need to sign the arbitration clause as their signature in the contract will suffice.[70] The Italian Supreme Court explained: "*a separate signature for the arbitral clause would be a too heavy burden.*"[71] In contrast, separate agreements shall, as a general rule, be signed by the parties.[72]

51. A conflict may arise if the main contract only makes a generic reference to a certain document (e.g., general conditions of a party or a charter party) which contains an arbitration clause but not expressly to the latter. In *Tradax Export v. Amoco Iranian Oil Company*, the Swiss Federal Tribunal took a liberal approach, holding that a general reference to a separate document containing an arbitration clause was sufficient to comply with the formal requirements under the NYC[73] and, by analogy, with the ones under the ECICA.

52. Another conflict may arise in cases in which only one party signed the document referring to the arbitration agreement (e.g., an arbitration clause in a sales confirmation or a purchase order). It is widely accepted, if the other party's consent can be found in a different document, the signature of such a party will not be necessary since agreements contained in an exchange of letters, telegrams or communications by teleprinter do not need to be signed by the parties.[74] Unlike the ECICA, Article 7 option I of the UNCITRAL Model Law provides the following reference on this point: "*[t]he reference in a contract to any document containing an arbitration clause constitutes an*

68. Julian D. M. Lew, Loukas A. Mistelis and Stefan M. Kröll, *Comparative International Commercial Arbitration*, p. 132, mn 7-10 (Kluwer Law International, 2003); Dominique Hascher, *European Convention on International Commercial Arbitration of 1961: Commentary*, in Vol. XXXVI, Yearbook Commercial Arbitration, 509, p. 514 (Albert Jan van den Berg ed., Kluwer Law International, 2011).
69. Julian D. M. Lew, Loukas A. Mistelis and Stefan M. Kröll, *Comparative International Commercial Arbitration*, p. 134, mn 7-14 (Kluwer Law International, 2003).
70. Nikolaus Pitkowitz, *Is There Still a Scope of Application of the European Convention on International Commercial Arbitration?*, in Austrian Yearbook on International Arbitration, 93–108, p. 106 (Klausegger and others eds., Manz, 2013).
71. *Societa Atlas General Timbers S.p.a. v. Agenzia Concordia Line, S.p.a.*, Supreme Court Plenary Session (*Corte di Cassazione Sezioni Unite*), 18 May 1978, in Vol. V, Yearbook Commercial Arbitration 1980, pp. 267–268 (Pieter Sanders ed., Kluwer Law International, 1980).
72. Nikolaus Pitkowitz, *Is There Still a Scope of Application of the European Convention on International Commercial Arbitration?*, in Austrian Yearbook on International Arbitration, 93–108, p. 106 (Klausegger and others eds., Manz, 2013).
73. *Tradax Export SA (Panama) v. Amoco Iran Oil Company*, Federal Tribunal (Tribunal Fédéral), 7 February 1984, Vol. XI, Yearbook Commercial Arbitration (1986).
74. Julian D. M. Lew, Loukas A. Mistelis and Stefan M. Kröll, *Comparative International Commercial Arbitration*, p. 139, mn 7-28 (Kluwer Law International, 2003); Nikolaus Pitkowitz, *Is There Still a Scope of Application of the European Convention on International Commercial Arbitration?*, in Austrian Yearbook on International Arbitration, 93–108, p. 106 (Klausegger and others eds., Manz, 2013); *see also SA X v. Mr. Y*, Supreme Court (*Tribunal Supremo*), 30 January 1986, in Vol. XIII, Yearbook Commercial Arbitration, p. 512 (Albert Jan van den Berg ed., 1998).

arbitration agreement in writing, provided that the reference is such as to make that clause part of the contract."[75] This reference, in a contemporary document, such as the UNCITRAL Model Law, suggests that, in practice, this situation has been an often conflicting issue in arbitration proceedings.

53. In some cases, courts have considered the absence of one party's signature in the main contract containing the arbitration clause or in other documents (e.g., broker's notes or sales confirmation) referring to the arbitration clause does not comply with the written form requirement; therefore, the agreements are not covered by the ECICA.

54. In *X (Hungary) v. Y (Germany)*, the parties concluded a contract for the sale of sunflower seeds, which referred to the Standard Conditions of the German Grain Trade. The Hungarian seller did not sign the contract. When the seller failed to supply the sunflower seeds, the German buyer commenced arbitration proceedings. The arbitral tribunal found that it did not have jurisdiction over the dispute for lack of a valid arbitration clause because the seller had not signed the contract.[76]

55. In *X (Italy) v. Y (Germany)*, an Italian broker firm drew up two contracts for the delivery of prunes, which referred to the General Conditions of the Hamburg Commodity Exchange, which contained an arbitration clause. The German counterpart signed the contract-duplicates and returned them to the Italian brokers' firm. The Court of Appeal of Hamburg analyzed whether a valid arbitration agreement had been concluded between the parties. The Court considered that the formal requirements of Article I(2)(a) had not been met because the General Conditions containing the arbitration clause only appeared in the broker's note, which had been signed exclusively by the German buyer.[77]

56. In *Epis-Centre v. Aguicersa*, the parties concluded a sales transaction upon the issuance of two notes by a broker and two subsequent sales confirmations issued by Epis-Centre. The broker's notes and the sales confirmations referred to a standard contract which contained an arbitration clause. Aguicersa never signed these documents. When the dispute arose between the parties, Epis-Centre commenced arbitration proceedings. The award was issued in favor of Epis-Centre and the latter sought enforcement in Spain. The Spanish Supreme Court denied enforcement, holding that the arbitration agreement did not comply with the formal written requirement under the NYC and, by analogy, with the one under the ECICA, as the documents were never been signed by one of the parties.[78]

75. UNCITRAL, Model Law on International Commercial Arbitration (1985), with amendments as adopted in 2006, General Assembly resolution 61/33, Article 7(6), option 1.
76. *X (Hungary) v. Y (Germany)*, Waren-Verein der Hamburger Börse, Award, 7 December 1995.
77. *Italian company v. German (F.R.) firm*, Court of Appeal of Hamburg (*Oberlandesgericht*), 22 September 1980, in Vol. V, Yearbook Commercial Arbitration, pp. 262–263 (Pieter Sanders ed., 1980).
78. *Unión de Cooperativas Agrícolas Epis-Centre v. Aguicersa, SL*, Supreme Court (*Tribunal Supremo*), 1678/199, 7 July 1998, in Vol. XXVII, Yearbook Commercial Arbitration, pp. 546–550 (Albert Jan van den Berg ed., 2002).

57. Courts have also taken into consideration the intention of the parties, to conclude an arbitration agreement was valid, notwithstanding the fact that one parties' signature was lacking. In *Thyssen v. Barna*, the parties exchanged certain telexes for a commercial transaction referring to a former charter party, which contained an arbitration clause, concluded between them. Thyssen made changes to the terms of the former charter party but never expressed its intention to modify the arbitration clause. Barna agreed with the changes made by Thyssen and replied: "*Thank you for your telex no. 660; the charterers agree, thus we have a contract with no open issues.*"[79] Based on these telexes, the Spanish Supreme Court held:

> These communications clearly show the common intention of the parties to submit disputes which could arise under their charter party to arbitration. Among their [contractual] conditions is an arbitral clause such as the arbitral clause in the charter party previously agreed between them, which was the basis on which the charter party at issue was negotiated (...) Hence, we must conclude that Thyssen has met the requirement of Art. IV together with Art. II and with Art. 1(2) (a) of the [ECICA].[80]

[b] Alternative Form Requirement

58. As an alternative form, the last part of Article I(2)(a) of the ECICA provides for the possibility of applying a less stringent standard in certain cases. This possibility resembles Article VII(1) of the NYC. Article VII(1) expressly refers to the application of the "*more-favourable-right provision*" only regarding the enforcement stage of the award. Nevertheless, it has been suggested that it should also be applicable to arbitration agreements.[81]

59. The last part of Article I(2)(a) of the ECICA provides that "*in relations between States whose laws do not require that an arbitration agreement be made in writing, any arbitration agreement concluded in the form authorized by these laws*" is valid also under the Convention. The English Arbitration Act of 1996 to name one example recognizes the validity of oral agreements if they are "*recorded by one of the parties, or by a third party with the authority of the parties to the agreement.*"[82]

60. The Highest Regional Court of Bavaria, when applying this provision emphasized the requirement that the legal orders of both affected States must provide for a more lenient standard:

> Art. I(2)(a) of this Convention allows for oral arbitration agreements only when both legal systems involved provide for this possibility. It is not sufficient that only

79. *Thyssen Haniel Logistic International GmbH v. Barna Consignataria SL*, Supreme Court (*Tribunal Supremo*), 14 July 1998, in Vol. XXVI, Yearbook Commercial Arbitration, pp. 851-853 (Albert Jan van den Berg ed., 2001).
80. *Ibid.*
81. Albert Jan van den Berg, *The New York Arbitration Convention of 1958*, p. 87 (Kluwer Law and Taxation, 1981).
82. English Arbitration Act 1996, England, 17 June 1996 (The Stationery Office Limited), Section 5, para. 4.

the law of one party or the [applicable] rules of arbitration have less stringent formal requirements.[83]

61. However, there is also case law to the contrary. Some domestic courts have only given consideration to the domestic law system of one of the parties' Contracting State, in order to apply a less stringent standard.[84]

62. Although it holds true that most domestic law systems require an arbitration agreement in writing,[85] the alternative form requirement is rarely applicable, in light of the amended text of Article 7(2), option 1 of the UNCITRAL Model Law.[86] It could be expected, that in the future, a larger number of domestic law systems will allow other forms of arbitration agreements, such as oral and tacit agreements.

63. Finally, while the last part of Article I(2)(a) of the ECICA, on the one hand, facilitates the enforcement of arbitration agreements, on the other hand, it somewhat contradicts the ECICA's purpose to promote the establishment of a uniform and delocalized legal regime, governing international commercial arbitration.

II ASPECTS NOT COVERED BY THE PROVISION

[A] Retroactivity

64. Retroactive application is relevant when applying the Convention. According to Article 8 of the VCLT, international conventions do not have a retroactive effect on the contractual relations of the parties "*unless a different intention appears from the treaty or is otherwise established.*"[87] Article 6 of the Geneva Convention of 1927 provides: "*The present Convention applies only to arbitral awards made after the coming-into-force of the Protocol on Arbitration Clauses [...].*"[88] Unlike the Geneva Convention of 1927, the ECICA and the NYC are noncommittal on the retroactive application of their provisions.

83. *Exporter (Yugoslavia) v. Importer (Germany)*, Higher Court of Appeal of Bavaria (*Bayerisches Oberstes Landesgericht*), 4Z Sch 16/02, 12 December 2002, in Vol. XXIX, Yearbook Commercial Arbitration, pp. 761–766 (Albert Jan van den Berg ed., 2004). (Unofficial translation from Kluwer Arbitration Law, original in German).
84. *Austrian seller v. German (F.R.) buyer*, Federal Supreme Court (*Bundesgerichtshof*), 25 May 1970 in Vol. II, Yearbook Commercial Arbitration, p. 236 (Pieter Sanders ed., 1977); *Seller v. Buyer*, Court of Appeal of Cologne (*Oberlandesgericht*), 16 December 1992, in Vol. XXI, Yearbook Commercial Arbitration, pp. 535–541 (Albert Jan van den Berg ed., 1996).
85. Julian D. M. Lew, Loukas A. Mistelis and Stefan M. Kröll, *Comparative International Commercial Arbitration*, p. 131, mn 7-6 (Kluwer Law International 2003).
86. Article 7(3), option I, defines arbitration agreement as follows "*[a]n arbitration agreement is in writing if its content is recorded in any or not form, whether the arbitration agreement or contract has been* ***concluded orally, by conduct, or by other means.***" (emphasis added) UNCITRAL, Model Law on International Commercial Arbitration (1985), with amendments as adopted in 2006, General Assembly resolution 61/33 Article 7.
87. VCLT, Article 28.
88. Geneva Convention of 1927, Article 6.

65. As for the NYC, its drafting history reveals disagreements regarding the possibility of retroactive application. Additionally, in practice, courts and tribunals have reached widely diverging conclusions on the question of retroactive application.[89] In *Sonatrach v. Ford*, the Court of Cassation of Belgium held that in the absence of a provision, which allows for the retroactive application of the NYC, the retroactive application of its provisions was not possible.[90] In contrast, other courts have concluded that, due to the procedural nature of the NYC's provisions, retroactive application is possible.[91]

66. These decisions could be applied by analogy to the ECICA, as both instruments lack an express provision on the matter and contain procedural rules. There are not a large number of cases which have dealt with retroactive application under the ECICA. However, in a case before the Spanish Supreme Court, the court *"declared that [the ECICA] applied to awards made before the date of adherence by a Contracting State."*[92]

[B] Seat of Arbitration in a Non-"Contracting State"

67. The seat of arbitration is not a factor for the application of the Convention.[93] Therefore, the Convention is applicable regardless of the fact that the arbitral proceedings took place in a non-Contracting State.[94] As provided by the Italian Supreme Court in *Damiano v. Tropfer*, for the application of the ECICA, it is irrelevant if the seat of the arbitration proceedings was not in a Contracting State:

> The [ECICA] is different because it departs from the old State-minded logic. This Convention makes use of the experience of mercantile arbitration and, in using a modern approach, denies the principle of a double connection of the arbitration, i.e., with the State a quo [i.e., where the arbitration takes or took place] and the State where recognition is sought. It does not even require a presupposition of the

89. Albert Jan van den Berg, *The New York Arbitration Convention of 1958*, p. 78 (Kluwer Law and Taxation, 1981).
90. *Société Nationale pour la Recherche, le Transport et la Commercialisation des Hydrocarbures (Sonatrach) v. Ford, Bacon and Davis Inc.*, Court of First Instance of Brussels (*Tribunal de Premiére Instance*), 6 December 1988, in Vol. XV, Yearbook Commercial Arbitration, pp. 370–377 (Albert Jan van den Berg ed., Kluwer Law International, 1990).
91. *Miserocchi v. Paolo Agnesi*, Supreme Court (*Corte di Cassazione*), 25 January 1977; *Total v. Achille Lauro*, cited in Albert Jan van den Berg, *The New York Arbitration Convention of 1958*, p. 79 (Kluwer Law and Taxation, 1981).
92. Dominique Hascher, *European Convention on International Commercial Arbitration of 1961: Commentary*, in Vol. XXXVI, Yearbook Commercial Arbitration, 509, p. 513 (Albert Jan van den Berg ed., Kluwer Law International 2011), citing Revista de la Corte Española de Arbitraje, p. 207 (1985).
93. Emmanuel Gaillard and John Savage eds., *Fouchard, Gaillard and Goldman on International Commercial Arbitration*, p. 141 (Kluwer Law International, 1999).
94. Dominique Hascher, *European Convention on International Commercial Arbitration of 1961: Commentary*, in Vol. XXXVI, Yearbook Commercial Arbitration, 509, p. 511 (Albert Jan van den Berg ed., 2011).

arbitral decision's effectiveness in the State where the arbitration took place or the law of which has been chosen.[95]

68. Nevertheless, it is important to analyze the effects of the Convention, on domestic courts and tribunals, acting in a non-Contracting State. As noted by Dominique Hascher, "*the assertion that the Convention is operative when arbitration proceedings take place in a non-Contracting State fails to take into account the potential impact of the law of the seat.*"[96] Accordingly, Hascher suggests it would be more prudent to conclude: "*the Convention's applicability is not guaranteed when the seat of the arbitration is situated in a non-Contracting State.*"[97]

69. In the case of domestic courts of a non-Contracting State, the provisions of the ECICA are not part of its legal system, therefore, they are not bound to apply them. For instance, the provision contained in Article VI of the ECICA, entitled "*Jurisdiction of Courts of Law,*" directed towards domestic courts, will not have a mandatory effect on them. Furthermore, if a provision of the law of the seat in a non-Contracting State, contradicts a provision of the ECICA, it may be assumed that domestic courts will give preference to the law of the seat.

70. For arbitrators, commonly used arbitration rules impose a duty on them to make every effort to issue an enforceable award.[98] A breach of the provisions of the ECICA may very likely render the award nonenforceable, in a Contracting State, and the arbitrators' duty will not be satisfied. Thus, it may follow that, if the subjective and objective conditions, for the application of the ECICA, are met arbitrators acting in a non-Contracting State will follow the ECICA's provisions.

71. Anyways, domestic courts and tribunals acting in a non-Contracting State may apply the provisions of the ECICA as "soft law" or as part of *lex mercatoria*, because "*they show an international trend on commercial arbitration.*"[99]

[C] Multiparty Proceedings

72. The ECICA does not contain a provision which specifically addresses multiparty proceedings, as most arbitration rules now do.[100] When all parties are located in a Contracting State, the Convention is applicable to the arbitration proceedings.

95. *Fratelli Damiano s.n.c. v. August Tropfer & Co.*, Supreme Court Plenary Session (*Corte di Cassazione Sezioni Unite*), 722, 8 February 1982, in Vol. IX, Yearbook Commercial Arbitration, pp. 418–420 (Pieter Sanders ed., 1984). (Unofficial translation from Kluwer Arbitration Law, original in Italian.)
96. Dominique Hascher, *European Convention on International Commercial Arbitration of 1961: Commentary*, in Vol. XXXVI, Yearbook Commercial Arbitration, 509, p. 511 (Albert Jan van den Berg ed., Kluwer Law International 2011).
97. Dominique Hascher, *European Convention on International Commercial Arbitration of 1961: Commentary*, in Vol. XXXVI, Yearbook Commercial Arbitration, 509, pp. 511–512 (Albert Jan van den Berg ed., Kluwer Law International 2011).
98. ICC Rules, Article 41; LCIA Rules, Article 32.2.
99. *Yugoslav Company, Buyer v. PDR Korea Company, Seller*, Award, 17 March 1982, in Vol. VIII, Yearbook Commercial Arbitration, pp. 128–132 (Pieter Sanders ed., 1983).
100. LCIA Rules, Article 8; ICC Rules, Articles 7–10.

However, in a multiparty proceeding, in which not all the parties involved are located in a Contracting State, it is questionable whether the Convention is only applicable vis-à-vis with the parties located in a Contracting State or, not applicable at all.

73. From the wording of Article I, it can be argued that for the ECICA to apply, all parties shall be located in a Contracting State.[101] In light of a literal interpretation of the Article, commentators have concluded, for a multiparty proceeding, in which at least one party is located in a non-Contracting State, that the ECICA shall not apply.[102] Courts have also rejected the application of the ECICA in cases where one of the parties involved is located in a non-Contracting State.[103]

74. However, there is case law to the contrary also on this point, which supports the application of the Convention even in cases where not all the parties involved were located in a Contracting State, at the time when the arbitration agreement was concluded.[104]

III RELATIONSHIP WITH OTHER LEGAL INSTRUMENTS

[A] The NYC and the ECICA

75. When a case falls within the scope of application of the ECICA and the NYC, the relationship between the instruments could be conceived as conflicting treaties [1], or as complementary instruments [2].

[1] Conflict of Treaties

76. If both instruments were to apply concurrently, one way of analyzing the overlapping provisions is by the terms of general rules of the conflict of treaties. The traditional principles are: *lex posterior derogat priori*, *lex specialis derogat generali*, and *la règle d'efficacité maximale*. The last mentioned principle is the most recent, hence, why it is not contemplated in the VCLT.[105]

---

101. Nikolaus Pitkowitz, *Is There Still a Scope of Application of the European Convention on International Commercial Arbitration?*, in Austrian Yearbook on International Arbitration, 93–108, p. 100 (Klausegger and others eds., Manz, 2013).
102. Florian Haugeneder, *The New Austrian Arbitration Act and the European Convention on International Commercial Arbitration*, 23(4) ARBITRATION INTERNATIONAL 646, p. 646 (2007); Nikolaus Pitkowitz, *Is There Still a Scope of Application of the European Convention on International Commercial Arbitration?*, in Austrian Yearbook on International Arbitration, 93–108, p. 100 (Klausegger and others eds., Manz, 2013).
103. *Pabalk Ticaret Ltd. Sirketi (Turkey) v. Norsolor SA (France)*, Supreme Court (*Cour de Cassation*), 9 October 1984 and Court of Appeal (*Cour d'Appel*), 19 November 1982, in Vol. XI, Yearbook Commercial Arbitration, pp. 484–491 (Albert Jan van den Berg ed., 1986); *Dutch seller v. German (F.R.) buyer*, Court of Appeal of Düsseldorf (*Oberlandesgericht*), 8 November 1971, in Vol. II, Yearbook Commercial Arbitration, pp. 237–238 (Pieter Sanders ed., 1977).
104. *See* cases in Section I A 4 above.
105. Albert Jan van den Berg, *The New York Arbitration Convention of 1958*, p. 91 (Kluwer Law and Taxation, 1981).

77. In particular, the principle of *lex posterior* prescribes that the provisions of a later treaty should prevail over those of an earlier treaty, concerning the same subject matter.[106] The principle of *lex posterior* is also relevant for treaty interpretation. According to Article 31(3)(a) of the VCLT, subsequent agreements on the same subject matter, which were concluded by the parties thereto, shall be taken into account for the interpretation of a treaty.[107]

78. In a few cases, courts have chosen to apply the ECICA over the NYC based on the principle of *lex posterior*. In *X (Austria) v. Y (Germany)*, the parties allegedly concluded an arbitration agreement in a sales confirmation, sent by the seller, which the buyer did not object. When analyzing the formal requirements of the arbitration agreement, the German Supreme Court decided to apply the last part of Article I(2)(a) of the ECICA, over Article II of the NYC, as: "*[t]his provision of the [ECICA], being of younger date than the [New York Convention], prevails.*"[108]

79. However, the VCLT also provides: "*when a treaty specifies that it is subject to, or that it is not to be considered as incompatible with, an earlier or later treaty, the provisions of that other treaty prevail.*"[109] The drafters of the ECICA were careful not to impair the general effectiveness of the NYC. Article X(7)[110] reflects this intention, as it provides "*[t]he provisions of the present Convention shall not affect the validity of multilateral or bilateral agreements concerning arbitration entered into by Contracting States.*" Therefore, the drafters intended both instruments to be complementarily and simultaneously applicable, not exclusively. Nonetheless, as will be discussed below, a simultaneous application may not be possible when certain provisions of both instruments overlap.

[2] Complementary Instruments

80. Although the subject matter of both instruments is international arbitration, generally the scope of the ECICA varies from the scope of the NYC. The NYC applies to the enforcement of the arbitration agreement and award. The ECICA covers a broader range of organizational aspects of arbitration proceedings. Most of the Conventions' provisions do not overlap; they complement each other and are "*integrally related.*"[111]

106. Ian Brownlie, *Principles of Public International Law*, p. 600 (6th ed., Oxford University Press, 2003).
107. VCLT, Article 31(3)(a).
108. *Austrian seller v. German (F.R.) buyer*, Federal Supreme Court (*Bundesgerichtshof*), 25 May 1970 in Vol. II, Yearbook Commercial Arbitration, p. 236 (Pieter Sanders ed., 1977).
109. VCLT, Article 30.
110. Nikolaus Pitkowitz, *Is There Still a Scope of Application of the European Convention on International Commercial Arbitration?*, in Austrian Yearbook on International Arbitration, 93–108, pp. 94–95 (Klausegger and others eds., Manz, 2013).
111. *Tradax v. Carapelli*, Court of Appeal of Florence (*Corte di Appello*), 22 October 1976, in Vol. III, Yearbook Commercial Arbitration, pp. 279–280 (Pieter Sanders ed., 1978).

81. As noted by van den Berg, "*[a]n indication of the complementary nature of the European Convention can be found already in its preamble which refers, in so many words, to the New York Convention.*"[112]

82. An additional example may be found in Article VI of the ECICA, which provides procedural actions regarding an arbitration agreement prior to the enforcement stage (e.g., conflict rules for determining the validity of an agreement, estoppel for raising a defense on the existence of an agreement)[113] whereas Article II(3) of the NYC, contains the provisions for the enforcement stage. Therefore, Article VI of the ECICA "*can be considered as an elaboration of Article II(3) of the [New York Convention] concerning the action for the enforcement of the arbitration agreement by a court.*"[114]

83. In Article IX, the ECICA refers indirectly to the enforcement of arbitration agreements and awards. Notably, the Article is an exception to the simultaneous applicability of both instruments. Article IX of the ECICA limits the scope of the grounds for setting aside an arbitral award, contained in Article V(1)(e) of the NYC.[115] Article IX does not include setting aside an award for violations of a Contracting State's public order, in the list for refusing enforcement or recognition of an award in another Contracting State. In such circumstances, the principle of *lex posterior* may apply, but only with respect to this provision.

84. Similarly, the written form requirements for the arbitration agreement are slightly different in both instruments. The ECICA covers arbitration agreements contained in an exchange of communications by teleprinter, between the parties; while the NYC does not. The difference could be overcome, according to the principle of *la règle d'efficacité maximale*, meaning:

> [I]f an award [or agreement] is unenforceable under one treaty which could be applied, but enforceable under another which could also be applied, the other treaty will be applicable, irrespective of whether it is an earlier or later treaty, an irrespective of whether it is more general or specific.[116]

85. Therefore, it may be submitted that the principle is the *rationale* behind the MFR-provision in Article VII of the NYC, the last part of Article I(2)(a), and Article X(7) of the ECICA.

---

112. Albert Jan van den Berg, *The New York Arbitration Convention of 1958*, p. 95 (Kluwer Law and Taxation, 1981).
113. *Ibid.*
114. *Ibid.*
115. Nikolaus Pitkowitz, *Is There Still a Scope of Application of the European Convention on International Commercial Arbitration?*, in Austrian Yearbook on International Arbitration, 93–108, p. 95 (Klausegger and others eds., Manz, 2013).
116. Albert Jan van den Berg, *The New York Arbitration Convention of 1958*, pp. 90–91 (Kluwer Law and Taxation, 1981).

[B] Domestic Law Systems and the ECICA

86. Domestic law systems usually have provisions regarding arbitration proceedings and the proceedings' relationship with domestic courts. Some of these provisions may conflict with provisions of the ECICA. A common conflict may arise, which relates to the formal requirements of an arbitration agreement. The conflict can be analyzed in accordance with the last part of Article I(2)(a) of the ECICA [1]. Other conflicts may result in relation to different stages of the arbitration proceedings. The conflicts can be analyzed according to the position of treaties in a domestic legal system, as well as certain principles of the conflict of laws [2].

[1] Conflict on the Formal Requirements of the Arbitration Agreement

87. Pursuant to the last part of Article I(2)(a), if a conflict arises between a domestic law provision and the ECICA, the latter will not supersede the former on the formal requirements of the arbitration agreement, if the domestic law requires less stringent requirements. This scenario is only possible, subject to the condition that all the Contracting States involved allow the said less stringent requirements. If the condition is not met and the arbitration agreement does not comply with the formal requirements of the ECICA, it does not automatically deem the arbitration agreement invalid; rather, the arbitration agreement will merely not be covered by the ECICA.

88. In cases where the formal requirements of the pertinent domestic law system are more stringent than those of the ECICA, then the conflict can be analyzed according to the position of international treaties in such a domestic law system or on the basis of the conflict of laws principles. This scenario is unlikely, as most domestic legal systems have adopted the UNCITRAL Model Law, which, pursuant to Article 7 option 1 therein, provides a flexible provision on the formal requirements of arbitration agreements.

[2] Other Conflicting Provisions

89. From an international perspective, as a general principle of international law, a State "*may not invoke the provisions of its internal law as justification for its failure to perform a treaty.*"[117] Pursuant to customary law, "*there is a general duty to bring internal law into conformity with obligations under international law.*"[118] However, a failure to bring about such conformity does not amount, in itself, to a breach of a treaty. Therefore, inconsistencies between the provisions of a treaty and those of domestic law may exist. In such situations, domestic courts will have to address the inconsistencies from a national perspective.

---

117. VCLT, Article 27.
118. Ian Brownlie, *Principles of Public International Law*, p. 35 (6th ed., Oxford University Press, 2003).

90. From a national perspective, once an international treaty is incorporated in a domestic law system, the prevalence of the treaty over a particular domestic law provision will depend on the position of the treaty within the hierarchy of such a domestic legal system.[119] When an inconsistency arises, if the international treaty is in a higher position than the domestic law provision, the provision of the former will prevail over the latter. However, as noted by Dr. Pitkowitz, a domestic law provision in a lower position may temporarily override the provision of a treaty: "*although unconstitutional, courts would still have to apply the later national law until invalidated by the constitutional court.*"[120]

91. In contrast, if the domestic law provision at stake is in a higher position than the international treaty (e.g., a constitutional provision), the domestic law provision will prevail over the treaty provision; but, in such an instance, a possible violation of the State's international obligations will have to be evaluated from an international perspective.

92. If the treaty and the relevant domestic law provision are in the same position, the inconsistency could be overcome by means of principles of conflict of laws. For instance, according to the principle *lex posterior*, when a domestic law provision is enacted, following the incorporation of an international treaty, the domestic law provision shall prevail.

93. Presently, a large number of domestic legal systems have adopted the UNCITRAL Model Law, which, in Article I(1), provides that the application of a domestic law on arbitration, in implementing the UNCITRAL Model Law, shall be subject to any agreement in force between the implementing State and any other State.[121] Therefore, the provisions of the ECICA are likely to prevail in most circumstances.

---

119. Nikolaus Pitkowitz, *Is There Still a Scope of Application of the European Convention on International Commercial Arbitration?*, in Austrian Yearbook on International Arbitration, 93–108, p. 98 (Klausegger and others eds., Manz, 2013).
120. *Ibid.*
121. UNCITRAL, Model Law on International Commercial Arbitration (1985), with amendments as adopted in 2006, General Assembly resolution 61/33 Article I(1).

ARTICLE II

Right of Legal Persons of Public Law to Resort to Arbitration

Lisa Beisteiner

INTRODUCTION

> *Article II—Right of Legal Persons of Public Law to Resort to Arbitration*
> 1. *In the cases referred to in Article 1, paragraph 1, of this Convention, legal persons considered by the law which is applicable to them as "legal persons of public law" have the right to conclude valid arbitration agreements.*
> 2. *On signing, ratifying or acceding to this Convention any State shall be entitled to declare that it limits the above faculty to such conditions as may be stated in its declaration.*

1. Article II of the ECICA explicitly recognizes the subjective arbitrability[1] of "legal persons of public law." The provision supersedes any limitations of the capacity of such persons to conclude arbitration agreements contained in the law governing their status ("the law applicable to them"): State entities may not rely on such restrictions in their national law to invalidate their consent to arbitration.

2. Article II is a substantive rule which is primarily addressed to the parties and the arbitral tribunal. Its historic purpose was to ensure the operability of arbitration agreements concluded by those—mainly public law—entities which at the time dominated trade in Eastern Europe. The scope of application of Article II is confined to international trade as referred to in Article I paragraph 1 of the ECICA. Therefore, public entities cannot derive subjective arbitrability from Article II in a non-trade

1. Emmanuel Gaillard and John Savage eds., *Fouchard, Gaillard and Goldman on International Commercial Arbitration*, p. 313, mn 534 and p. 322, mn 548 (Kluwer Law International, 1999).

context.[2] The same holds true for domestic cases: Public entities that are located within the jurisdiction of one and the same Contracting State cannot invoke Article II to submit to arbitration in a third State, even if the legal relationship between them is of a commercial nature.[3]

3. At the time the ECICA was concluded, public legal entities in a number of jurisdictions were not empowered to conclude arbitration agreements. Therefore, the major achievement of Article II consisted in leveling the playing field in international commercial arbitration within the Contracting States (I). The ECICA does not contain a definition of "legal person of public law," leaving open which entities are covered by its scope (II). In order not to discourage those States from becoming parties to the ECICA which at the time applied domestic restrictions to the right of "legal persons of public law" to conclude arbitration agreements, the drafters incorporated an express possibility of making a reservation in Article II paragraph 2 ECICA (III). Article II does not directly regulate the question of what representation requirements apply to State entities for the conclusion of arbitration agreements, nor the question of whether the conclusion of an arbitration clause constitutes a waiver of immunity from enforcement (IV).

I THE RELEVANCE OF THE PROVISION

4. At the time the ECICA was negotiated and drafted, international trade in Eastern Europe was dominated by the States and their instrumentalities, including State-owned companies.[4] The capacity of "legal persons of public law" to conclude arbitration agreements, i.e., the subjective arbitrability of such public law entities, was at the time subject to widely diverging treatment in the various jurisdictions.[5] Of the different regulatory approaches prevailing within the Contracting States at the time, Razumov identifies at least three categories:

- First, States where, according to the law, jurisprudence, or legal doctrine, the State and other legal entities of public law enjoy great freedom in concluding arbitration agreements.
- Second, States where the conclusion by the State and other legal persons of public law of arbitration agreements is almost completely forbidden.

2. Nikolaus Pitkowitz, *Is There Still a Scope of Application of the European Convention on International Commercial Arbitration?*, in Austrian Yearbook on International Arbitration, 93–108, p. 108 (Klausegger and others eds., Manz, 2013).
3. Dominique Hascher, *European Convention on International Commercial Arbitration of 1961: Commentary*, Vol. XXXVI, Yearbook Commercial Arbitration, 509, p. 516 (Albert Jan van den Berg ed., 2011).
4. Stefan Kröll, *The European Convention on International Commercial Arbitration: The Tale of a Sleeping Beauty*, in Austrian Yearbook on International Arbitration, 4, p. 11 (Klausegger and others eds., Manz, 2013).
5. Rudolf Kaiser, *Das Europäische Übereinkommen über die internationale Handelsschiedsgerichtsbarkeit vom 21. April 1961*, in Zürcher Studien zum Internationalen Recht, pp. 63–66, no. 39 (Fritzsche et al. eds., 1977).

- Third, States where the conclusion of arbitration agreements by public entities is restricted in domestic transactions but is permitted and practiced in international commercial transactions.[6]

5. On top of that, even within these categories the exact legal regimes on subjective arbitrability of public entities varied considerably.[7] Due to these differences and the additional fact that such internal rules were not always easily discernible, private users of arbitration faced considerable uncertainty when concluding arbitration agreements with "legal persons of public law" of another Contracting State.

6. Domestic restrictions on subjective arbitrability of public entities, primarily to secure the supervision of the administrative courts over State entities, were not confined to Eastern European jurisdictions. For instance, at the time the ECICA was concluded, the French domestic legal system contained in Article 2060 of the Civil Code a prohibition of the conclusion of arbitration agreements for States and their public entities:

> One may not enter into arbitration agreements in [...] controversies concerning public bodies and institutions and more generally in all matters in which public policy is concerned.[8]

7. A similar prohibition applied—and in some cases still applies—in other laws influenced by France at the time.[9] For instance, under Belgian law, legal persons of public law were prohibited from concluding arbitration agreements.[10] A provision qualifying the subjective arbitrability of legal persons of public law still persists in the Belgian *Code Judiciaire* today.[11]

6. Konstantin Leonidovich Razumov, *The Law Governing the Capacity to Arbitrate*, in Planning Efficient Arbitration Proceedings: The Law Applicable in International Arbitration, ICCA Congress Series, Vol. 7, pp. 260–267 (Albert Jan van den Berg ed., Kluwer Law International, 1996).
7. *Ibid.*
8. 1972 French Civil Code, Article 2060, first sentence, translated by Georges Rouhette, Professor of Law, with the assistance of Dr. Anne Rouhette-Berton.
9. Stefan Kröll, *The European Convention on International Commercial Arbitration: The Tale of a Sleeping Beauty*, in Austrian Yearbook on International Arbitration, 4, p. 11 (Klausegger and others eds., Manz, 2013).
10. Emmanuel Gaillard and John Savage eds., *Fouchard, Gaillard and Goldman on International Commercial Arbitration*, p. 142, mn 283 (Kluwer Law International, 1999); Article 1672, para. 2 of the Belgian *Code Judiciaire* as applicable in the *Bentler v. Belgium* award, quoted by Jan Paulsson, *May a State Invoke its Internal Law to Repudiate Consent to International Arbitration*, 2(1) Arbitration International 90, p. 91 (1986).
11. Article 1676, para. 3 *Code Judiciaire* ("*Sans préjudice des lois particulières, les personnes morales de droit public ne peuvent conclure une convention d'arbitrage que lorsque celle-ci a pour objet le règlement de différends relatifs à une convention. La convention d'arbitrage est soumise aux mêmes conditions quant à sa conclusion que la convention qui fait l'objet de l'arbitrage. En outre, les personnes morales de droit public peuvent conclure une convention d'arbitrage en toutes matières déterminées par la loi ou par arrêté royal délibéré en Conseil des ministres. Cet arrêté peut également fixer les conditions et les règles à respecter relatives à la conclusion de la convention.*").

8. In 1975, the French legislator introduced an additional paragraph to Article 2060 of the Civil Code to soften the prohibition, which however still required an authorization by decree:

> [C]ategories of public entities of an industrial or commercial character may be authorized by decree to enter into arbitration agreements.[12]

9. Whilst Article 2060 of the French Civil Code does not specify whether it also refers to international constellations or to domestic transactions only, in *Galakis c. Trésor Public* the French *Cour de Cassation* confined its application to domestic transactions.[13] The case referred to a sea shipping of goods contract concluded between the French Ministry of the Merchant Navy and a Greek merchant. The contract contained an arbitration clause. When the dispute arose between the parties, France objected to the validity of the arbitration agreement. However, the French *Cour de Cassation* ruled that the prohibition did not apply to international commercial contracts and consequently upheld the validity of the arbitration clause.[14]

10. Against the backdrop of this heterogeneous legal landscape across Europe (and beyond), the primary relevance of Article II paragraph 1 lies in the legal certainty it grants to the users of international arbitration: Within the scope of the ECICA, an arbitration agreement concluded by a "legal person of public law" of another Contracting State will be deemed valid despite any contrary provisions of the applicable domestic law. The only exception is where such domestic restrictions have been expressly "declared" as a reservation under Article II paragraph 2.[15]

11. As a provision of public international law contained in an international treaty, Article II expressly vests public legal entities of the Contracting States with the capacity to enter into arbitration agreements. As such, it constitutes an innovative attempt at harmonizing the domestic legal systems of the Contracting States with regard to the subjective arbitrability of public entities.[16] Whilst comparable national provisions, as, e.g., Article 177 paragraph 2 of the Swiss Arbitration Law (i.e., Swiss Federal Statute on Private International Law) rest upon the same underlying principle, they cannot directly confer such power to enter into arbitration agreements upon foreign entities. Instead, e.g., Article 177 Swiss Arbitration Law is based on the general principle of *non venire contra factum proprium* and stipulates that Swiss-seated tribunals and Swiss

---

12. 1972 French Civil Code as amended by Act No. 75-596 of 9 July 1975, Article 2060, second sentence, translated by Georges Rouhette, Professor of Law, with the assistance of Dr. Anne Rouhette-Berton.
13. Stefan Kröll, *The European Convention on International Commercial Arbitration: The Tale of a Sleeping Beauty*, in Austrian Yearbook on International Arbitration, 4, p. 11 (Klausegger and others eds., Manz, 2013); *see also* Bertrand Moreau, with the collaboration of d'Éloïse Glucksmann and Pierre Feng, *Arbitrage International*, paras 83–84 (June 2016).
14. *Galakis c. le Trésor public*, N.256, *Cour de Cassation*, chb. Civ. 1ère, 2 May 1966.
15. Stefan Kröll, *The European Convention on International Commercial Arbitration: The Tale of a Sleeping Beauty*, in Austrian Yearbook on International Arbitration, 4, p. 11 (Klausegger and others eds., Manz, 2013).
16. As set out in the Austrian government bill introducing the ECICA, Article II was intended to prompt the relevant States to amend their domestic laws accordingly, Government Bill 187 and Supplement, X GP, 27 June 1963 (*Regierungsvorlage und Beilagen*) (AT), p. 16.

courts are not bound by any domestic restrictions—notwithstanding their validity—of the subjective arbitrability of State entities contained in foreign internal law.[17] Article 177 reads:

> A state, or an enterprise held by, or an organization controlled by a state, which is party to an arbitration agreement, cannot invoke its own law in order to contest its capacity to arbitrate or the arbitrability of a dispute covered by the arbitration agreement.

12. In this vein, Article II paragraph 1 ECICA expresses a general principle of international arbitration law according to which public entities may not rely on their own internal law to frustrate the validity of an international arbitration agreement.[18] This has been *inter alia* acknowledged *obiter* in the 1983 landmark case *Benteler v. Belgium*,[19] which resounded the opinion prevailing at the time already.[20] Even where the ECICA is not directly applicable, therefore, in practice its Article II paragraph 1 may be invoked in support of the general principle enshrined in this provision. Different intellectual approaches have been advocated to encapsulate this principle, including framing it as a rule of international public policy or basing it on the *non venire contra factum proprium* (or estoppel) principle.[21]

13. The *Benteler v. Belgium*[22] case was heard in Switzerland by three European arbitrators, who issued an interim award on jurisdiction. The dispute referred to a contract concluded between two German private parties, on the one side, and, on the other, a Belgian State mining company and the Belgian State, regulating the shareholding in and reorganization of the mining company (in essence, a joint venture agreement). The contract contained an arbitration clause. When the dispute arose, the German private party, Benteler,[23] resorted to arbitration. However, Belgium invoked its domestic law provisions in an attempt to nullify the arbitration agreement (Article 1672 of the Belgian *Code Judiciare*). Benteler referred to Article II of the ECICA and pointed out that whilst Belgium had made a reservation when ratifying the ECICA which limited the scope of Article II paragraph 1, this reservation expressly provided that the Belgian State was authorized to conclude arbitration agreements. In an interim award,

---

17. *See* in detail Stefan Kröll, *The European Convention on International Commercial Arbitration: The Tale of a Sleeping Beauty*, in Austrian Yearbook on International Arbitration, 4, p. 12 (Klausegger and others eds., Manz, 2013).
18. Stefan Kröll, *The European Convention on International Commercial Arbitration: The Tale of a Sleeping Beauty*, in Austrian Yearbook on International Arbitration, 4, p. 12 (Klausegger and others eds., Manz, 2013).
19. *Dipl. Ing. Erick Benteler KG, Helmut Benteler KG v. Belgian State, S.A. ABC*, Interim Award, 18 November 1993, in Vol. X, Yearbook Commercial Arbitration 1985, pp. 37–38 (Pieter Sanders ed., Kluwer Law International, 1985).
20. *See* Jan Paulsson, *May a State Invoke its Internal Law to Repudiate Consent to International Arbitration*, 2(1) ARBITRATION INTERNATIONAL 90 (1986). Also confer the ICC Award of 1971 referring in this respect to "international *ordre public*," ICC Case 1939, cited by Yves Derains, 1973 Revue de l'arbitrage 145.
21. Jan Paulsson, *May a State Invoke its Internal Law to Repudiate Consent to International Arbitration*, 2(1) ARBITRATION INTERNATIONAL 90, p. 91 (1986).
22. *See supra* fn. 19.
23. More precisely, the proceedings involved the two Western German parties Erich Benteler KG and Helmut Benteler KG.

the arbitral tribunal upheld its jurisdiction as it found the ECICA was applicable to the dispute and that Belgium could not invoke the provision in its own law prohibiting public persons from concluding arbitration agreements.[24] Consequently, the Belgian State was bound to the arbitration agreement. Whilst noting that different conceptual approaches (or techniques) exist to achieve the same result, the Tribunal affirmed the existence of a general principle of the "common law of arbitration" that a State may not use its national law to contest the validity of an arbitration clause.[25] It should not go unnoticed—and it was in fact mentioned by the Tribunal—that at the time the draft legislation at the place of arbitration (Switzerland) contemplated the introduction of a rule to the same effect as Article II paragraph 1 ECICA (i.e., what was to become Article 177 of the Swiss Arbitration Law; *see supra* paragraph 11).

II THE NOTION OF "LEGAL PERSONS OF PUBLIC LAW"

14. Not only the State itself but also other "legal persons of public law" are granted subjective arbitrability under Article II paragraph 1 ECICA. The ECICA does not provide a definition of "legal persons of public law." The theory of legal person of public law can be traced back to French administrative law,[26] where the notion is broad in scope, encompassing: the State, territorial formations, public institutions, associations for pursuing public interest, including the subjects of private law vested with public functions and authorities.[27] The interpretation standard applicable to the term "legal person of public law" employed in Article II paragraph 1, however, is an autonomous one, i.e., detached from domestic legal norms.[28] Interpretation must center on the ordinary meaning of the term and, notably, give due consideration to the purpose of the rule.

15. The ordinary meaning of the term "legal person" as common to most jurisdictions is that of an entity which is the bearer of legal rights and can be the subject of legal obligations.[29] The ordinary meaning of the term "public law," on the other hand, has been defined as:

24. Dominique Hascher, *European Convention on International Commercial Arbitration of 1961: Commentary*, Vol. XXXVI, Yearbook Commercial Arbitration, 509, p. 517 (Albert Jan van den Berg ed., 2011).
25. *Confer* Jan Paulsson, *May a State Invoke Its Internal Law to Repudiate Consent to International Arbitration*, 2(1) ARBITRATION INTERNATIONAL 90, p. 91 (1986).
26. Oleg Jastrebov, *The Use of the Category of "Legal Persons of Public Law"* in Foreign Legal Instruments, 20(11) MIDDLE-EAST JOURNAL OF SCIENTIFIC RESEARCH 1541, p. 1542 (2014).
27. *Ibid.*
28. In *Benteler v. Belgium*, the Tribunal when analyzing the term "international commerce" posited that *"[i]t is in accordance with [the ECICA's] purpose to accept that the legal notions and terms used in the Convention have in principle the connotation which is theirs in the relationship of international commerce. It would indeed be contrary to the very object of the Convention to admit that its terms have to be interpreted according to notions of domestic law, because such an interpretation would lead to the very type of difficulties the Convention's drafters wanted to avoid." Dipl. Ing. Erick Benteler KG, Helmut Benteler KG v. Belgian State, S.A. ABC*, Interim Award, 18 November 1993, Vol. 1(2), JOURNAL OF INTERNATIONAL ARBITRATION, pp. 184–190 (Kluwer Law International, 1984).
29. Malcom N. Shaw, *International Law*, p. 195 (Cambridge University Press, 2008).

> [T]he branch or department of law which is concerned with the state in its political or sovereign capacity, including constitutional and administrative law, and with the definition, regulation, and enforcement of rights in cases where the state is regarded as the subject of the right or object of the duty [...] and the law of the state, considered in its quasi private personality [...].[30]

16. Accordingly, the ordinary meaning of the notion "legal person of public law" encompasses a wide variety of entities. The purpose of the ECICA, notably of Article II paragraph 1, to create a harmonized substantive rule on subjective arbitrability also militates in favor of a broad interpretation of the term.

17. In this vein, commentators to the ECICA have rightly advocated a broad interpretation of the notion of "legal persons of public law" in Article II, comprising "*not only public corporations but also States and any public agencies.*"[31] Under this reading, the term is not restricted to the State, or "organs of the State" as defined in Article 4 of the ILC Draft Articles on Responsibility of States for Internationally Wrongful Acts ("ILC Articles").[32] Rather, beyond Article 4 ILC Articles (i.e., organs of the State, whether exercising legislative, executive, judicial, or other functions and whether organs of the central government or of a territorial unit of the State), the definition of "legal persons of public law" in Article II of the ECICA will, in particular, also cover entities referred to in Article 5[33] (i.e., persons exercising powers of governmental authority) and may even extend to Article 8[34] (persons controlled by the State) of the ILC Articles.[35]

18. In an ICC case, the sole arbitrator stretched the scope of "legal persons of public law" under Article II paragraph 1 so as to extend to certain international organizations.[36] It is worthwhile noting that Dominique Hascher, when referring to this case in his commentary to Article II of the ECICA, remarks that the sole arbitrator treated the

---

30. Henry Campbell Black, M.A., *Black's Law Dictionary*, pp. 1106–1107 (5th ed., West 1979).
31. Dominique Hascher, *European Convention on International Commercial Arbitration of 1961: Commentary*, Vol. XXXVI, Yearbook Commercial Arbitration, 509, p. 516 (Albert Jan van den Berg ed., 2011); *see also* Nikolaus Pitkowitz, *Is There Still a Scope of Application of the European Convention on International Commercial Arbitration?*, in Austrian Yearbook on International Arbitration, 93–108, p. 108 (Klausegger and others eds., 2013), advocating a "broad" interpretation; Jens Adolphsen, in Münchener Kommentar zur Zivilprozessordnung, Vol. 3, §1061, Appendix 2 European Convention, Article II, mn 1 (4th ed., Krüger & Rauscher eds., C.H. Beck, 2013), equally in favor of a "broad" interpretation also comprising local states and state agencies or enterprises.
32. Draft Articles on Responsibility of States for Internationally Wrongful Acts with Commentaries 2001, Article 4.
33. *Ibid.*, Article 5.
34. *Ibid.*, Article 8.
35. Florian Haugeneder, *The New Austrian Arbitration Act*, 23(4) ARBITRATION INTERNATIONAL 645, p. 651 (2007), defines legal persons of public law as "*persons not governed by the private law of a country, including the State*" with reference to *Benteler v. Belgium*, Interim Award, X YBCA 37.
36. *International Organization A v. Company B*, ICC Award No. 2091, 14 May 1972, in 1975 Rev. Arb. 252, pp. 252–258, commentary by Philippe Fouchard pp. 258–267; *see also* Dominique Hascher, *European Convention on International Commercial Arbitration of 1961: Commentary*, Vol. XXXVI, Yearbook Commercial Arbitration, 509, pp. 516–517 (Albert Jan van den Berg ed., 2011); referring to the case as an "*interesting attempt*" to extend the ambit of Article II.

international organization as a legal person of "public **international** law." The term "legal persons of public international law" certainly encompasses international organizations. It is, of course, broader than the term "legal persons of public law" as employed by the drafters of the ECICA. It is, therefore, doubtful whether indeed international organizations should be covered by Article II as a general rule.

III POSSIBLE RESERVATION UNDER ARTICLE II PARAGRAPH 2

19. Under Article II paragraph 2, the Contracting States can limit the right contained in paragraph 1 by way of a declaration upon signing, ratifying, or acceding to the Convention. Any such limitation will then be easily and early on available to the private counterparty.[37] Conversely, if a Contracting State does not limit the right of its "legal persons of public law" to conclude arbitration agreements by one of the three possibilities set forth in paragraph 2, such State cannot thereafter invoke its domestic law to deny the validity of arbitration agreements concluded by its public entities.

20. Whilst the ECICA does not contain any express prohibition or limitation on making reservations to (certain provisions of) the Convention (*confer* Article 19 VCLT), Article II paragraph 2 is the only reservation which is expressly provided for therein. In particular, the final clauses of Article X do not expressly allow for (further) reservations.[38]

21. The express possibility to make a reservation under Article II paragraph 2 was included in order to accommodate the interests of those civil law States which were strongly opposed to the content of Article II and would otherwise not have become parties to the ECICA.[39] This was, e.g., the case of the signatory State Belgium which made the following declaration upon its accession to the ECICA in 1975:

> In accordance with Article II paragraph 2, of the Convention, the Belgian Government declares that in Belgium only the State has, in the cases referred to in Article I, paragraph 1, the faculty to conclude arbitration agreements.[40]

37. Rudolf Kaiser, *Das Europäische Übereinkommen über die internationale Handelsschiedsgerichtsbarkeit vom 21. April 1961*, in Zürcher Studien zum Internationalen Recht, p. 67 (Fritzsche et al. eds., No. 39, 1977).
38. Nikolaus Pitkowitz, *Is There Still a Scope of Application of the European Convention on International Commercial Arbitration?*, in Austrian Yearbook on International Arbitration, 93–108, p. 108 (Klausegger and others eds., Manz, 2013), refers to it as "the only possible reservation to the European Convention."
39. Dominique Hascher, *European Convention on International Commercial Arbitration of 1961: Commentary*, Vol. XXXVI, Yearbook Commercial Arbitration, 509, p. 517 (Albert Jan van den Berg ed., 2011).
40. European Convention on International Commercial Arbitration, Geneva, 21 April 1961, UNTS, Vol. 484, p. 349, Declarations and Reservations, available at https://treaties.un.org/pages/ViewDetails.aspx?src=TREATY&mtdsg_no=XXII-2&chapter=22&clang=_en (last visited 12 September 2017).

22. In the case of Belgium, therefore, only the State has the capacity to conclude arbitration agreements. Upon its accession to the ECICA in 2003, Latvia made the following declaration, deviating somewhat from the Belgian reservation:

> In accordance with Article II, paragraph 2, of the [ECICA], the Republic of Latvia declares that Article II, paragraph 1, does not apply for state authorities and local government authorities.[41]

23. Latvia withdrew this reservation on 23 December 2013. As far as can be seen, its internal restriction on the subjective arbitrability of state entities (as contained in Article 5(1)(2) of the Latvian Arbitration Act[42]) is still in force. However, the Supreme Court of Latvia has ruled that the restriction set forth in Article 5(1)(2) excludes State-owned private companies because, under Latvian law, these companies are not considered State institutions.[43]

24. Whereas Hungary ratified the ECICA in 1963 without reservation, its internal law formerly contained a substantive limitation of the arbitrability of disputes involving State-held assets in Hungary (including shares).[44]

25. Contrary to initial concerns that Article II might be undermined by a generous use of the possibility to make reservations to this provision,[45] as of today no Contracting State other than Belgium upholds a reservation under Article II paragraph 2 ECICA.

---

41. European Convention on International Commercial Arbitration, Geneva, 21 April 1961, UNTS, Vol. 484, p. 349, Declarations and Reservations, available at https://treaties.un.org/pages/ViewDetails.aspx?src=TREATY&mtdsg_no=XXII-2&chapter=22&clang=_en (last visited 10 May 2018).
42. Leg. cit reads in relevant part "*Any civil dispute may be referred for resolution to an arbitral institution if the parties have voluntarily agreed and concluded an arbitration agreement, with the exception of a dispute: [...] 2) in which at least one party is a State or local government institution or if the award of the arbitral institution may affect the rights of State or a local government institutions; [...].*" Latvian Arbitration Act, entered into force on 1 January 2015, with amendments introduced by the Judgment of the Satversme [Constitutional] Court of 28 November 2014 and the Law of 6 October 2016, which entered into force on 3 November 2016, published in the "Latvijas Vēstnesis", 204 (5776), on 20 October 2016. Translation provided in *The Arbitration Law*, ICCA International Handbook on Commercial Arbitration (Jan Paulsson and Lise Bosman eds., Kluwer Law International).
43. Ģirts Lejinš and Eva Kalnina, *National Report for Latvia (2018)*, in ICCA International Handbook on Commercial Arbitration, pp. 1-44 (Jan Paulsson and Lise Bosman eds., Law International 1984, Supplement No. 92, December 2016), referring to Decision 46 of the Supreme Court of the Republic of Latvia of 29 October 2013.
44. Article 17(3) of "Act CXCVI of 2011 on National Assets"; Gabor Bardos, *The Award and the Courts, Hungary: New Rules on Arbitration Related to National Assets,* in Austrian Yearbook on International Arbitration, p. 181 (Klausegger and Klein et al. eds., 2013). The relevant provision was repealed with effect as from 19 March 2015, by Sections 33 and 35 of the Act VII of 2015 on the investment related to the maintenance of the capacity of the Nuclear Plant of Paks, as well as on the amendment of certain connected Acts; confer Csongor István Nagy, *The Lesson of a Short-Lived Mutiny: The Rise and Fall of Hungary's Controversial Arbitration Regime in Cases Involving National Assets,* 26(2) AMERICAN REVIEW OF INTERNATIONAL ARBITRATION p. 239 (2016).
45. Frédéric-Edouard Klein, *Europäisches Übereinkommen über Handelsschiedsgerichtsbarkeit,* 76(5/6) Zeitschrift für Zivilprozess, p. 347 (1963).

IV THE AMBIT OF ARTICLE II

[A] Internal Rules on Authority to Represent the State?

26. Article II regulates the question of subjective arbitrability. Under a narrow reading of the provision, it does not specify who has the authority to represent a State and what formalities are required for a legal person of public law to validly give its consent to enter into an arbitration agreement.[46] Therefore, a State may try to rely on these internal formalities to deny the validity of the arbitration agreement concluded by a "legal person of public law." In fact, national provisions on the formalities to be complied with by public entities when entering into arbitration agreements may create the same legal uncertainty as national limitations of their subjective arbitrability. Under a narrow interpretation of Article II, the ECICA would not invalidate any such additional formal requirements, such as the signature of a second minister, the approval by the parliament or by a supervisory authority, or other formalities.

27. Under Article 27 of the VCLT "*[a] party may not invoke the provisions of its internal law as justification for its failure to perform a treaty.*"[47] The ratio of this provision applies all the more in public-private contracts. Indeed, it would defeat the purpose of Article II paragraph 1 ECICA to request a foreign private party to perform extensive due diligence into the authority of a State's representative or into the required domestic formalities before concluding an arbitration agreement with a "legal person of public law."

28. Therefore, whilst Article II paragraph 1 does not directly apply to the representation and formal requirements provided by national law for the conclusion of arbitration agreements, where those formalities go beyond what is normally required to bind the respective State in a commercial transaction (i.e., where they are "discriminatory")[48] or

46. Stefan Kröll, *The European Convention on International Commercial Arbitration: The Tale of a Sleeping Beauty*, in Austrian Yearbook on International Arbitration, 4, p. 12 (Klausegger and others eds., Manz, 2013); Florian Haugeneder, *The New Austrian Arbitration Act*, 23(4) ARBITRATION INTERNATIONAL, 645, p. 651 (2007); Hans-Jakob Maier, Europäisches Übereinkommen und UN-Übereinkommen über die Internationale Schiedsgerichtsbarkeit, p. 9 (1966); Apparently different opinion, Peter Schlosser, *Kommentar zur Schiedsgerichtsordnung*, para. 404 (Stein and Jonas eds., 2014) ("*Article II [...] also guarantees the absence of limitations of the power of representation of representatives who are authorized to conclude the substantive-law agreement containing the arbitration clause.*"); similar apparently, qualifying representation formalities under public law as rules which need to be declared under Article II, para. 2, *Fouchard*, as cited by Rudolf Kaiser, *Das Europäische Übereinkommen über die internationale Handelsschiedsgerichtsbarkeit vom 21 April 1961*, in Zürcher Studien zum Internationalen Recht, p. 67 No. 15 (Fritzsche et al. eds., No. 39, 1977), (who on his part advocates a narrow reading of Article II).

47. VCLT, Article 27; *see also* the Swiss Federal Private International Law Act specifically provides in Article 177(2) that a State party to an arbitration agreement "*cannot rely on its own law to contest the arbitrability of a dispute or its own capacity to be a party to an arbitration.*"

48. Florian Haugeneder, *The New Austrian Arbitration Act*, 23(4) ARBITRATION INTERNATIONAL 645, p. 651 (2007) ("*[C]onditions considerably more onerous than the requirements for representation in normal commercial matters are arguably contrary to Article II if their effect is to substantially restrict the practical possibility of persons of public law concluding arbitration agreements.*").

where such formalities could not have been reasonably contemplated by the private counterparty (i.e., where the foreign private party has relied in good faith on the valid conclusion of the arbitration agreement),[49] they must be deemed at variance with Article II paragraph 1 ECICA.[50] This follows from a broad and purposeful interpretation of Article II.[51] Additional support may be found in Article 46 VCLT, under which a State cannot invalidate a treaty to which it has consented based on a purported violation of its internal regulations regarding the competence to conclude treaties, unless the violation was manifest (i.e., objectively evident to any State acting in accordance with normal practice and in good faith) and if the internal rule was of fundamental importance. The general principle expressed therein must apply all the more in dealings of the State or State entity with a private counterparty.[52] Whereas a foreign private party which intends to conclude an arbitration agreement with a "legal person of public law" will, therefore, be required to prior perform a reasonable due diligence on the requisite formalities on the part of the "legal person of public law" under the latter's internal rules, the standard for such due diligence should not be set too high.

[B] Waiver of Immunity from Execution?

29. Article II addresses restrictions of the capacity of public entities to conclude arbitration clauses and, hence, relates to the jurisdiction of the arbitral tribunal. When a State or a State organ concludes an arbitration agreement in the framework of international trade, the State will regularly be held to have renounced its jurisdictional immunity.[53] Article II ECICA does not take a position on whether the conclusion of an arbitration clause also constitutes a waiver of immunity from execution and enforcement. In fact, it may be less clear whether consent to arbitration is tantamount to a renunciation of immunity from enforcement.[54] A separate waiver may be required;

49. Stefan Kröll, *The European Convention on International Commercial Arbitration: The Tale of a Sleeping Beauty*, in Austrian Yearbook on International Arbitration, 4, p. 12 (Klausegger and others eds., Manz, 2013).
50. Also *see* Ernst Mezger, *Das Europäische Übereinkommen über die Handelsschiedsgerichtsbarkeit*, 29 RabelsZ, 231, p. 252 (1965), advocating against an undermining of Article II, para. 1, by way of internal representation provisions, which would lead to an "unbearable legal uncertainty."
51. Stefan Kröll, *The European Convention on International Commercial Arbitration: The Tale of a Sleeping Beauty*, in Austrian Yearbook on International Arbitration, 4, p. 12 (Klausegger and others eds., Manz, 2013).
52. Also *see* in this regard Jan Paulsson, *May a State Invoke Its Internal Law to Repudiate Consent to International Arbitration*, 2(1) ARBITRATION INTERNATIONAL, 90, p. 91 (1986).
53. Bertrand Moreau, with the collaboration of d'Éloïse Glucksmann and Pierre Feng, *Arbitrage International*, para. 87 (June 2016).
54. Jacques Moury, *L'incidence de la stipulation d'une clause compromissoire sur l'immunité d'exécution de l'Etat étranger*, D. 2001. 2139, para. 7; Bertrand Moreau, with the collaboration of d'Éloïse Glucksmann and Pierre Feng, *Arbitrage International*, para. 88 (June 2016).

whether express or tacit, such waiver must be clear and unambiguous.[55] Not all arbitral tribunals have considered the conclusion of an arbitration agreement by the State or its entities as such clear and unambiguous waiver from execution.[56]

55. *State Entities in International Arbitration*, in IAI Series on International Arbitration, p. 121 (Emmanuel Gaillard and Jennifer Younan eds., Juris Publishing Inc., 2008).

56. *Ibid*. "*Though the issue of immunity from jurisdiction of the arbitral tribunal has been resolved and rendered moot by consistent adjudications by arbitral tribunals and national courts, the issue of immunity to execution still remains unresolved with no uniform practice in sight*." Samarth Sagar, "*Waiver of Sovereign Immunity" Clauses in Contracts: An Examination of Their Legal Standing and Practical Value in Enforcement of International Arbitral Awards*, 31(5) JOURNAL OF INTERNATIONAL ARBITRATION, 609, p. 610 (Kluwer Law International, 2014).

ARTICLE III

Right of Foreign Nationals to Be Designated as Arbitrators

Gerold Zeiler

INTRODUCTION

> *Article III—Right of Foreign Nationals to be designated as Arbitrators*
>
> *In arbitration covered by this Convention, foreign nationals may be designated as arbitrators.*

1. Article III allows individuals of a different nationality from that of the parties to the dispute or from the place of arbitration to be appointed as arbitrators in proceedings covered by the Convention.[1] At the time when the ECICA was drafted, the domestic law of certain countries such as Italy, Greece, Portugal, and Spain prohibited foreigners to act as arbitrators. Therefore, "*Article III … was inserted in the Convention in order to bring the legislation of these countries onto harmony with that of the vast majority of countries.*"[2]

2. Article III uses the word "may" instead of "shall," which makes clear that it is not a mandatory provision but rather a discretionary power of the parties or the appointing authority, as the case may be.

3. Additionally, the wording of Article III does not distinguish between foreign nationals of a Contracting State from those of a non-Contracting State. Therefore, as

1. "*Art. III is intended to permit the choice of arbitrators which are not necessarily nationals of any* ***State concerned in the arbitration proceedings***" (emphasis added) Dominique Hascher, *European Convention on International Commercial Arbitration of 1961: Commentary*, in Vol. XXXVI, Yearbook Commercial Arbitration, 509, p. 517 (Albert Jan van den Berg ed., 2011).
2. P. I. Benjamin, *The European Convention on International Commercial Arbitration*, 37 BRITISH YEARBOOK INTERNATIONAL LAW 478, p. 487 (1961).

noted by the Italian Supreme Court in *Damiano v. Tropfer*, "*for the purpose of deciding whether the European Convention is applicable to the arbitral matter at issue, the nationality of the arbitrator, i.e. whether or not he belongs to a State which has ratified the Convention,* ***is irrelevant.***"[3]

4. The relevance of this provision in the development of international arbitration is the acknowledgment that impeding foreign nationals to be appointed as arbitrators may, first, affect the perception among arbitration users of the neutrality of arbitrators and, second, limit the number of arbitrators suitable for a particular case.

5. A key element of international arbitration is neutrality,[4] as recognized by a Court of Appeal in Frankfurt:

> Certainly, in respect to arbitral clauses in international trade, one of the primary reasons for the acceptance of an arbitral tribunal is the greater confidence in its neutrality and the mistrust of the parties of the national domestic courts of either contracting partner.[5]

6. The neutrality of an arbitrator is sometimes seen as related to his/her nationality.[6] Parties sometimes will be more likely to acknowledge the neutrality of arbitrators if they are nationals of countries other than the litigants. Such a perception is important for the acceptance and success of international arbitration as a dispute resolution mechanism. The parties to a dispute coming from different countries "*are wary of placing the decision in the hands of the judiciary of their counterpart's country, out of fear that common nationality might result in national judges favoring their compatriots.*"[7] Neutrality is, therefore, one of the reasons why parties coming from different countries choose arbitration over domestic courts.

7. Although common nationality does not necessarily lead to a bias, there is a general assumption that the judge/arbitrator and the party sharing its nationality will likely also share certain values, interests, or ideologies which could tend to lack neutrality.[8] Consequently, and even though being of a different nationality does not guarantee

3. *Fratelli Damiano s.n.c. v. August Tropfer & Co.*, Italian Supreme Court, Plenary Session (*Corte di Cassazione, Sezioni Unite*), No. 722, 8 February 1982, in Vol. IX, Yearbook Commercial Arbitration, pp. 418–420 (Pieter Sanders ed., 1984). (Unofficial English translation from Kluwer Arbitration, original in Italian) (emphasis added).
4. Gary Born, *International Commercial Arbitration*, Introduction, p. 1 (2nd ed., Kluwer Law International, 2014).
5. *Polish foreign trade state enterprise v. FR German manufacturer*, Court of Appeal of Frankfurt (*Oberlandesgericht*), 24 September 1985, in Vol. XV, Yearbook Commercial Arbitration 1990, pp. 666–670 (Albert Jan van den Berg ed., 1990). (Unofficial English translation from Kluwer Arbitration, original in German).
6. Pierre Lalive, *On the Neutrality of the Arbitrator and the Place of Arbitration*, Swiss Essays on International Arbitration 23, p. 24 (1984).
7. Lee Ilhyung, *Practice and Predicament: The Nationality of the International Arbitrator (With Survey Results)*, 31(3) Fordham International Law Journal, 603, p. 603 (2008).
8. Pierre Lalive, *On the Neutrality of the Arbitrator and the Place of Arbitration*, Swiss Essays on International Arbitration 23, p. 25 (1984).

neutrality, it helps to reduce an "unhealthy atmosphere of doubt and fear"[9] among the arbitration users.

8. The possibility of diversity of nationality between the arbitrators and the parties, provided in Article III, is nowadays contained in a large number of arbitration rules.[10] Some rules provide it as a stringent requirement which is subject to certain exceptions,[11] while others do solely as a factor to be taken into consideration when appointing, particularly, a sole arbitrator or the chairman of the arbitral tribunal.[12] In the case of party-appointed arbitrators, the perception is sometimes that "*each party is likely to select an arbitrator of the same nationality, with the understanding that the party-appointed arbitrator will inform the tribunal of the appointing party's legal and business culture.*"[13]

9. The connection between nationality and neutrality of the arbitrator may appear to be overly simplistic. Under the same rationale, other factors, such as the residence of an arbitrator, could be defined as disqualifying elements. Thus, different nationality as a mandatory rule might be seen as too rigid or superficial. On the other hand, choosing arbitrators with a nationality different from the parties' may help to avoid the perception of partiality.

10. Some arbitration rules limit the selection of arbitrators to individuals included in a list approved by an arbitral institution. It has been argued that such rules are not affected by Article III of the ECICA.[14]

11. Finally, if the appointment of foreign arbitrators were not allowed, the range of candidates for a particular case would be restricted and the quality of the arbitration proceedings possibly compromised. It would be difficult to guarantee that in every Contracting State there is an arbitrator with the qualifications required for the case at stake or with the time to accept the appointment as an arbitrator. In contrast, granting the parties a possibility to choose an arbitrator from any nationality, as Article III of the ECICA does, broadens the range of possibilities to find an arbitrator who possesses qualifications uniquely suited for the case.

---

9. *Ibid.*
10. Nigel Blackaby et al., *Redfern and Hunter on International Arbitration*, p. 250, mn 4.61 (6th ed., 2015).
11. For instance, Article 13(5) of the ICC Rules provides, subject to certain exceptions, that: "*[t]he sole arbitrator or the chairman of an arbitral tribunal shall be of a nationality other than those of the parties.*" This requirement is not absolute as the parties may agree otherwise, ICC Rules, Article 13(5); *see also* LCIA Rules, Article 6(1).
12. Article 28 of the China International Economic and Trade Arbitration Commission ("CIETAC") Rules mentions the nationality of the parties as factor to be taken into consideration when appointing arbitrators.
13. Lee Ilhyung, *Practice and Predicament: The Nationality of the International Arbitrator (With Survey Results)*, 31(3) Fordham International Law Journal, 603, pp. 603–604 (2008).
14. Dominique Hascher, *European Convention on International Commercial Arbitration of 1961: Commentary*, in Vol. XXXVI, Yearbook Commercial Arbitration, 509, p. 517 (Albert Jan van den Berg ed., 2011).

ARTICLE IV
Organization of the Arbitration

Markus Schifferl

INTRODUCTION

Article IV- Organization of the Arbitration

(1) The parties to an arbitration agreement shall be free to submit their disputes:
   (a) to a permanent arbitral institution; in this case, the arbitration proceedings shall be held in conformity with the rules of the said institution;
   (b) to an ad hoc *arbitral procedure; in this case, they shall be free inter alia:*
      (i) to appoint arbitrators or to establish means for their appointment in the event of an actual dispute;
      (ii) to determine the place of arbitration; and
      (iii) to lay down the procedure to be followed by the arbitrators.

(2) Where the parties have agreed to submit any disputes to an ad hoc *arbitration, and where within thirty days of the notification of the request for arbitration to the respondent one of the parties fails to appoint his arbitrator, the latter shall, unless otherwise provided, be appointed at the request of the other party by the President of the competent Chamber of Commerce of the country of the defaulting party's habitual place of residence or seat at the time of the introduction of the request for arbitration. This paragraph shall also apply to the replacement of the arbitrator(s) appointed by one of the parties or by the President of the Chamber of Commerce above referred to.*

(3) Where the parties have agreed to submit any disputes to an ad hoc *arbitration by one or more arbitrators and the arbitration agreement contains no indication regarding the organization of the arbitration, as mentioned in paragraph 1 of this article, the necessary steps shall be taken by the arbitrator(s) already appointed, unless the parties are able to agree thereon and without prejudice to the case referred to in paragraph 2 above. Where the parties cannot agree on the appointment of the sole arbitrator or where the arbitrators appointed cannot agree on the measures to be taken, the claimant shall apply for the necessary action, where the place of arbitration has been agreed upon by the parties, at his option to the President of the Chamber of Commerce of the place of arbitration agreed upon or to the President of the competent Chamber of*

Commerce of the respondent's habitual place of residence or seat at the time of the introduction of the request for arbitration. Where such a place has not been agreed upon, the claimant shall be entitled at his option to apply for the necessary action either to the President of the competent Chamber of Commerce of the country of the respondent's habitual place of residence or seat at the time of the introduction of the request for arbitration, or to the Special Committee whose composition and procedure are specified in the Annex to this Convention. Where the claimant fails to exercise the rights given to him under this paragraph the respondent or the arbitrator(s) shall be entitled to do so.

(4) When seized of a request the President or the Special Committee shall be entitled as need be:
  (a) to appoint the sole arbitrator, presiding arbitrator, umpire, or referee;
  (b) to replace the arbitrator(s) appointed under any procedure other than that referred to in paragraph 2 above;
  (c) to determine the place of arbitration, provided that the arbitrator(s) may fix another place of arbitration;
  (d) to establish directly or by reference to the rules and statutes of a permanent arbitral institution the rules of procedure to be followed by the arbitrator(s), provided that the arbitrators have not established these rules themselves in the absence of any agreement thereon between the parties.

(5) Where the parties have agreed to submit their disputes to a permanent arbitral institution without determining the institution in question and cannot agree thereon, the claimant may request the determination of such institution in conformity with the procedure referred to in paragraph 3 above.

(6) Where the arbitration agreement does not specify the mode of arbitration (arbitration by a permanent arbitral institution or an ad hoc *arbitration) to which the parties have agreed to submit their dispute, and where the parties cannot agree thereon, the claimant shall be entitled to have recourse in this case to the procedure referred to in paragraph 3 above to determine the question. The President of the competent Chamber of Commerce or the Special Committee shall be entitled either to refer the parties to a permanent arbitral institution or to request the parties to appoint their arbitrators within such time-limits as the President of the competent Chamber of Commerce or the Special Committee may have fixed and to agree within such time-limits on the necessary measures for the functioning of the arbitration. In the latter case, the provisions of paragraphs 2, 3 and 4 of this article shall apply.*

(7) Where within a period of sixty days from the moment when he was requested to fulfill one of the functions set out in paragraphs 2, 3, 4, 5 and 6 of this Article, the President of the Chamber of Commerce designated by virtue of these paragraphs has not fulfilled one of these functions, the party requesting shall be entitled to ask the Special Committee to do so.

I OVERVIEW

1. Article IV grants the parties autonomy to agree on the form and specifics of their arbitration proceedings. In particular, Article IV paragraph 1 expressly gives the parties the choice to agree on institutional arbitration (lit (a)) or on ad hoc arbitration (lit (b)). However, the largest part of the Article's wording aims to safeguard the parties' agreement by providing a fallback option in case the arbitration agreement is incomplete or defective or a party does not cooperate during the proceedings.

2. The peculiar complexity of Article IV provides an interesting insight into the differences the drafters of the ECICA had to overcome at height of the Cold War when negotiating a mechanism that ensures the enforcement of arbitration agreements without the intervention of domestic courts. As the former ideological barriers have, by and large, ceased to exist, some authors consider Article IV as outdated.[1]

3. However, Article IV still has some practical relevance, which a knowledgeable arbitration practitioner might be able to put to good use. This mainly applies to the possibility to uphold and remedy an otherwise unworkable arbitration clause pursuant to Article IV paragraph 5.[2]

II AD HOC ARBITRATION

[A] General Overview

4. Pursuant to Article IV paragraph 1 lit (b), the parties shall be free to refer their dispute to ad hoc arbitration. The term ad hoc arbitration is usually defined in the negative, namely an arbitration that is not administered by an administrative arbitral institution.[3] Hence, it is a catch-all phrase for any arbitration that is not institutional.

5. Under the ECICA, parties to ad hoc arbitrations are free to determine the number of arbitrators, their qualifications and way of their appointment, as well as the specific rules under which they wish to conduct their arbitration. As to the latter, the parties may refer to a specific set of rules such as the UNCITRAL Arbitration Rules, to a national arbitration law or even draft their own procedural code, which—not surprisingly—is extremely rare. This raises the interesting question whether mandatory provisions of the arbitration law at the place of the arbitration, e.g., a legal obligation that an arbitral tribunal must have either one or three arbitrators, have to be adhered to or whether they are replaced by ECICA allowing the parties to freely determine the number of arbitrators.

6. In cases where the parties cannot find agreement, e.g., on the appointment of arbitrators, the ECICA ultimately provides for such decisions to be taken by an appointing authority. During the negotiations leading to the ECICA, finding a suitable appointing authority was subject to great debate. Both Eastern and Western Blocs were concerned as to the appointing authority's neutrality, leading to all kinds of tentative solutions. At one point, the negotiating parties nearly agreed that all decisions should be put to the Executive Secretary of the Economic Commission for Europe, who should act as the representative of the Secretary-General of the United Nations. On second

---

1. Florian Haugeneder, *The New Austrian Arbitration Act and the European Convention on International Commercial Arbitration*, 23(4) Arbitration International, 646, p. 655 (2007).
2. *See* below III.B.
3. Pieter Sanders, *Commentary on UNCITRAL Arbitration Rules*, 2 Yearbook Commercial Arbitration, 172, 2.4 (1977); Ulrich G. Schroeter, *Ad Hoc or Institutional Arbitration: A Clear-Cut Distinction? A Closer Look at Borderline Cases*, 10(2) Contemporary Asia Arbitration Journal, 141, p. 146 (2017).

thought, the regular involvement of such senior public official to issues of a purely private nature was discarded.[4] Ultimately, the parties agreed on the complicated procedure outlined below.[5]

[B] Substitute Appointment of Arbitrator

7. One of the major issues in ad hoc arbitration is the fact that there is no arbitral institution that appoints or replaces an arbitrator in case one of the arbitration parties does not cooperate.

8. Article IV paragraph 2 contains a fallback option in case one of the parties fails to appoint its arbitrator within thirty days of the notification of the request for arbitration to the respondent. If not otherwise provided for by the parties,[6] the President of the competent Chamber of Commerce of the country of the defaulting party's habitual place of residence or seat at the time of the notification of the request for arbitration shall effect the appointment at the request of the other, non-defaulting party. When the President of the competent Chamber of Commerce fails to comply with this mandate, upon request the mandate will be transferred to the Special Committee whose composition is set out in Annex I of the ECICA. In case the defaulting party no longer has its place of residence or seat in a Member State of the ECICA, the other party may apply to the President of the Special Committee to take the necessary action.[7] Furthermore, when the ECICA was drafted, multiparty arbitration proceedings were not common and, therefore, not considered. Hence, in such situations, the application of Article IV paragraph 2 may raise difficult questions.

9. Article IV paragraph 3 sets out another complicated fallback option in case the parties cannot agree on the appointment of a sole arbitrator. Here, the claimant shall apply for the substitute appointment to either the President of the Chamber of Commerce[8] of the agreed place of arbitration or to the President of the competent Chamber of Commerce of the respondent's habitual place of residence or seat at the time of the notification of the request for arbitration. If no place of arbitration has been agreed upon, the claimant at its option shall be entitled to apply to the President of the competent Chamber of Commerce of the respondent's habitual place of residence or seat at the time of the notification of the request for arbitration, or in the alternative to the Special Committee.[9]

---

4. Lazare Kopelmanas, *La Place De La Convention Europeenne Sur L'arbitrage Commercial International Du 21 Avril 1961 dans L'évolution Du Droit International De L'arbitrage*, 7 Annuaire Français de Droit International. pp. 331–354, p. 335 (1961).
5. *Ibid.*; P. I. Benjamin, *The European Convention on International Commercial Arbitration*, 37 British Yearbook International Law 478, p. 483 (1961).
6. If parties agree to submit their ad hoc arbitration to the UNCITRAL Arbitration Rules, which is rather common for international ad hoc arbitrations, the appointing authority is to be determined pursuant to Article 6 UNCITRAL Arbitration Rules.
7. Florian Haugeneder, *The New Austrian Arbitration Act and the European Convention on International Commercial Arbitration*, 23(4) Arbitration International, 646, p. 656 (2007).
8. *See* below section V.
9. *See* commentary to Annex I of the ECICA.

10. An interesting question arises as to the relation between Article IV paragraphs 2 and 3 and the procedure for the substitute appointment of arbitrators under the arbitration law at the place of arbitration, which usually confers this power to a State court.[10] Which appointing authority to address within the scope of application of the ECICA, the competent court under the national arbitration law at the seat of arbitration or the authority designated under the ECICA? This is not merely a theoretical problem, as a French court case demonstrates. In the underlying arbitration to this French court case, the Court of First Instance of Milan as the court at the place of arbitration appointed a substitute arbitrator for a French party to the arbitration while the chairperson was appointed by the Turin Chamber of Commerce. After the arbitral award was rendered in Italy, the French Court of Appeal of Lyon denied the award's enforcement as the arbitral tribunal was not composed in line with Article IV of the ECICA. The French Court of Appeal held that, pursuant to Article IV paragraph 2, the substitute appointment for the French party should have been made by the President of the French Chamber of Commerce.[11] While this decision has been criticized because France and Italy are parties to the Paris Agreement which modified the content of Article IV paragraph 2 vis-à-vis its Contracting States and, hence, the applicability of the original text of Article IV paragraph 2 was questionable,[12] it illustrates a potential pitfall Article IV might pose before an overly formalistic court with regard to the enforcement and recognition but also for the setting aside of an arbitral award.[13]

[C] Determination of Procedural Rules

11. Article IV paragraph 3 affirms the principle of party autonomy. If the parties had not already agreed on the organization of the arbitral proceedings in their arbitration agreement, they may still do so in course of the arbitration and after the appointment of the arbitrator(s). If the parties cannot agree, the necessary steps shall be taken by the arbitrator(s) already appointed.

12. If for any reason the appointed arbitrators cannot reach an agreement on the necessary steps, one has to differentiate. In case the parties have agreed on the place of arbitration, the claimant may apply to the President of the Chamber of Commerce either at the place of arbitration or at the place of the respondent's habitual place of residence or seat at the time of the notification of the request for arbitration. When there is no agreement on the place of arbitration, the Claimant may also apply to the Special Committee.[14]

10. For example the Austrian Supreme Court for arbitrations seated in Austria.
11. France No. E4, *SA France-Embryon v. Renato Argonauta*, Court of Appeal of Lyon, 4 July 1991, in Vol. XIX, Yearbook Commercial Arbitration, pp. 859–862 (Albert Jan van den Berg ed., 1994).
12. Emmanuel Gaillard and John Savage eds., *Fouchard, Gaillard and Goldman on International Commercial Arbitration*, pp. 524, 525, mn 926 (Kluwer Law International, 1999).
13. Florian Haugeneder, *The New Austrian Arbitration Act and the European Convention on International Commercial Arbitration*, 23(4) Arbitration International, 646, p. 657 (2007).
14. *See* commentary to Annex I of the ECICA.

13. Finally, where the claimant fails to exercise the rights provided to it under paragraph 3, the respondent or the arbitrator(s) shall be entitled to exercise those rights. Hence, the procedure just laid out also applies for the unusual, although possible, case where the claimant fails to cooperate in reaching an agreement on the organization of the proceedings.[15]

III INSTITUTIONAL ARBITRATION

[A] General Overview

14. Pursuant to Article IV paragraph 1 lit (a), the parties shall be free to refer their dispute to a "permanent arbitral institution." This does not point to or encompass a permanent decision-making body such as the ICJ. Rather, as case law on the similar term "permanent arbitral bodies" used in the NYC shows,[16] Article IV paragraph 1 lit (a) refers to administrative arbitral institutions such as the ICC, Stockholm Chamber of Commerce (SCC) or Vienna International Arbitration Center ("VIAC"). These arbitral institutions merely administer arbitration proceedings but leave the decision of the dispute to arbitral tribunals appointed on a case by case basis.

[B] Determination of the Arbitral Institution

15. Pursuant to Article IV paragraph 5, the procedure set out in Article IV paragraph 3 also applies where the parties have decided to submit their disputes to institutional arbitration but failed to determine the institution and subsequently cannot agree thereon. Again, one has to distinguish two possible situations.

16. In case the parties have agreed on the place of arbitration, the claimant may at its option apply to the President of the Chamber of Commerce[17] of the place of arbitration or to the President of the Chamber of Commerce of the respondent's habitual place of residence or seat at the time of the introduction of the request for arbitration to determine the arbitral institution. Where the parties have not agreed on a place of arbitration, the claimant shall be entitled at its option to apply to the President of the Chamber of Commerce of the respondent's habitual place of residence or seat or to the Special Committee.[18]

15. P. I. Benjamin, *The European Convention on International Commercial Arbitration*, 37 British Yearbook International Law 478, p. 483 (1961).
16. *Equating "permanent arbitral bodies" under Article I(2) of the 1958 New York Convention with arbitral institutions*, in Wei Sun & Melanie Willems, *Arbitration in China*: A Practitioner's Guide,10, p. 12 (Wolters Kluwer 2015). Belgium No. E5, *Société Lorraine de Matériel Radio-électrique (SLORA) v. NV Barco Electronic, NV Barco and others*, Rechtbank van Koophandel (Commercial Court), Kortrijk, 337/91, 1 October 1993, the arbitration clause referred to the International Chamber of Commerce of Paris.
17. *See* below section V.
18. *See* commentary to Annex I of the ECICA.

17. Whether the claimant can also use Article IV paragraph 5 to remedy an ambiguous arbitration clause is open to debate.[19] The author knows of at least one case, where this has been successful. Confronted with an ambiguous arbitration clause referring to two different arbitral institutions, the President of the Austrian Federal Economic Chamber determined the "correct" arbitral institution. Such scope of applicability of Article IV paragraph 5 is also affirmed in German literature[20] and judicature.[21] Specifically, the Court of Appeal of Hamburg held that:

> According to Swiss and German legal interpretation an arbitral clause is null and void where it refers the dispute to the decision of an arbitral tribunal which does not exist, or where it is not unambiguously determined or determinable to which of more arbitral tribunals the dispute is referred. However, the European Convention, which is applicable to the parties, takes priority here. The Convention provides in its Art. IV(5) in conjunction with (3), on the validity of the arbitration agreement, for a procedure to determine the competent arbitral tribunal in lieu of the parties.[22]

18. On this basis, Article IV paragraph 5 provides an option to uphold the validity of an arbitration agreement, which might otherwise have been null and void.[23]

[C] Determination of the Institutional Rules

19. Article IV paragraph 1 lit (b) stipulates that in the case of an agreement on institutional arbitration, the arbitration proceedings shall be held in conformity "with the rules of the said institution." Most administrative arbitral institutions grant the parties a certain leeway to modify their arbitration rules if these modifications respect the spirit of the institutional rules.[24]. Such modifications do not violate Article IV. The question remains whether Article IV allows the parties to determine an arbitral institution to administer the arbitration under different (institutional) rules. If the arbitral institution is willing to do that, which likely will not be the case, the parties' wish should be respected as long as due process is not affected.

---

19. Julian D. M. Lew, Loukas A. Mistelis and Stefan Kröll, *Comparative International Commercial Arbitration*, p. 343 (Wolters Kluwer, 2003).
20. H. Raeschke-Kessler, *Neuere Entwicklungen im Bereich der Internationalen Schiedsgerichtsbarkeit*, NJW, 3041, p. 3044 (1988). *See also*, Peter Schlosser, *Das Recht der internationalen privaten Schiedsgerichtsbarkeit*, pp. 286–287 (2nd ed. Mohr Siebeck1989).
21. Germany No. E11, *German party v. Austrian GmbH*, Court of Appeal of Hamburg, 15 November 1995, in Vol. XXI, Yearbook Commercial Arbitration, pp. 845–850 (Albert Jan van den Berg ed., 1996) (citations omitted).
22. Germany No. E11, *German party v. Austrian GmbH*, Court of Appeal of Hamburg, 15 November 1995, in Vol. XXI, Yearbook Commercial Arbitration, pp. 845–850 (Albert Jan van den Berg ed., 1996) (citations omitted).
23. Dominique Hascher, *European Convention on International Commercial Arbitration of 1961: Commentary*, in Vol. XXXVI, Yearbook Commercial Arbitration, 509, p. 522 (Albert Jan van den Berg ed., 2011).
24. Cf. Jason Fry, Simon Greenberg and Francesca Mazza, *The Secretariat's Guide to ICC Arbitration*, mn 3-17 (ICC Publication No. 729E, 2012).

IV NO AGREEMENT ON THE MODE OF ARBITRATION

20. Article IV paragraph 6 stipulates that where the arbitration agreement does not specify the mode of arbitration (ad hoc arbitration or institutional arbitration) and the parties cannot agree thereon, the claimant shall be entitled to have recourse to the procedure referred to in Article IV paragraph 3 to determine this question. Accordingly, the President of the competent Chamber of Commerce[25] or the Special Committee shall be entitled either to refer the parties to a permanent arbitral institution or to set forth the procedural steps for an ad hoc arbitration to take place. In the latter case, the President of the competent Chamber of Commerce or the Special Committee, as the case may be, shall request the parties to appoint their arbitrators within such time limits as the President of the competent Chamber of Commerce or the Special Committee may have fixed and to agree within such time limits on the necessary measures for the functioning of the arbitration.

21. The practical importance of Article IV paragraph 6 is limited as the term "ad hoc arbitration" is usually defined in the negative, namely an arbitration that is not administered by an administrative arbitral institution.[26] Hence, most if not nearly all arbitration agreements that do not designate an arbitral institution are ad hoc arbitration agreements.

V COMPETENCES OF THE PRESIDENT RESPECTIVELY THE SPECIAL COMMITTEE

22. Article IV paragraph 4 sets out that when seized of a request the President of the competent Chamber of Commerce or the Special Committee shall be entitled, as need be: (i) to appoint the sole arbitrator, presiding arbitrator, umpire, or referee;[27] (ii) to replace the arbitrator(s) appointed under any procedure other than that referred to in Article IV paragraph 2; (iii) to determine the place of arbitration, provided that the arbitrator(s) may fix another place of arbitration; and (iv) to establish directly or by reference to the rules and statutes of a permanent arbitral institution the rules of procedure to be followed by the arbitrator(s), provided that the arbitrators have not established these rules themselves in the absence of any agreement thereon between the parties.

---

25. *See* section V below.
26. Pieter Sanders, *Commentary on UNCITRAL Arbitration Rules*, 2 Yearbook Commercial Arbitration, 172, 2.4 (1977); Ulrich G. Schroeter, *Ad Hoc or Institutional Arbitration—A Clear-Cut Distinction? A Closer Look at Borderline Cases*, 10(2) Contemporary Asia Arbitration Journal, 141, p. 146 (2017).
27. An "umpire" is an arbitrator who gives a ruling as sole arbitrator where the two arbitrators appointed by the parties disagree on the merits of the dispute. A "referee" is an arbitrator who gives a casting vote between the other two arbitrators appointed by the parties, thereby being bound to follow the opinion of one of them. The term "presiding arbitrator" is commonly also referred to as the "chairperson" of the arbitral tribunal. P. I. Benjamin, *The European Convention on International Commercial Arbitration*, 37 British Yearbook International Law 478, pp. 483–484, fn. 2 (1961).

23. Pursuant to Article X paragraph 6 ECICA, each Member State has to communicate to the Secretary-General of the United Nations a list of the Chambers of Commerce or other institutions in their country, who will exercise this function. To give a few examples, Azerbaijan has communicated the Economic Court of the Republic of Azerbaijan, Croatia the Permanent Arbitration Court of the Croatian Chamber of Commerce and Slovakia the Slovak Chamber of Commerce and Industry.

24. The composition and procedure of the Special Committee are set out in an Annex to the ECICA. The whole system was set up to balance the influence of the former Western and Eastern Blocs. Therefore, it is quite complicated and, from today's perspective, anachronistic.[28] Furthermore, while the first Special Committee was installed in 1965, it was only renewed every four years as provided for in the Annex until 1993.[29] Hence, currently there is no Special Committee. Even during its existence, only two applications were submitted to the Special Committee requesting its intervention.[30]

28. Lazare Kopelmanas, *La Place De La Convention Europeenne Sur L'arbitrage Commercial International Du 21 Avril 1961 dans L'évolution Du Droit International De L'arbitrage*, 7 Annuaire Français de Droit International. pp. 331–354 (1961).
29. Ottoarndt Glossner, *The Institutional Appointment of Arbitrators: The Special Committee of the European Convention on Commercial Arbitration of Geneva, 21 April 1961*, 12(1) Arbitration International, pp. 95–100, p. 96 (1 March 1996).
30. *Ibid.*, p. 97.

ARTICLE V
Plea as to the Arbitral Jurisdiction

Lisa Beisteiner

INTRODUCTION

> *Article V Pleas as to the Arbitral Jurisdiction*
>
> *(1) The party which intends to raise a plea as to the arbitrator's jurisdiction based on the fact that the arbitration agreement was either non-existent or null and void or had lapsed shall do so during the arbitration proceedings, not later than the delivery of its statement of claim or defence relating to the substance of the dispute; those based on the fact that an arbitrator has exceeded his terms of reference shall be raised during the arbitration proceedings as soon as the question on which the arbitrator is alleged to have no jurisdiction is raised during the arbitral procedure. Where the delay in raising the plea is due to a cause which the arbitrator deems justified, the arbitrator shall declare the plea admissible.*
>
> *(2) Pleas to the jurisdiction referred to in paragraph 1 above that have not been raised during the time-limits there referred to, may not be entered either during a subsequent stage of the arbitral proceedings where they are pleas left to the sole discretion of the parties under the law applicable by the arbitrator, or during subsequent court proceedings concerning the substance or the enforcement of the award where such pleas are left to the discretion of the parties under the rule of conflict of the court seized of the substance of the dispute or the enforcement of the award. The arbitrator's decision on the delay in raising the plea, will, however, be subject to judicial control.*
>
> *(3) Subject to any subsequent judicial control provided for under the* lex fori, *the arbitrator whose jurisdiction is called in question shall be entitled to proceed with the arbitration, to rule on his own jurisdiction and to decide upon the existence or the validity of the arbitration agreement or of the contract of which the agreement forms part.*

1. Article V addresses objections against the arbitrators' jurisdiction raised in the arbitration proceedings based on the nonexistence of a valid arbitration agreement or the excess of the arbitrators' mandate (Article VI ECICA, conversely, addresses jurisdictional objections raised before the State court based on the existence of a valid arbitration agreement). The purpose of Article V is to resolve, at an early stage in the proceedings, jurisdictional objections concerning the consent of the parties to arbitrate and the limits of the arbitrators' mandate as agreed by the parties. In this respect, the provision aims at discouraging a party from delaying the completion of the arbitration proceedings or obstructing the enforcement of the award.[1] Article V presupposes the (potential) inexistence of a valid arbitration agreement, referring to a situation which is not literally covered by the ambit of the ECICA as defined in its Article I; in this respect, therefore, Article I requires extensive interpretation.[2] Conversely, some commentators have submitted that the ECICA would not apply at all in case of arbitration agreements which do not fulfill the form requirements set out in its Article I.[3]

2. Article V only covers certain types of objections (I) and sets forth the time limits that apply to each of them (II). If the objections are not raised within the time limits provided, the affected party's right to object will be precluded (III). As a fundamental principle underlying the ECICA, Article V encapsulates the principle of competence-competence which means the arbitrators are empowered to (preliminarily) rule on their own jurisdiction and to proceed with the arbitration even if their jurisdiction is contested (IV).

I PLEAS COVERED BY THE PROVISION

3. Article V paragraph 1 specifies which objections are covered by the time limits and consequences set forth in the provision. Unlike Article VI of the ECICA, the objections referred to in Article V shall be raised before the arbitrators, not the domestic courts, to challenge the arbitrators' jurisdiction to resolve the dispute. Objections to the jurisdiction of the tribunal other than those set out in Article V paragraph 1 are not covered by Article V as, e.g., objections to the improper constitution or composition of the tribunal.[4]

4. The first type of objection contemplated by Article V paragraph 1 concerns challenges against the arbitration agreement on the grounds that the agreement is *"non-existent, null and void or had lapsed."* The wording differs from Article II(3) of the NYC which provides for the competence of domestic courts if the arbitration agreement

1. P. I. Benjamin, *The European Convention on International Commercial Arbitration*, 37 British Yearbook International Law 478, p. 488 (1961).
2. Peter Schlosser, in Friedrich Stein and Martin Jonas, Kommentar zur Zivilprozessordnung, Vol. 10, Annex to § 1061, para. 409 (23rd ed., Bork & Roth eds., 2014).
3. Different opinion, with further references, Roman Mallmann, Die Bedeutung der Schiedsvereinbarung im Verfahren zur Anerkennung und Vollstreckbarerklärung ausländischer Schiedssprüche, 3 SchiedsVZ, 152, p. 158 (2004).
4. Jens Adolphsen, in Münchener Kommentar zur Zivilprozessordnung, Vol. 3, § 1061, Appendix 2 European Convention, mn 7 (4th ed., Krüger & Rauscher eds., C.H. Beck, 2013). De lege ferenda critically, Ernst Mezger, Das Europäische Übereinkommen über die Handelsschiedsgerichtsberkeit, 29 RabelsZ 231, p. 266 (1965).

is "*null and void, inoperative or incapable of being performed.*"[5] In contrast, when aligning the language used in Article IX(1) of the ECICA, the drafters were cautious, as far as possible, not to depart from the terms utilized in the NYC.[6]

5. Neither the text of the ECICA nor its drafting history specify further details on the interpretation of the grounds for challenging the arbitration agreement. The ground "nonexistent" has been interpreted as covering "*cases in which the contract simply does not contain an arbitration clause or where the litigants are not subject to an arbitration agreement* [in the form set out in Article I(2)(a) of the ECICA]."[7]

6. The words "null and void" are "usually coupled together" in the English version of international arbitration rules[8] and conventions,[9] although they have the same meaning,[10] which is invalidity *ab initio* (i.e., from its conclusion).[11] In fact, the French version of Article V simply refers to "*la nullité (...) de la convention d'arbitrage.*" An arbitration agreement may be interpreted as "null and void" due to a formal or a substantive defect. A formal defect exists whenever the arbitration agreement lacks one of the requirements set forth in Article I(2)(a) of the ECICA.[12] A substantive defect may arise where the consent to arbitrate is tainted with "misrepresentation, duress, fraud or undue influence."[13] Subjective defects may also pertain to the subject matter of the arbitration agreement or the legal capacity of the parties to arbitrate.[14]

7. The phrase "had elapsed" covers cases where the arbitration agreement, although initially valid, has ceased to have effects. The effects of an arbitration agreement may lapse due to a variety of reasons, such as the termination of the arbitration clause (in mutual agreement or unilaterally for due cause), the expiry of its agreed term, or the

---

5. NYC, Article II(3). *See also* UNCITRAL Model Law, Article 8(1) which follows the wording of the NYC instead of the ECICA.
6. "*During the drafting of Article IX, a proposal to depart form the terms of the NYC was rejected because of the drafters' desire to follow the text of Article V of the NYC as closely as possible.*" Dominique Hascher, *European Convention on International Commercial Arbitration of 1961: Commentary*, in Vol. XXXVI, Yearbook Commercial Arbitration, 509, p. 536 (Albert Jan van den Berg ed., 2011).
7. Dominique Hascher, *European Convention on International Commercial Arbitration of 1961: Commentary*, in Vol. XXXVI, Yearbook Commercial Arbitration, 509, p. 524 (Albert Jan van den Berg ed., 2011).
8. For instance ICC Arbitration Rules, Article 6(9); ICDR Arbitration Rules, Article 18(3); VIAC Arbitration Rules, Article 28(1).
9. NYC, Article II(3).
10. Albert Jan van den Berg, *The New York Arbitration Convention of 1958*, p. 155 (Kluwer Law International, 1981).
11. Dominique Hascher, *European Convention on International Commercial Arbitration of 1961: Commentary*, in Vol. XXXVI, Yearbook Commercial Arbitration, 509, p. 524 (Albert Jan van den Berg ed., 2011).
12. *See* commentary to Article 1(2)(a) of the ECICA.
13. Albert Jan van den Berg, *The New York Arbitration Convention of 1958*, p. 155 (Kluwer Law International, 1981).
14. *See*, however, below paras 12 and 13 on the limitation of the preclusive effect of Article V to "waivable" defects.

waiver of the arbitration agreement where a matter subject to an arbitration clause is referred to a State court without timely objection to the court's lack of jurisdiction.[15]

8. Pursuant to the principle of separability which is widely accepted in international arbitration,[16] the arbitration agreement will not be affected by the status of the main agreement. Therefore, the performance, novation, rescission or invalidity of the main contract will not necessarily impact the validity or operability of the arbitration agreement.[17] The principle of separability is not expressly contained in the ECICA, nor was its inclusion contemplated during the drafting period.[18] Article V(3) provides that the arbitrators are empowered "to decide upon the existence or the validity of the arbitration agreement **or** of the contract of which the agreement forms part." However, it does not expressly specify that a finding on the invalidity of the main contract will not impact the validity of the arbitration agreement. Against the prevailing view under which the ECICA does not regulate the principle of separability of the arbitration clause from the main agreement,[19] this language has been interpreted by some as encapsulating the principle of separability.[20]

9. The second type of objection addressed by Article V paragraph 1 ECICA refers to cases where the arbitrator exceeds "his terms of reference": The notion of "terms of reference" denotes the submission by the parties of a specific dispute to arbitration. The arbitrator's jurisdiction will then be limited to judging upon the dispute as submitted to arbitration. Under the second objection, therefore, there is a valid arbitration clause, but the arbitrators exceed the specific submission to arbitration as delineated by the parties' prayers for relief based on this clause: Accordingly, as Dominique Hascher formulates, the notion "terms of reference" connotes "*the mandate of the arbitral tribunal as defined by the parties and not to the scope of the*

15. Dominique Hascher, *European Convention on International Commercial Arbitration of 1961: Commentary*, in Vol. XXXVI, Yearbook Commercial Arbitration, 509, p. 524 (Albert Jan van den Berg ed., 2011).
16. *Bermudian Company v. Spanish Company*, Final Award, ICC Case No. 5485, 18 August 1987, in Vol. XIV, Yearbook Commercial Arbitration, pp. 156–173 (Albert Jan van den Berg ed., 1989).
17. Germany No. E25, *Principal (Czech Republic) v. Sales agent (Germany)*, Court of Appeal of Dresden, 11 Sch 07/08, 18 February 2009 in Vol. XXXV, Yearbook Commercial Arbitration, pp. 582–584 (Albert Jan van den Berg ed., 2010). In this case, the Dresden Court of Appeal held that the invalidity of the main contract does not necessarily affect the validity of the arbitration agreement, unless the ground for the invalidity of the main contract could also be extended to the arbitration agreement.
18. Dominique Hascher, *European Convention on International Commercial Arbitration of 1961: Commentary*, in Vol. XXXVI, Yearbook Commercial Arbitration, 509, p. 525 (Albert Jan van den Berg ed., 2011), who also submits that the question of severability is governed by the law determined under Article VI(2) ECICA as applicable to the existence and validity of the arbitration clause.
19. For example, Rudolf Kaiser, *Das Europäische Übereinkommen über die Internationale Handelsschiedsgerichtsbarkeit*, in Zürcher Studien zum Internationalen Recht, p. 113 (Fritzsche et al. eds., Kraus-Reprint, 1977); Jens Adolphsen, in Münchener Kommentar zur Zivilprozessordnung, Vol. 3, § 1061, Appendix 2 European Convention, mn 18 (4th ed., Krüger & Rauscher eds., C.H. Beck, 2013).
20. For instance, Ernst Mezger, Das Europäische Übereinkommen über die Handelsschiedsgerichtsberkeit, 29 RabelsZ 231, p. 264 (1965).

arbitration clause."[21] Whilst some institutional rules, such as the ICC Arbitration Rules,[22] provide for a separate procedural document called "terms of reference" which is indeed intended to set out (amongst other things) the mandate of the arbitrators, many other rules do not provide for formal terms of reference to be established.[23] The arbitrators will then have to refer to the initial exchange of submissions to analyze the mandate given to them by the parties in the specific case (their "submission to arbitration").[24]

10. Beyond the parties' submission to arbitration, it has been suggested that the second objection would also comprise objections to an excess of authority (power) of the tribunal (confer the equally authentic French text: "*la question litigieuse excéderait les pouvoirs de l'arbitre*"), e.g., objections to the authority (power) of the tribunal to grant a certain relief.[25] This approach has merits to the extent the tribunal's authority (powers) are indeed directly determined by the parties, e.g., where the parties restrict the power of the tribunal to grant interim relief, or—arguably—where they authorize the tribunal to decide *ex aequo et bono*.[26] It may be supported by comparing the—apparently broader—notion of "terms of reference" in Article V of the ECICA, covering the tribunal's mandate and, arguably, its authority as vested by the parties on the one hand, and the reference in Article IX(1) of the ECICA to the "terms of the submission to arbitration," which was intended to follow the wording of Article V NYC, on the other hand.

11. The law applicable by the arbitrators to decide on the existence and validity of the arbitration agreement is not expressly set out in Article V. It was suggested that the arbitrators apply by analogy the conflict of laws rules as defined in Article VI(2) for the courts in order to determine the law applicable to this question.[27]

---

21. Dominique Hascher, *European Convention on International Commercial Arbitration of 1961: Commentary*, in Yearbook Commercial Arbitration, Vol. XXXVI, 509, p. 524 (Albert Jan van den Berg ed., 2011). Florian Haugeneder, *The New Austrian Arbitration Act*, 23(4) Arbitration International 645, p. 654 (2007).
22. ICC Arbitration Rules, Article 23; *see also* the Rules of Arbitration of the Euro-Arab Chambers of Commerce, Article 23-7.
23. Confer Julian D. M. Lew, Loukas A. Mistelis and Stefan M. Kröll, *Comparative International Commercial Arbitration*, pp. 530, 531, mn 21-27 (Kluwer Law International, 2003); Emmanuel Gaillard and John Savage eds., *Fouchard, Gaillard and Goldman on International Commercial Arbitration*, p. 667, mn 1230 (Kluwer Law International, 1999).
24. Nigel Blackaby et al., *Redfern and Hunter on International Arbitration*, p. 378, mn 6.57 (5th ed., Oxford 2009).
25. Confer, in this regard, Peter Schlosser, in Friedrich Stein and Martin Jonas, Kommentar zur Zivilprozessordnung, Vol. 10, Annex to § 1061, para. 410 (23rd ed., Bork & Roth eds., 2014).
26. Confer Regional Court of Hamburg BB Beilage 1999, Nr 4, 19–22, which held that the second objection applied to the question of whether the tribunal could apply principles of *lex mercatoria* to its decision on the merits; different opinion, based on the fact that this would concern the standard of decision-making, Peter Schlosser, in Friedrich Stein and Martin Jonas, Kommentar zur Zivilprozessordnung, Vol. 10, Annex to § 1061, para. 410 (23rd ed., Bork & Roth eds., 2014).
27. Dominique Hascher, *European Convention on International Commercial Arbitration of 1961: Commentary*, in Vol. XXXVI, Yearbook Commercial Arbitration, 509, p. 526 (Albert Jan van den Berg ed. 2011); Jens Adolphsen, in Münchener Kommentar zur Zivilprozessordnung, § 1061, Appendix 2 European Convention, Vol. 3, mn 17 (Krüger & Rauscher eds., C.H. Beck ed., 2013).

12. Not all defects of the arbitration agreement[28] are covered by the preclusive effect[29] of Article V, but only those "left to the [()sole()] discretion of the parties." This concerns defects of the arbitration agreement which may be waived by the parties and are not to be addressed ex officio. The ECICA has refrained from spelling out the law applicable to this assessment. Rather, under Article V paragraph 2, the applicable law to determine which objections are "left to the [()sole()] discretion of the parties" depends on the stage at which the objection is raised: Whenever the plea was raised during the arbitration proceedings, the applicable law will be the "law applicable by the arbitrator." Whenever an objection is raised during the subsequent court proceedings concerning the substance or the enforcement of the award, the applicable law will be "the rule of conflict of the court seized," i.e., the conflict of laws rules to be applied by the respective domestic court.[30] Therefore, the question of whether an objection can be waived may well be answered differently by the tribunal and the (different) court(s). Some commentators have advocated for the analogous application of the applicable law rule set forth in Article VI paragraph 2 in the analysis of the procedural relevance of any such defect.[31] Others refer to the procedural law applicable to the arbitration as the relevant law.[32]

13. It was set out that nonwaivable jurisdictional objections will *"generally pertain to public policy."*[33] This will include substantive defects based on the invalidity of the arbitration agreement due to a party's incapacity to arbitrate (provided such incapacity is deemed part of public policy) or the nonarbitrability of the matter in dispute (objective arbitrability).[34]

II TIME LIMITS FOR RAISING A PLEA

14. Regarding the first type of objection (lack of valid arbitration agreement), the party contesting the jurisdiction of the tribunal shall raise the objection not later than (i.e., at the latest at the same time as) the delivery of its statement of claim or defense relating

28. There appears to be little scope of application for this rule with regard to the second type of objection set out in Article V para. 1, which by definition concerns the mandate (and, arguably, authority) granted to the tribunal by the parties.
29. *See* below Section III.
30. According to Jens Adolphsen, in Münchener Kommentar zur Zivilprozessordnung, Vol. 3, § 1061, Appendix 2 European Convention, mn 10 (4th ed., Krüger & Rauscher eds., C.H. Beck, 2013), this will be the relevant procedural law, i.e., the *lex fori* of the court.
31. Peter Schlosser, in Friedrich Stein and Martin Jonas, Kommentar zur Zivilprozessordnung, Vol. 10, Annex to § 1061, para. 417 (23rd ed., Bork & Roth eds., 2014), who also points out that in principle the law applicable to the arbitration agreement will be relevant.
32. Jens Adolphsen, in Münchener Kommentar zur Zivilprozessordnung, § 1061, Appendix 2 European Convention, Vol. 3, mn 9 (4th ed., Krüger & Rauscher eds., C.H. Beck, 2013).
33. Dominique Hascher, *European Convention on International Commercial Arbitration of 1961: Commentary*, in Vol. XXXVI, Yearbook Commercial Arbitration, 509, p. 525 (Albert Jan van den Berg ed. 2011). More narrowly, Ernst Mezger, Das Europäische Übereinkommen über die Handelsschiedsgerichtsberkeit, 29 RabelsZ 231, p. 265 (1965), who refers to such lack of jurisdiction as is based on "mandatory law."
34. Confer Florian Haugeneder, *The New Austrian Arbitration Act*, 23(4) ARBITRATION INTERNATIONAL 645, p. 655 (2007).

to the substance of the dispute. The term "statement of claim or defense" refers to the initial (typically but not necessarily written[35]) submissions by the parties on the substance of the dispute rather than on jurisdictional aspects. The "statement of defense" denotes the first defense to the claim, as opposed to any subsequent defense in the further course of the proceedings.[36] It has been submitted that the term "statement of claim" refers to a counterclaim raised in the arbitration.[37] The language "statement of claim" may also imply that the claimant, upon initiating the arbitration and discussing the merits of his claim, will be barred from subsequently raising any jurisdictional objections based on the nonexistence of a valid arbitration clause. A plea under Article V paragraph 1 first option needs to be raised before entering the first discussion of the merits of the case, which may also be done in a short initial communication prior to a formal written submission as envisaged by any applicable institutional rules. The terminology used by the parties or the arbitration rules for the parties' submissions, such as "statement of claim" or, under the LCIA Arbitration Rules, e.g., "statement of case"[38] is of no import in this regard.

15. The second type of objection (excess of the arbitrators' mandate or, arguably, authority as granted by the parties in their submission to arbitration) needs to be raised during the arbitration proceedings as soon as the "question" on which the arbitrator is alleged to have no jurisdiction "is raised," i.e., as soon as the respective request for relief going beyond the arbitrator's mandate or powers is raised. This includes the raising of new claims, including of counterclaims, as well as the amendment of existing claims; further, the raising of requests which exceed the powers of the arbitrators as granted by the parties. The sole fact that additional factual or legal "questions" are being introduced into the proceedings does not call for an objection under Article V paragraph 1 second option.[39]

16. The provision does not specify whether the jurisdictional objection must be raised in a written[40] or an oral communication. As a matter of law, therefore, an oral plea will suffice; a different reading would unduly extend the preclusion norm of Article V. However, to put the objection on file for a later stage of the arbitration or subsequent court proceedings, the parties are well advised to and typically will raise the objection in writing.

---

35. Jens Adolphsen, in Münchener Kommentar zur Zivilprozessordnung, Vol. 3, § 1061, Appendix 2 European Convention, mn 3 (4th ed., Krüger & Rauscher eds., C.H. Beck, 2013) asserts, albeit without further explanation, that where an oral discussion is mandatory, no preclusion shall occur until such oral hearing.
36. Dominique Hascher, *European Convention on International Commercial Arbitration of 1961: Commentary*, in Vol. XXXVI, Yearbook Commercial Arbitration, 509, p. 524 (Albert Jan van den Berg ed., 2011).
37. Florian Haugeneder, *The New Austrian Arbitration Act*, 23(4) ARBITRATION INTERNATIONAL, 645, p. 654 (2007).
38. LCIA Arbitration Rules, Article 15.
39. In a similar vein, Peter Schlosser, in Friedrich Stein and Martin Jonas, Kommentar zur Zivilprozessordnung, Vol. 10, Annex to § 1061, para. 410 (23rd ed., Bork & Roth eds., 2014).
40. Reference to the "delivery of its statement of claim or defence" might indicate a written plea.

17. The principle and time limits set forth in Article V are reflected in many national arbitration laws and institutional rules in similar terms.[41]

18. Where the arbitrator concludes, within his or her discretion, that the delay is justified (more precisely: "*the delay in raising the plea is due to a cause which the arbitrator deems justified*"), he must (arg.: "shall") admit the belated plea (Article V paragraph 1 last sentence).[42] Article V does not give any guidance on when a delay may be considered justified and the approaches of national laws on the issue will vary considerably. The arbitrators' decision on whether a delay *is deemed justified* or not is not subject to judicial control.[43] The arbitrator's decision on *whether there was a delay* in raising the plea, however, is subject to judicial control (Article V paragraph 2 last sentence): The court (typically the enforcement court) is authorized to review whether there was indeed an objective delay as established by the tribunal and, if it finds to the contrary, to rule on the jurisdictional objection in the court proceedings.[44] Where the tribunal fails to decide on the timeliness of the jurisdictional objection (e.g., because it deems the objection has no merit anyways and, therefore, leaves the issue of timeliness open), the court will equally be entitled to decide on the objective delay.[45]

III CONSEQUENCES OF RAISING A PLEA BELATEDLY

19. The consequence of not raising an objection within the specified time limits, contained in Article V(2), is that the respective party will be barred from raising the objection (i) during a subsequent stage of the arbitral proceedings or (ii) "in court proceedings concerning the substance or the enforcement of the award."[46] As such, the

41. *See*, above all, UNCITRAL Model Law, Article 16(1); German Code of Civil Procedure (ZPO), Section 1040(2); Austrian Code on Civil Procedure (ZPO), Section 592 para. 2; Netherlands Code of Civil Procedure, Article 1052(2), to name a few.
42. In the same vein, Jens Adolphsen, in Münchener Kommentar zur Zivilprozessordnung, Vol. 3, § 1061, Appendix 2 European Convention, mn 3 (4th ed., Krüger & Rauscher eds., C.H. Beck, 2013).
43. Jens Adolphsen, in Münchener Kommentar zur Zivilprozessordnung, Vol. 3, § 1061, Appendix 2 European Convention, mn 12 (4th ed., Krüger & Rauscher eds., C.H. Beck, 2013).
44. Ernst Mezger, Das Europäische Übereinkommen über die Handelsschiedsgerichtsberkeit, 29 RabelsZ 231, p. 266 (1965); Jens Adolphsen, in Münchener Kommentar zur Zivilprozessordnung, Vol. 3, § 1061, Appendix 2 European Convention, mn 13 (4th ed., Krüger & Rauscher eds., C.H. Beck, 2013).
45. *See* below [para. 26 (Wünsche case)].
46. Dominique Hascher, *European Convention on International Commercial Arbitration of 1961: Commentary*, in Vol. XXXVI, Yearbook Commercial Arbitration, 509, p. 524 (Albert Jan van den Berg ed., 2011); Germany No. 82/E16, *K Trading Company (Syria) v. Bayerischen Motoren Werke AG (Germany)*, Higher Court of Appeal of Bavaria, 4Z Sch 005-04, 23 September 2004, in Vol. XXX, Yearbook Commercial Arbitration, pp. 568–573 (Albert Jan van den Berg ed., 2005); Spain No. 28, *Nobulk Cargo Services Ltd. v. Compañía Española de Laminación S.A.*, Spanish Supreme Court, Not Indicated, 27 February 1991, in Vol. XXI, Yearbook Commercial Arbitration, pp. 678–680 (Albert Jan van den Berg ed., Kluwer Law International, 1996); Spain No. 6 / E3, *X S.A. v. Y*, Spanish Supreme Court, Not Indicated, 14 January 1983, in Vol. XI, Yearbook Commercial Arbitration, pp. 523–524 (Albert Jan van den Berg ed., Kluwer Law International, 1986).

"estoppel rule"[47] of Article V is an emanation of the principle of procedural efficiency: It bars opportunistic behavior under which the parties may wait and see how their case develops on the merits before they decide to raise the jurisdictional objection they hold "on stock." Rather, under the ECICA, if the jurisdictional objection is not raised in a timely manner, the respective right is lost.[48]

20. The wording of the ECICA limits the preclusive effect of Article V paragraph 2 to the pending arbitration, as well as to court proceedings (1) on the same subject matter ("concerning the substance"), or (2) on an enforcement (which must also include recognition) of the award. Under the ECICA, as it seems, the jurisdictional plea, therefore, is not precluded in subsequent proceedings to set aside the award.[49] Failure to timely object to the arbitrators' jurisdiction at the arbitration stage would then not cure the defect in the arbitration agreement (to the extent the objection was waivable). Rather, the party could still bring an action for setting aside the award. Certainly, such reading of the ECICA is not helpful considering the purpose of Article V. Accordingly, some commentators appear to also apply Article V to setting aside proceedings.[50]

21. A different question relates to whether only the jurisdictional plea which was effectively raised in the arbitration will be preserved, or if the raising of any objection preserves the party's right to subsequently object to the jurisdiction of the tribunal also based on other grounds.[51]

22. In *Buyer (Austria) v. Seller (Serbia and Montenegro)*, an award was issued in favor of the seller who sought enforcement of the award in Austria. The buyer, in turn, objected that the award violated public policy, *inter alia*, on the grounds of the invalidity of the arbitration agreement due to a forged signature. The case was eventually submitted to the Austrian Supreme Court which reasoned that the buyer had waived its right to raise the objection of the invalidity of the arbitration agreement because such objection had not been raised within the time limits set forth in Article V.[52]

---

47. Dominique Hascher, *European Convention on International Commercial Arbitration of 1961: Commentary*, in Vol. XXXVI, Yearbook Commercial Arbitration, 509, p. 524 (Albert Jan van den Berg ed., 2011).
48. Accordingly, Peter Schlosser, in Friedrich Stein and Martin Jonas, Kommentar zur Zivilprozessordnung, Vol. 10, Annex to § 1061, para. 414 (23rd ed., Bork & Roth eds., 2014), stresses that Article V ECICA does not contemplate the tacit conclusion of an arbitration agreement.
49. Dominique Hascher, *European Convention on International Commercial Arbitration of 1961: Commentary*, in Vol. XXXVI, Yearbook Commercial Arbitration, 509, p. 525 (Albert Jan van den Berg ed., 2011).
50. Florian Haugeneder, *The New Austrian Arbitration Act*, in 23(4) Arbitration International 645, p. 654 (2007), who—albeit without discussing the issue—extends the preclusive effect of Article V ECICA to annulment claims; further *confer* Jens Adolphsen, in Münchener Kommentar zur Zivilprozessordnung, Vol. 3, § 1061, Appendix 2 European Convention, mn 17 (4th ed., Krüger & Rauscher eds., C.H. Beck, 2013).
51. Advocating this second approach, Peter Schlosser, in Friedrich Stein and Martin Jonas, Kommentar zur Zivilprozessordnung, Vol. 10, Annex to § 1061, para. 415 (23rd ed., Bork & Roth eds., 2014).
52. *Buyer (Austria) v. Seller (Serbia and Montenegro)*, Austrian Supreme Court, 3Ob221/04b, 26 January 2005, in Vol. XXX, Yearbook Commercial Arbitration, pp. 421–436 (Albert Jan van den Berg ed., 2005).

23. Similarly, in *K Trading Company v. BMW*, an award was rendered in favor of K Trading which sought enforcement of the award in Germany. BMW objected the enforcement of the award alleging the invalidity of the arbitration clause. However, the Higher Court of Appeal found that BMW was estopped from objecting to the validity of the arbitration agreement between the parties because BMW had participated in the arbitration without raising any such objection.[53]

24. In *Seller (France) v. Buyer (Germany)*, an award was issued in France in favor of the seller who thereafter sought enforcement of the award in Germany. During the arbitration, the buyer had—without success—raised a jurisdictional objection. The Munich Court of Appeal refused enforcement due to the lack of a valid arbitration agreement. The Federal Supreme Court confirmed the Court of Appeal's decision and rejected the seller's argument that the buyer's failure to challenge the award in the country of origin within the time limits for an appeal set out in French procedural law, would preclude the buyer from raising the objection at the enforcement stage in Germany:

> The European Convention does not provide for a further preclusion for failure to file, against the arbitral award, an appeal to be filed within a given time limit. Since Defendant argued from the beginning in the arbitration that there was no arbitration agreement, the plea of lack of jurisdiction is admissible under the European Convention.[54]

25. In any event, the arbitrator's decision on the delay in raising the plea will be subject to judicial control.

26. In *Wünsche Handelsgesellschaft v. Coop. S. Maria srl*, Wünsche commenced arbitration proceedings against S. Maria. S. Maria disputed the validity of the arbitration clause between the parties, for the first time, at the hearing before the arbitral tribunal. The award was issued in favor of Wünsche. However, S. Maria requested the setting aside of the award before the Court of First Instance of Hamburg on the grounds that the arbitration clause had referred the dispute to an arbitral tribunal constituted under different institutional rules. According to the Court of Appeal's reasoning, under Article V(2) ECICA the court was exclusively entitled to rule on the tribunal's decision on the delay of the objection. However, in the case at hand the arbitral tribunal had not ruled on the delay of the objection as it had found the objection unfounded. The Court of Appeal reasoned that as a result of doing so the arbitral tribunal had admitted the objection and that the court was not authorized to revisit the objection's admissibility. The German Supreme Court disagreed with the Court of Appeal's decision on this point. The Supreme Court reasoned that, under Article V, the court's power to review an arbitrators' decision on the admissibility of the plea was not limited to decisions

53. Germany No. 82/E16, *K Trading Company (Syria) v. Bayerischen Motoren Werke AG (Germany)*, Higher Court of Appeal of Bavaria, 4Z Sch 005-04, 23 September 2004, in Vol. XXX, Yearbook Commercial Arbitration, pp. 568–573 (Albert Jan van den Berg ed., 2005).
54. Germany No. 136, *French Seller v. German Buyer, Oberlandesgericht*, Munich, 23 November 2009 and Bundesgerichtshof, 16 December 2010 in Vol. XXXVI, Yearbook Commercial Arbitration, pp. 273–276, para. 28 (Albert Jan van den Berg ed.,2011).

which were actually rendered on the admission of the jurisdictional objection. Otherwise, the arbitrators, by not deciding on the admissibility of a late plea because they found the plea groundless anyway, would frustrate the power of the courts to examine the timeliness of the plea. In consequence, the admissibility must be decided by the court when the arbitrator has left the issue open.[55]

27. Therefore, in the absence of a decision by the arbitrators on the delay in raising the objection, the court will nevertheless be authorized to decide on the timeliness of the plea.

28. The preclusive effect of Article V paragraph 2 ECICA only applies to a party who had an opportunity to present its case. Beyond that, the wording and drafting history of the ECICA suggest that it applies only to those parties who in fact made an appearance in the arbitration, i.e., not in ex parte proceedings (arg.: "*The party which intends to raise a plea [...] the delivery of its claim or defence [...]*").[56] An argument to militate in favor of the latter approach is that a party who does not participate in the arbitration at all does not generate any legitimate expectation that it would agree to submit to the tribunal's jurisdiction.[57] There are arguments to equally apply Article V paragraph 2 ECICA in ex parte proceedings, because (and as long as) the nonparticipating party had an opportunity to present its case but chose not to participate in the arbitration and, hence, not to raise its jurisdictional objection. Such reading would bar a recalcitrant party from holding on stock jurisdictional objections by refusing to participate in the arbitration. On the other hand, Article V is a preclusion norm and should, as such, not be interpreted extensively.

IV PRINCIPLE OF COMPETENCE-COMPETENCE

29. Article V(3) provides for the principle of competence-competence (*Kompetenz-Kompetenz*) which is presently recognized by most modern arbitration statutes,[58] and

55. Germany No. E7, *Wünsche Handelsgesellschaft v. Coop. S. Maria srl, German Supreme Court*, Not Indicated, 2 December 1982, in Vol. XV, Yearbook Commercial Arbitration, pp. 660–665 (Albert Jan van den Berg ed., 1990).
56. Dominique Hascher, *European Convention on International Commercial Arbitration of 1961: Commentary*, in Vol. XXXVI, Yearbook Commercial Arbitration, 509, p. 524 (Albert Jan van den Berg ed., 2011). Jens Adolphsen, in Münchener Kommentar zur Zivilprozessordnung, Vol. 3, § 1061, Appendix 2 European Convention, mn 6 (4th ed., Krüger & Rauscher eds., C.H. Beck, 2013); Peter Schlosser, in Friedrich Stein and Martin Jonas, Kommentar zur Zivilprozessordnung, Vol. 10, Annex to § 1061, para. 413 (23rd ed., Bork & Roth eds., 2014), for instance, emphasizes that the defendant should not be forced to participate in the arbitration in order to avert preclusion of his jurisdictional objection. Roman Mallmann, Die Bedeutung der Schiedsvereinbarung im Verfahren zur Anerkennung und Vollstreckbarerklärung ausländischer Schiedssprüche, 3 SchiedsVZ, 152, p. 159 (2004).
57. Roman Mallmann, Die Bedeutung der Schiedsvereinbarung im Verfahren zur Anerkennung und Vollstreckbarerklärung ausländischer Schiedssprüche, 3 SchiedsVZ, 152, p. 158 (2004).
58. UNCITRAL Model Law, Article 16(1). The principle can also be found in non-Model Law countries such as Switzerland and England. China is an exception as the decision on jurisdiction lies within the competence of either the arbitral institution chosen by the parties or of the domestic courts. Julian D. M. Lew, Loukas A. Mistelis and Stefan M. Kröll, *Comparative International Commercial Arbitration*, p. 333, mn 14-17, fn. 8 (Kluwer Law International, 2003).

institutional arbitration rules.[59] The NYC is an exception, as it does not expressly provide for the principle of competence-competence. A precedent of the principle can be found in Article 36(6) of the ICJ Statute[60] which allows the Court to rule on its own jurisdiction. The principle of competence-competence protects the arbitration against obstruction or delay by one party.[61] It was regarded as an innovative step at the time (one commentator remarked that Article V of the ECICA was "*breaking new ground*"[62]).

30. Under the principle of competence-competence, the arbitrators are empowered to determine the existence, validity, and scope of the arbitration agreement, without the need to invoke the jurisdiction of a domestic court.[63] It enables the arbitral tribunal to continue the proceedings even where the existence or validity of the arbitration agreement has been challenged by one of the parties before the tribunal or before a domestic court. Article VI of the ECICA reinforces this principle as it provides that whenever arbitration proceedings have been initiated, any subsequent challenge to the arbitrators' jurisdiction[64] brought before the domestic courts shall, in principle, be stayed until the arbitrators have rendered their award (this has been referred to as limited negative *Kompetenz-Kompetenz*[65]).[66] Whilst the tribunal faced with a jurisdictional objection is "entitled" by the ECICA to continue the arbitration proceedings, it is under no obligation to do so.[67]

31. The principle entails what one may perceive a theoretical contradiction since it implies that arbitrators should also be entitled to decide on their own jurisdiction

59. ICC Arbitration Rules, Article 6(3); LCIA Arbitration Rules, Article 23(1); ICDR Arbitration Rules, Article 18(1); VIAC Arbitration Rules, Article 28(1).
60. United Nations, *Statute of the International Court of Justice*, 18 April 1946, Article 36(6) provides "*In the event of a dispute as to whether the Court has jurisdiction, the matter shall be settled by the decision of the Court.*"
61. William W. Park, *Determining an Arbitrator's Jurisdiction: Timing and Finality in American Law*, 8 Nevada Law Journal 135, p. 138 (16 January 2008); Dominique Hascher, *European Convention on International Commercial Arbitration of 1961: Commentary*, in Vol. XXXVI, Yearbook Commercial Arbitration, 509, p. 525 (Albert Jan van den Berg ed., 2011); Stefan Kröll, *The European Convention on International Commercial Arbitration: The Tale of a Sleeping Beauty*, in Austrian Yearbook on International Arbitration, 4, p. 10 (Klausegger and others eds., Manz, 2013).
62. Ernst Mezger, Das Europäische Übereinkommen über die Handelsschiedsgerichtsberkeit, 29 RabelsZ 231, p. 262 (1965).
63. Julian D. M. Lew, Loukas A. Mistelis and Stefan M. Kröll, *Comparative International Commercial Arbitration*, p. 334, mn 14-19 (Kluwer Law International, 2003); *Bermudian Company v. Spanish Company*, Final Award, ICC Case No. 5485, 18 August 1987, in Vol. XIV, Yearbook Commercial Arbitration, pp. 156–173 (Albert Jan van den Berg (ed.), Kluwer Law International, 1989).
64. In detail, Article VI extends to any claims by which the court is "*subsequently asked to deal with the same subject-matter between the same parties or with the question whether the arbitration agreement was non-existent or null and void or had lapsed*"; *see* commentary to Article VI of the ECICA.
65. Stefan Kröll, *The European Convention on International Commercial Arbitration: The Tale of a Sleeping Beauty*, in Austrian Yearbook on International Arbitration, 4, p. 10 (Klausegger and others eds., Manz, 2013).
66. *See* commentary to Article VI of the ECICA.
67. Jens Adolphsen, in Münchener Kommentar zur Zivilprozessordnung, Vol. 3, § 1061, Appendix 2 European Convention, mn 16 (4th ed., Krüger & Rauscher eds., C.H. Beck, 2013).

where the parties never (validly) agreed to submit to arbitration.[68] This problem is overcome by the fact that the tribunal's decision is subject to the subsequent judicial control (if any) as provided for under the *lex fori* of the domestic court seized with such request.[69] The principle of competence-competence as framed by the ECICA is, thus, in general, not absolute. Conversely, the ECICA does not prevent the national law (*lex fori*) from framing the competence-competence of the tribunal as an absolute principle.[70] The ECICA does not require the Contracting States to establish any judicial control of the tribunal's decision on jurisdiction, except for the tribunal's decision on a delay in raising the jurisdictional plea. The *lex fori* referenced in Article V(3) ECICA refers to the law of the domestic court where the judicial control (notably challenge or review) is sought, which will typically be the place of arbitration or enforcement.[71]

32. Following the tribunal's decision, the domestic court seized to review such a decision on the nonexistence or invalidity of the arbitration agreement must follow the special rule on the applicable law set forth in Article VI of the ECICA.

68. Julian D. M. Lew, Loukas A. Mistelis and Stefan M. Kröll, *Comparative International Commercial Arbitration*, p. 332, mn 14-13, 14-14 (Kluwer Law International, 2003).
69. Emmanuel Gaillard and John Savage eds., *Fouchard, Gaillard and Goldman on International Commercial Arbitration*, pp. 400–401, mn 659–660 (Kluwer Law International, 1999).
70. This was the case under the former German arbitration law, under which the tribunal's decision on its own jurisdiction was final and not reviewable under certain circumstances; *see*, with further references, Stefan Kröll, *The European Convention on International Commercial Arbitration: The Tale of a Sleeping Beauty*, Austrian Yearbook on International Arbitration, 4, p. 10 (Klausegger and others eds., Manz, 2013).
71. Stavros Brekoulakis, *Arbitrability and Conflict of Jurisdictions: The (Diminishing) Relevance of Lex Fori and Lex Loci Arbitri*, in Conflict of Laws in International Arbitration, p. 117 (Franco Ferrari and Stefan Kröll eds., Sellier International Publishers, 2010).

ARTICLE VI

Jurisdiction of Courts of Law

Alfred Siwy

INTRODUCTION

Article VI—Jurisdiction of courts of law

1. *A plea as to the jurisdiction of the court made before the court seized by either party to the arbitration agreement, on the basis of the fact that an arbitration agreement exists shall, under penalty of estoppel, be presented by the respondent before or at the same time as the presentation of his substantial defence, depending upon whether the law of the court seized regards this plea as one of procedure or of substance.*
2. *In taking a decision concerning the existence or the validity of an arbitration agreement, courts of Contracting States shall examine the validity of such agreement with reference to the capacity of the parties, under the law applicable to them, and with reference to other questions:*
   - *(a) under the law to which the parties have subjected their arbitration agreement;*
   - *(b) failing any indication thereon, under the law of the country in which the award is to be made;*
   - *(c) failing any indication as to the law to which the parties have subjected the agreement, and where at the time when the question is raised in court the country in which the award is to be made cannot be determined, under the competent law by virtue of the rules of conflict of the court seized of the dispute.*

   The courts may also refuse recognition of the arbitration agreement if under the law of their country the dispute is not capable of settlement by arbitration.
3. *Where either party to an arbitration agreement has initiated arbitration proceedings before any resort is had to a court, courts of Contracting States subsequently asked to deal with the same subject-matter between the same parties or with the question whether the arbitration agreement was non-existent or null and void or had lapsed, shall stay their ruling on the arbitrator's jurisdiction until the arbitral award is made, unless they have good and substantial reasons to the contrary.*

> 4. *A request for interim measures or measures of conservation addressed to a judicial authority shall not be deemed incompatible with the arbitration agreement, or regarded as a submission of the substance of the case to the court.*

1. Article V together with Article VI of the ECICA regulates the relationship between the arbitration proceedings and domestic courts. Article VI focuses on challenges to the jurisdiction of domestic courts where there is an arbitration agreement and regulates the intervention of domestic courts in the arbitration proceedings.[1] First, it imposes a strict deadline for raising jurisdictional objections based on the existence of an arbitration agreement (I). Second, it designates the applicable law governing the substantive validity of the arbitration agreement (II). Third, it addresses the issue regarding lis pendens, when a party initiates arbitration proceedings and domestic court proceedings are initiated by the other party (III). Finally, it allows the parties to request interim measures before domestic courts (IV).

I TIME LIMIT FOR RAISING A JURISDICTIONAL OBJECTION BEFORE DOMESTIC COURTS

2. When a party to an arbitration agreement initiates domestic court proceedings, paragraph 1 of Article VI imposes a time limit for the other party to raise a jurisdictional objection before such a court on the grounds of the existence of an arbitration agreement.

3. According to paragraph 1, a plea as to the jurisdiction of the court shall be presented by the respondent before or at the same time as the presentation of his substantial defense, depending upon whether the law of the court seized regards this plea as one of procedure or of substance.

4. The time limits for raising a jurisdictional objection, therefore, depend on whether such an objection is considered a procedural or substantive issue (the latter of which seems rather uncommon). The objection "*must be made by the respondent before presenting his substantial defence where the court seised regards this plea as one of procedure.*"[2] It must be raised "*at the same time as the presentation of the substantial defence where such court regards the plea as one of substance.*"[3] In both scenarios, "*the failure to raise the plea within the time-limits operates as an estoppel.*"[4] Therefore, the party which fails to challenge the jurisdiction of the domestic court on time is precluded from raising the objection in a further stage.[5]

---

1. Stefan Kröll, *The European Convention on International Commercial Arbitration: The Tale of a Sleeping Beauty,* in Austrian Yearbook on International Arbitration, 4, p. 13 (Klausegger and others eds., Manz, 2013).
2. P. I. Benjamin, *The European Convention on International Commercial Arbitration,* 37 British Yearbook International Law 478, p. 489 (1961).
3. *Ibid.*
4. *Ibid.*
5. Florian Haugeneder, *The New Austrian Arbitration Act and the European Convention on International Commercial Arbitration,* 23(4) Arbitration International, 646, p. 653 (2007); Dominique Hascher, *European Convention on International Commercial Arbitration of 1961:*

5. As the point in time when the plea should be raised depends on domestic law certain contradictions may be encountered. First, in Austrian Law, Article 584 of the Code of Civil Procedures *"requires that the objection be brought together with the first submission of oral or written pleadings on the matter."*[6] Austrian Law at the same time considers the objection to the jurisdiction as a procedural matter. Contrary to Article 584, under Article VI of the ECICA when the court seized *"considers the objection of lack of jurisdiction a question of procedure"* the objection shall be raised *"**before** … the defense on the merits is submitted."* The rule enshrined in Article 584 would only be compatible if Austrian law considered the matter to be one of substantive law, which is not the case. This has the consequence that within the scope of application of the ECICA, a plea as to the jurisdiction of the court would be belated if made in one submission together with the reply on the merits.

6. This reasoning was followed by the Italian Supreme Court in *Cifuindus v. OFAG*. In this case, the parties concluded an agreement for, *inter alia*, the supply of electro-mechanic ceramic parts which contained an arbitration clause. When the dispute arose between the parties, OFAG applied for an injunction against Cifuindus before the Court of First Instance of Milan. Cifuindus counterclaimed the injunction and, in its statement of defense on the merits, objected to the jurisdiction of Italian courts based on the arbitration clause. When the matter reached the Supreme Court, it held that under Italian law the objection on lack of jurisdiction is a procedural matter. Hence, the Supreme Court found that, according to Article VI of the ECICA, Cifuindus' jurisdictional objection was belated:

> In the case at issue, Cifuindus did not object to the lack of jurisdiction, on the grounds of a foreign arbitration clause, when replying to the injunction: he has defended itself on the merits of the case and has filed a counterclaim .... On the other hand, the [ECICA] provides in Art. VI that a plea based on an arbitration agreement must be raised before or at the moment the defense on the merits is submitted, depending on whether the law of the competent court considers the objection of lack of jurisdiction a question of procedure or substance. Since Italian law considers this objection to be of a procedural nature, Cifuindus' objection was indeed precluded since Cifuindus had submitted its defence on the merits without **first** raising the point of lack of jurisdiction.[7]

7. Second, it may also be the case, that the pertinent domestic law system allows a party to raise the jurisdictional plea at a later stage than the submission of the defense of the merits. For instance, German arbitration law provides that a party may raise the defense until the first oral hearing. By this point, the party may have already presented

Commentary, in Vol. XXXVI, Yearbook Commercial Arbitration, 509, p. 527 (Albert Jan van den Berg ed., 2011); Julian D. M. Lew, Loukas A. Mistelis and Stefan Kröll, *Comparative International Commercial Arbitration*, p. 340 (Wolters Kluwer, 2003).

6. Florian Haugeneder, *The New Austrian Arbitration Act and the European Convention on International Commercial Arbitration*, 23(4) Arbitration International, 646, p. 653 (2007).

7. *SpA Cifuindus v. OFAG-Ofendau und Feuerungstechnik AG*, Italian Supreme Court (*Corte di Cassazione*), 5071, 16 October 1985, in Il Foro Italiano, Vol. 108, No. 11 (November 1985), pp. 2871/2872–2875/2876 (Societa Editrice Il Foro Italiano ARL) (Unofficial English translation, original in Italian); *see also* Jurisprudence No. 5071, Giust civ. Mass. 1985, fasc. 10, foro it. 1985, I, 2872.

its defense on the merits.[8] This situation also contradicts the wording of Article VI(1) because even assuming that German Law considers the objection as a matter of substance, the limit to raise the objection is *"at the moment the defense on the merits is submitted."*

8. The solution of these two contradictions will depend on the conflict of laws rules applied, for instance, in legal systems where a treaty is hierarchically above federal laws, the provisions of the ECICA shall prevail.[9]

II APPLICABLE LAW FOR DOMESTIC COURTS TO ANALYZE THE SUBSTANTIVE VALIDITY OF THE ARBITRATION AGREEMENT

9. As discussed above, Article I(2)(a) regulates the form requirements of the arbitration agreement. Article VI(2) of the ECICA provides the applicable law, pertaining to the capacity of the parties [A], and other substantive questions on the existence or the validity of the arbitration clause [B].

[A] Capacity of the Parties

10. For the arbitration agreement to be valid, the parties shall have the legal capacity to contract. As a general rule, *"any natural or legal person who has capacity to enter into a valid contract has the capacity to enter into an arbitration agreement."*[10] The rules governing the capacity of the parties vary from State to State.[11] For instance, arbitration law in France *"aims to determine the validity of the arbitration agreement on the basis of the parties' intent without any reference to national law."*[12] These variations could lead to different outcomes and, as a result, lead to uncertainty.

11. Few arbitration laws regulate the law applicable to the capacity of the parties in a pre-award stage;[13] the ECICA is one of these rules.[14] According to paragraph 2 of Article VI of the ECICA, the party's capacity is analyzed by domestic courts, under the law applicable to the parties. The NYC and some domestic law systems deal with this issue

8. Article 1032(1) ZPO. Stefan Kröll, *The European Convention on International Commercial Arbitration: The Tale of a Sleeping Beauty*, in Austrian Yearbook on International Arbitration, p. 15 (Klausegger and others eds., Manz, 2013).
9. *See* above commentary to Article I of the ECICA, section III.B.
10. Nigel Blackaby et al., *Redfern and Hunter on International Arbitration*, p. 81, mn 2.31 (6th ed., Oxford, 2015).
11. *Ibid.*
12. Julian D. M. Lew, Loukas A. Mistelis and Stefan Kröll, *Comparative International Commercial Arbitration*, p. 118 (Wolters Kluwer, 2003).
13. The UNCITRAL Model Law only regulates the incapacity of the parties but does not refer to the applicable law, Julian D. M. Lew, Loukas A. Mistelis and Stefan Kröll, *Comparative International Commercial Arbitration*, p. 117, fn. 64 (Wolters Kluwer, 2003).
14. Julian D. M. Lew, Loukas A. Mistelis and Stefan Kröll, *Comparative International Commercial Arbitration*, p. 117 (Wolters Kluwer, 2003).

in the context of the enforcement stage.[15] Whether in a pre-award or in a post-award stage, all of these instruments refer to the law applicable to the parties but fail "*to give any further information as to how to determine the 'law applicable to the [parties]'.*"[16] The traditional view favors the application of the choice of law method and refers to different factors depending on whether the party is a natural [1] or a legal person [2].

12. The Convention does not contain any conflict of laws rules designating the law governing the capacity of the parties to enter into arbitration agreements. Hence, the court seized of the matter will apply its own conflict of laws rules to determine the applicable law.

[1] Natural Persons

13. In civil law countries, the capacity of natural persons is commonly "*governed by their national law or if they are stateless or have a refugee status, by the law of their domicile or residence.*"[17] For instance, in *X buyer (German) v. Y seller (Yugoslav)*, the Court of Appeal in Bremen held that the arbitration agreement was not valid, as it found the Yugoslav seller lacked a foreign trade authorization to conclude arbitration agreements under the Yugoslav law in force at that time:

> According to Art. VI(2) of the [ECICA] concluded between Germany and the former Socialist Federal Republic of Yugoslavia and applicable to its successor state Croatia, and according to general German conflict of laws, the legal capacity of the seller is to be ascertained according to **its personal law**.[18]

14. In contrast, in common law countries, the law of the domicile or the habitual residence of the parties will generally prevail.[19] The law governing the main contract may also play a relevant role in certain countries, such as the U.S.A.[20]

15. Article V(I)(a) of the NYC; Hong Kong, Arbitration Ordinance, Section 44(2)(a), Germany ZPO, Article 1059(2)(1)(a).
16. Emmanuel Gaillard and John Savage eds., *Fouchard, Gaillard and Goldman on International Commercial Arbitration*, p. 242 (Kluwer Law International, 1999).
17. *Ibid.*; Julian D. M. Lew, Loukas A. Mistelis and Stefan Kröll, *Comparative International Commercial Arbitration*, p. 118 (Wolters Kluwer, 2003).
18. *Buyer v. Seller*, Supreme Court (*Bundesgerichtshof*), 23 April 1998, in Albert Jan van den Berg (ed.), Vol. XXIV, Yearbook Commercial Arbitration, pp. 928–934 (Kluwer Law International, 1999) (emphasis added, unofficial English translation from Kluwer Arbitration, original in German); *German party v. Austrian GmbH*, Court of Appeal of Hamburg (*Oberlandesgericht*), 15 November 1995, in Albert Jan van den Berg (ed.), Vol. XXI, Yearbook Commercial Arbitration, pp. 845–850 (Kluwer Law International, 1996).
19. Emmanuel Gaillard and John Savage eds., *Fouchard, Gaillard and Goldman on International Commercial Arbitration*, p. 244 (Kluwer Law International, 1999); Julian D. M. Lew, Loukas A. Mistelis and Stefan Kröll, *Comparative International Commercial Arbitration*, p. 118 (Wolters Kluwer, 2003).
20. Emmanuel Gaillard and John Savage eds., *Fouchard, Gaillard and Goldman on International Commercial Arbitration*, p. 244 (Kluwer Law International, 1999).

[2] Legal Persons

15. In most civil law countries, the capacity of a legal person is governed by the law where the company has its main place of business.[21] In contrast, in common law countries the law of the company's place of incorporation is generally the applicable law.[22]

16. A legal person acts through its representatives. The powers of the representatives are generally governed by the law of their source;[23] therefore, their capacity is also regulated by the rules contained in Article VI(2).[24] In some cases, a special power-of-attorney might be needed, while in others, a general power-of-attorney will suffice.[25]

[B] Other Substantive Questions

17. The validity of the arbitration agreement may be affected by other factors such as misrepresentation, fraud, ambiguity, mistake, insolvency of the parties, among others.[26] Article VI(2) contains a special conflict of laws rule to determine the applicable law for these cases. According to its wording, the first law that is taken into consideration is the one to which the parties have subjected the arbitration agreement. Therefore, besides issues regarding the capacity of the parties, the autonomy of the parties shall be the primary connecting factor.[27] When there is no indication as to the law chosen by the parties, it is provided that the law of the place where the award will be rendered (i.e., the place of arbitration) shall be applied.[28] In the absence of choice

21. *Ibid.*; Julian D. M. Lew, Loukas A. Mistelis and Stefan Kröll, *Comparative International Commercial Arbitration*, p. 118 (Wolters Kluwer, 2003).
22. Emmanuel Gaillard and John Savage eds., *Fouchard, Gaillard and Goldman on International Commercial Arbitration*, p. 245 (Kluwer Law International, 1999); Julian D. M. Lew, Loukas A. Mistelis and Stefan Kröll, *Comparative International Commercial Arbitration*, p. 118 (Wolters Kluwer, 2003).
23. Emmanuel Gaillard and John Savage eds., *Fouchard, Gaillard and Goldman on International Commercial Arbitration*, p. 246 (Kluwer Law International, 1999); Nigel Blackaby et al., *Redfern and Hunter on International Arbitration*, p. 82, mn 2.35 (6th ed., Oxford, 2015).
24. Dominique Hascher, *European Convention on International Commercial Arbitration of 1961: Commentary*, in Vol. XXXVI, Yearbook Commercial Arbitration, 509, p. 529 (Albert Jan van den Berg ed., 2011).
25. Emmanuel Gaillard and John Savage eds., *Fouchard, Gaillard and Goldman on International Commercial Arbitration*, p. 249 (Kluwer Law International, 1999).
26. Julian D. M. Lew, Loukas A. Mistelis and Stefan Kröll, *Comparative International Commercial Arbitration*, pp. 149–150 (Wolters Kluwer, 2003).
27. Stefan Kröll, *The European Convention on International Commercial Arbitration: The Tale of a Sleeping Beauty*, in Austrian Yearbook on International Arbitration, 4, p. 14 (Klausegger and others eds., Manz, 2013); P. I. Benjamin, *The European Convention on International Commercial Arbitration*, 37 British Yearbook International Law 478, p. 490 (1961); *SA France-Embryon v. Renato Argonauta*, Court of Appeal of Lyon (*Cour d'Appel*), 4 July 1991, in Vol. XIX, Yearbook Commercial Arbitration, pp. 859–862 (Albert Jan van den Berg ed., 1994).
28. *Haegens Bouw v. N.V. Theuma Deurenindustrie*, Court of Appeal of Brussels (*Hof van Beroep*), 15 October 1992, in Vol. XVIII, Yearbook Commercial Arbitration, pp. 612–615 (Albert Jan van den Berg ed., 1993). In this case reference was made to the Convention although the Netherlands are not a party to it; *Cerámicas Casao, S.A. (Spain) v. I.A.G. Impianti Automazione Gestione srl (Italy)*, Supreme Court (*Tribunal Supremo*), 558/2007, 17 May 2007, in Vol. XXIII, Yearbook

of law by the parties, the place of arbitration becomes the "strongest connecting factor" to the arbitration clause.[29]

18. If the place of arbitration cannot be determined at the time when the objection is raised, reference should be made to the conflict of laws rules of the State of the domestic court seized.[30] The connecting factors employed can include, among others: the origin of the parties; the law governing the main contract; the place where most of the main contract is going to be performed; the place where the arbitration agreement was concluded; or a combination of them.[31] These factors may vary from State to State and, therefore, a different result could be reached depending on which court is seized, which causes uncertainty.

[C] Arbitrability of the Subject Matter

19. The last sentence of Article VI(2)(c) refers to the arbitrability of the dispute. According to the provision, domestic courts may refuse the recognition of an arbitration clause "*if under the law of their country the dispute is not capable of settlement by arbitration.*"

20. Nonarbitrability is a restriction of party autonomy imposed by domestic law systems regarding matters that cannot be decided in arbitration.[32] Its main purpose is to safeguard the exclusive jurisdiction of their national courts on specific types of disputes because: of public policy or order reasons; or the authority of arbitrators is restricted to the rights and obligations of the parties to the dispute, and, as a general rule, they cannot interfere with the status of third parties.[33]

21. In the enforcement stage, the applicable law to determine the arbitrability of the subject matter, according to the NYC, is the law of the place of arbitration.[34] However,

---

Commercial Arbitration, pp. 698–702 (Albert Jan van den Berg ed., 2008); *Licensing Projects (Spain) v. Pirelli & C. SpA (Italy)*, Court of Appeal of Barcelona (*Court of Appeal*), 86/2009, 29 April 2009, in Vol. XXXV, Yearbook Commercial Arbitration, pp. 452–453 (Albert Jan van den Berg ed., 2010); *see also*, Bundesgerichtshof, 20 March 1980, BGHZ 77, p. 32.

29. Julian D. M. Lew, Loukas A. Mistelis and Stefan Kröll, *Comparative International Commercial Arbitration*, p. 122 (Wolters Kluwer, 2003).
30. Dominique Hascher, *European Convention on International Commercial Arbitration of 1961: Commentary*, in Vol. XXXVI, Yearbook Commercial Arbitration, 509, p. 529 (Albert Jan van den Berg ed., 2011); P. I. Benjamin, *The European Convention on International Commercial Arbitration*, 37 British Yearbook. International Law 478, p. 490 (1961); Stefan Kröll, *The European Convention on International Commercial Arbitration: The Tale of a Sleeping Beauty*, in Austrian Yearbook on International Arbitration, 4, p. 14 (Klausegger and others eds., Manz, 2013).
31. Julian D. M. Lew, Loukas A. Mistelis and Stefan Kröll, *Comparative International Commercial Arbitration*, p. 124 (Wolters Kluwer, 2003).
32. Loukas A. Mistelis, *Arbitrability: International and Comparative Perspectives*, in Arbitrability: International and Comparative Perspectives, International Arbitration Law Library, Vol. 19, pp. 1–18 (Loukas A. Mistelis and Stavros L. Brekoulakis eds., Kluwer Law International, 2009).
33. Laurence Shore, *The United States' Perspective on "Arbitrability,"* in Arbitrability: International and Comparative Perspectives, International Arbitration Law Library, Vol. 19, pp. 69–84 (Loukas A. Mistelis and Stavros L. Brekoulakis eds., Kluwer Law International, 2009).
34. Article V(2)(a) of the NYC.

in the case of Article VI(2)(c) of the ECICA, the applicable law at the pre-award stage is the national law of the domestic court seized.

22. Some commentators have considered that the approach taken by the ECICA is not entirely correct, as not every domestic court seized is competent to rule on the arbitrability of the subject matter. Prof. Stavros L. Brekoulakis notes the domestic law of the seized court will be relevant only where there is a conflict of jurisdiction between such a court and the arbitral tribunal in order to safeguard its exclusive jurisdiction over the particular dispute.[35] However, "*if there is no jurisdictional conflict, the national law of the place of referral will be irrelevant, and these national courts should arguably refrain from determining the arbitrability of the dispute.*"[36] Therefore, the domestic laws on the arbitrability of the court seized should only apply where, without the arbitration clause, such a court would have jurisdiction.

III THE PRINCIPLE OF LIS PENDENS

23. The principle of lis pendens serves to protect the defendants or respondents to have to defend themselves twice in the same matter and to establish legal certainty and predictability by avoiding conflicting decisions.[37] A party may initiate court proceedings, *inter alia,* in an attempt to escape from its obligation to submit a dispute to arbitration or "*because it genuinely challenges the validity of the arbitration agreement.*"[38]

24. Article VI(3) of the ECICA regulates the principle of lis pendens between arbitration and domestic court proceedings. According to this provision, when a party has initiated arbitration proceedings and a domestic court is successively asked to deal with the same subject matter between the same parties, or with the question of whether the arbitration agreement is nonexistent, null and void, or has lapsed, the latter shall stay its ruling on the arbitrator's jurisdiction until the arbitral award is rendered. Only after the award has been rendered, can the court resume proceedings.[39] The provision, therefore, establishes the *Kompetenz-Kompetenz* of the Tribunal.

25. This provision will apply if certain conditions are met [A] and if the seized court founds the exception of "good and substantial reasons" is not applicable [B].

35. Stavros L. Brekoulakis, *Revisiting the Revisited Lex Fori,* in Arbitrability: International and Comparative Perspectives, International Arbitration Law Library, Vol. 19, pp. 99–120 (Loukas A. Mistelis and Stavros L. Brekoulakis eds., Kluwer Law International, 2009).
36. *Ibid.*
37. Denice Forstén, *Parallel Proceedings and the Doctrine of Lis Pendens in International Commercial Arbitration: A Comparative Study Between the Common Law and Civil Law Traditions* (Uppsala Universitet, 2015), available at www.diva-portal.org/smash/get/diva2:813565/FULLTEXT01.pdf (last visited 22 January 2018).
38. Julian D. M. Lew, Loukas A. Mistelis and Stefan Kröll, *Comparative International Commercial Arbitration,* p. 362 (Wolters Kluwer, 2003).
39. Dominique Hascher, *European Convention on International Commercial Arbitration of 1961: Commentary,* in Vol. XXXVI, Yearbook Commercial Arbitration, 509, p. 531 (Albert Jan van den Berg ed., 2011).

[A] Conditions That Are Required to Be Met

26. For the principle of lis pendens to apply under the ECICA, the arbitration proceedings shall: [1] be initiated before domestic court proceedings and [2] comply with certain other conditions.

[1] Initiation of Arbitration Proceedings Before Domestic Court Proceedings

27. According to the wording of Article VI(3), it must first be determined when the arbitral proceedings commenced. The majority view is arbitration proceedings commence with the request for arbitration.[40] The same applies if the request was submitted to the President of the competent Chamber of Commerce, according to Article IV(2).[41] The main purpose of the request for arbitration is that one party notifies the other of its intention to resort to arbitration, "*[giving] notice to the other party to appoint its arbitrator and to set out its position in the proceedings.*"[42] Therefore, the request for arbitration, despite the fact that the arbitral tribunal has not been constituted, shall be considered the commencement of arbitration proceedings, "*[o]therwise, the respondent would have had an opportunity to appeal to a court instead of appointing an arbitrator.*"[43] The form and content of the request will depend on the applicable arbitration rules to the case at stake.

28. Article VI(3) only regulates cases in which arbitration proceedings are initiated prior to court proceedings. However, it does not regulate the other possible scenario, i.e., where court proceedings are initiated before arbitration proceedings. Nevertheless, in *Domingo, Saltor v. Mecánicas Automatismos*, the Barcelona Court of Appeal decided to apply the principle of lis pendens contained in Article VI(3) *a contrario sensu*:

> [...]once a party has introduced a claim before a Spanish court, the other party, which has initiated arbitral proceedings on the same matter or dispute, must await the decision of the court (Art. VI(3) of the [ECICA] *a contrario sensu*).[44]

---

40. Emmanuel Gaillard and John Savage eds., *Fouchard, Gaillard and Goldman on International Commercial Arbitration*, p. 656 (Kluwer Law International, 1999).
41. Alice Fremuth-Wolf, *The European Convention on International Arbitration as a Tool to Remedy Pathological Arbitration Agreements- "There's Still Life in the Old Dog Yet,"* in Austrian Yearbook on International Arbitration, 61, p. 73 (Klausegger and others eds., Manz, 2013).
42. Emmanuel Gaillard and John Savage eds., *Fouchard, Gaillard and Goldman on International Commercial Arbitration*, p. 656 (Kluwer Law International, 1999).
43. Dominique Hascher, *European Convention on International Commercial Arbitration of 1961: Commentary*, in Vol. XXXVI, Yearbook Commercial Arbitration, 509, p. 530 (Albert Jan van den Berg ed., 2011).
44. *Domingo Torm Colóm v. Saltor SA (Andorra) and Mecánicas y Automatismos SA*, Court of Appeal of Barcelona (*Audencia Provincial*), 22 January 1991, in Vol. XX, Yearbook Commercial Arbitration, pp. 1068–1074 (Albert Jan van den Berg ed., 1995). (Unofficial English translation from Kluwer Arbitration, original in Spanish). The court applied the Convention even though one of the parties was located in Andorra which is not a party thereto.

29. The application of Article VI(3) *a contrario sensu* may conflict with some domestic law provisions, providing that arbitration proceedings may be initiated even if court proceedings are pending.[45] The result of this conflict will depend on the conflict of laws rule applied for solving the inconsistency.[46] Further, the application contradicts the fundamental principle of *Kompetenz-Kompetenz*. The section should, therefore, not be applied in such constellations.

30. Under Article II(3) of the NYC, domestic courts have the obligation to refer the parties to arbitration if one of the parties invokes the existence of an arbitration clause unless it finds that said agreement is null and void, inoperative, or incapable of being performed. This provision, unlike Article VI(3) of the ECICA, does not establish any time restriction and, therefore, it can be invoked despite the arbitration proceedings not being initiated.[47]

[2] Same Dispute

31. The provision requires that both the tribunal and the court are seized by the "*same subject matter between the same parties.*" Legal systems vary with regard to the determination of the same subject matter, in particular also between civil and common law countries.[48] The ECICA, however, does not provide any guidance as to what the same subject matter actually is.

32. In civil law countries, the most commonly accepted conditions are the following: "*(i) the dispute shall deal with the same subject-matter; (ii) the disputes are between the same parties; and (iii) involve the same cause of action.*"[49] If these conditions are met, the civil law rule for deciding which court shall deal with the dispute is the first-in-time rule. In other words, the domestic court that was seized first shall continue with its proceedings, and the subsequent court seized shall decline jurisdiction.[50]

33. In contrast, in common law countries it is more likely that the domestic court that was seized first shall decide on the matter, unless it considers there is another available forum which has jurisdiction and is more appropriate for solving the dispute at stake.[51]

45. For instance, Article 584(1) of the Austrian Code of Civil Procedure.
46. *See* above commentary to Article I of the ECICA, section III.B.
47. Florian Haugeneder, *The New Austrian Arbitration Act and the European Convention on International Commercial Arbitration*, 23(4) ARBITRATION INTERNATIONAL 646, p. 652 (2007).
48. Denice Forstén, *Parallel Proceedings and the Doctrine of Lis Pendens in International Commercial Arbitration: A Comparative Study Between the Common Law and Civil Law Traditions*, p. 48 (Upssala University Master's Thesis in Procedural Law, 2015).
49. Alice Fremuth-Wolf, *The European Convention on International Arbitration as a Tool to Remedy Pathological Arbitration Agreements- "There's Still Life in the Old Dog Yet,"* in Austrian Yearbook on International Arbitration, 61, p. 73 (Klausegger and others eds., Manz, 2013).
50. For instance, Italian Code of Civil Procedures, Article 39.1.
51. Ronald A. Brand and Scott R. Jablonski, *Forum Non Conveniens: History, Global Practice, and Future under the Hague Convention on Choice of Court Agreements*, p. 1 (Oxford University Press 2007); *Spiliada Maritime Corp. v. Cansulex Ltd* [1987] A.C. 460.

34. In practice, the lack of any definition of the "same subject matter" may cause considerable uncertainties, e.g., in situations in which a party relies on some additional facts in one case but not in the other while the core of case remains the same or invokes different legal rules but applied to the same fact and asking for the same relief, e.g., a claim for payment based either on performance of a contract or damages. National laws do not provide for uniform answers in such situations. As Article VI(3) is addressed at the courts, they will in practice apply the national rules on lis pendens to determine whether the disputes are on the same subject matter.

[B] Exception Due to "Good and Substantial Reasons"

35. Article VI(3) provides an exception to the principle of lis pendens in favor of arbitration when the seized domestic court founds there are good and substantial reasons to not stay its proceedings. The Convention does not clarify what constitutes "good and substantial reasons"; therefore, it is a discretionary power of the seized domestic court.

36. Commentators have considered, for instance, a "*good and substantial reason exists if there is obviously no valid arbitration agreement*,"[52] or in case of "*the existence of res judicata or collateral estoppel precluding arbitration proceedings or of a pending litigation shortly awaiting a final decision.*"[53] In any case, this notion should be applied in exceptional circumstances[54] and interpreted narrowly, as it is an exception to the general rule.[55]

IV INTERIM MEASURES

37. The intervention of judicial authorities during the course of the arbitration proceedings is sometimes necessary. The main reason is judicial authorities have resources, such as coercive powers, that are lacking in an arbitration tribunal.[56] The granting of interim or conservatory measures is one case where intervention might be necessary.

38. The ECICA contemplates this possibility by establishing, in Article VI(4), that a request before judicial authorities for interim measures or measures of conservation be compatible with arbitration proceedings, even though the latter are taking place in

52. Julian D. M. Lew, Loukas A. Mistelis and Stefan Kröll, *Comparative International Commercial Arbitration*, p. 348 (Wolters Kluwer, 2003).
53. Dominique Hascher, *European Convention on International Commercial Arbitration of 1961: Commentary*, in Vol. XXXVI, Yearbook Commercial Arbitration, 509, p. 530 (Albert Jan van den Berg ed., 2011).
54. Julian D. M. Lew, Loukas A. Mistelis and Stefan Kröll, *Comparative International Commercial Arbitration*, p. 348 (Wolters Kluwer, 2003).
55. Dominique Hascher, *European Convention on International Commercial Arbitration of 1961: Commentary*, in Vol. XXXVI, Yearbook Commercial Arbitration, 509, p. 530 (Albert Jan van den Berg ed., 2011).
56. Margaret L. Moses, *The Principles and Practice of International Commercial Arbitration*, p. 87 (2nd ed., Cambridge, 2012).

another State. In *Bahia v. Eintacar*, arbitration proceedings were commenced between the parties in Switzerland. Eintacar requested interim measures in Spain, and the domestic court seized granted them. On appeal, the court confirmed the lower court's ruling providing: "*[according to the text Article VI(4) of the ECICA] we may conclude that it is possible for a Spanish judge to adopt interim measures in support of arbitration, even though the arbitral proceedings are taking place in a different country.*"[57]

39. A request for interim or conservatory measures shall not be regarded as an implicit waiver of the requesting party's arbitration rights. The content of this provision has been observed by a large number of contemporary arbitration rules.[58]

40. Although the terms "interim measures" and "measures of conservation" are used interchangeably,[59] the wording of Article VI(4) of the ECICA suggests they have different meanings, as they are connected by the disjunctive word "or." Some commentators have classified interim measures as those of a provisional nature, not necessarily protective, and measures of conservation as those of a protective nature, not necessarily provisional.[60] In contrast, the UNCITRAL Model Law provides a different classification of the measures from the ECICA.[61] Article 17 of the UNCITRAL Model Law distinguishes between interim measures and preliminary orders. According to the provision, an interim measure is any temporary measure, in the form of an award or in any other form, intended to protect the ability of a party to obtain a final award.[62] A preliminary order is "*essentially the same as an interim measure with one major exception: it is obtained* ex parte—*that is, the tribunal has heard from only one of the parties.*"[63]

41. In *Pama v. Shultz*, the parties concluded a contract for the purchase of certain machinery which contained an arbitration clause. When the dispute arose between the parties, Pama commenced arbitration and simultaneously lodged an action before a domestic court in Verona, seeking a suspension of payment by Schultz until an arbitral award was rendered. The domestic court held that, according to Article VI(4) of the ECICA, the granting of interim measures by a domestic court is not incompatible with arbitration and should not be regarded as a submission of the case's substance to domestic courts. In the end, the domestic court did not grant the requested interim measures because Pama's request did not meet all necessary conditions under Italian

57. *Bahia Industrial, S.A. v. Eintacar-Eimar, S.A.*, District Court of Cadiz (*Audiencia Provincial*), 12 June 1991, in Vol. XVIII, Yearbook Commercial Arbitration, pp. 616–618 (Albert Jan van den Berg ed., 1993).
58. 2003 Japan Arbitration Law, Article 15; 1998 German Arbitration Act, §1033; ICDR Rules, Article 21(3), ICC Rules, Article 28(2).
59. Emmanuel Gaillard and John Savage eds., *Fouchard, Gaillard and Goldman on International Commercial Arbitration*, pp. 709 and 710 (Kluwer Law International, 1999).
60. *Ibid.*, p. 709.
61. UNCITRAL Model Law, Article 17.
62. Margaret L. Moses, *The Principles and Practice of International Commercial Arbitration*, p. 106 (2nd ed., Cambridge, 2012).
63. *Ibid.*, pp. 106–107.

law for interim measures.[64] Therefore, the mere request of interim measures to a domestic court does not suffice. The request shall comply with certain conditions depending on the domestic law of the court seized, such as urgency and irreparable harm.

42. The words "judicial authority" in Article VI(4) includes domestic courts and any other authority with the competence and power to grant provisional orders.[65]

64. *Pama Industrie S.p.A. v. Shultz Steel Company, Banca Nazionale del Lavoro*, Magistrate's Court of Verona (*Pretura*), 22 April 1985, in Vol. XII, Yearbook Commercial Arbitration, pp. 494–495 (Albert Jan van den Berg ed., 1987).
65. Dominique Hascher, *European Convention on International Commercial Arbitration of 1961: Commentary*, in Vol. XXXVI, Yearbook Commercial Arbitration, 509, p. 531 (Albert Jan van den Berg ed., 2011).

ARTICLE VII

Applicable Law

Alfred Siwy

INTRODUCTION

> *Article VII—Applicable law*
>
> 1. *The parties shall be free to determine, by agreement, the law to be applied by the arbitrators to the substance of the dispute.*
>   *Failing any indication by the parties as to the applicable law, the arbitrators shall apply the proper law under the rule of conflict that the arbitrators deem applicable. In both cases the arbitrators shall take account of the terms of the contract and trade usages.*
> 2. *The arbitrators shall act as* amiables compositeurs *if the parties so decide and if they may do so under the law applicable to the arbitration.*

1. Article VII determines the law applicable to the merits of a particular dispute. The provision is a rudimentary conflict of laws provision which—in the first degree—operates independently from any domestic law system.[1] Hence, the law chosen by the parties applies by virtue of Article VII(1), not due to any conflict of laws rule of the *lex arbitri*. The conflict of laws rules of domestic legal systems are relevant only in the absence of such choice by virtue of Article VII(1) (second paragraph), which provides for the application of the conflict of laws rule deemed appropriate by the tribunal.

2. Hence, the arbitrators will apply the law chosen by the parties (I). In the absence of such an agreement, the arbitrators will apply the law determined by the conflict of laws rule they deem applicable (II). In both cases, the arbitrators shall apply the terms of the

---

1. P. I. Benjamin, *The European Convention on International Commercial Arbitration*, 37 BRITISH YEARBOOK INTERNATIONAL LAW 47, p. 491 (1961).

contracts and trade usages as an international factor (III). Additionally, if certain conditions are met, Article VII provides for a decision *ex aequo et bono* (IV).

I THE WILL OF THE PARTIES AS THE MAIN FACTOR

3. The provisions of the ECICA show that its primary and guiding principle is party autonomy.[2] Article VII is not an exception; it provides that when deciding which law is applicable to the merits of the case, arbitrators shall respect the will of the parties.[3]

4. As stated by the tribunal in ICC Case No. 6850:

> The parties' authority of free choice of law is confirmed as an internationally valid principle by Article 7 of the [ECICA]. The parties are to be enabled to subject their legal relations to the law they choose, and to exclude the national law which would otherwise apply.[4]

5. Presently, most arbitration rules and conventions recognize the supremacy of the principle of party autonomy,[5] as it has become a cornerstone of international commercial arbitration.[6]

6. Article VII does not specify either the form of the parties' agreement on the applicable law [A] or the timing of its conclusion [B]. The parties are free to choose the law they favor more [C], although certain limits might restrict this selection [D].

[A] Form of the Parties' Agreement

7. Article VII does not specify which forms the agreement of the parties shall take. It is not specified whether the consent shall be expressly contained in the terms of the main contract or whether, in the absence of express terms, it may be extracted from an interpretation of the intention of the parties.[7] However, in the absence of any such requirement in the Convention and in light of the wording contained in Article VII (second paragraph) stating, "*any indication by the parties*," it is obvious that there are

---

2. Stefan Kröll, *The European Convention on International Commercial Arbitration: The Tale of a Sleeping Beauty*, in Austrian Yearbook on International Arbitration, 4, p. 9 (Klausegger and others eds., Manz, 2013); P. I. Benjamin, *The European Convention on International Commercial Arbitration*, 37 British Yearbook International Law 478, p. 491 (1961).
3. *Austrian buyer v. Czechoslovak foreign trade Company*, Award, CAC Case No. Rsp. 192/78, 27 May 1980, in Vol. XI, Yearbook Commercial Arbitration, p. 114 (Albert Jan van den Berg ed., 1986); *Consultant v. State agency and others*, Final Award, ICC Case No. 7047, in Vol. XXI, Yearbook Commercial Arbitration, pp. 79–98 (Albert Jan van den Berg ed., 1996).
4. ICC Case No. 6850.
5. French Code of Civil Procedures, Decree no. 2005-460, 13 May 2005, Article 1496, Russian Federation Law on International Commercial Arbitration, N 5338-1, 7 July 1993, Article 28(1); UNCITRAL Model Law, Article 28; ICC Rules, Article 17(1); LCIA Rules, Article 22(3); ICSID Convention, Article 42.
6. Nigel Blackaby et al., *Redfern and Hunter on International Arbitration*, p. 187, mn 3.97 (6th ed., 2015).
7. Emmanuel Gaillard and John Savage eds., *Fouchard, Gaillard and Goldman on International Commercial Arbitration*, pp. 787 and 788 (Kluwer Law International, 1999).

no form requirements for the parties' agreement. Indeed, the legislative history of this Article "*indicates that the drafters contemplated the possibility of an express as well as of an implied choice of law.*"[8] In the case of a tacit selection, the intention of the parties must be certain; "*this is a substantive requirement that the arbitrators cannot disregard.*"[9]

8. For the identification of a tacit agreement, the method of interpretation used by the arbitrators to determine the intention of the parties should reflect international law practice.[10] As a general rule, the place of arbitration does not amount to a tacit choice of law.[11]

[B] Time of the Conclusion of the Parties' Agreement

9. Article VII does not specify at which point in time the parties shall agree on the applicable law to the merits. Parties usually include a governing law clause in the main contract.[12] However, if the parties fail to do so, the parties can choose the applicable law not only at the time of signing the arbitration agreement but also at any other time before or even after the dispute has arisen.[13]

[C] Freedom of the Parties to Choose the Law They Favor

10. The ECICA does not impose a particular set of rules to govern the merits of a dispute, instead it grants the parties the freedom to choose any law they deem appropriate. The parties may select any law related to the parties, the main agreement, or a neutral law.[14]

11. The wording of Article VII refers to a "law" instead of "law(s)" or "rules of law"; the latter terms have been used by modern arbitration rules to allow the parties to select more than one legal system or nonnational sets of rules such as the UNIDROIT

---

8. Dominique Hascher, *European Convention on International Commercial Arbitration of 1961: Commentary*, in Vol. XXXVI, Yearbook Commercial Arbitration, 509, p. 532 (Albert Jan van den Berg ed., 2011).
9. Emmanuel Gaillard and John Savage eds., *Fouchard, Gaillard and Goldman on International Commercial Arbitration*, p. 788 (Kluwer Law International, 1999).
10. Julian D. M. Lew, Loukas A. Mistelis and Stefan Kröll, *Comparative International Commercial Arbitration*, p. 18 (Wolters Kluwer, 2003).
11. Emmanuel Gaillard and John Savage eds., *Fouchard, Gaillard and Goldman on International Commercial Arbitration*, p. 789 (Kluwer Law International, 1999).
12. Jason Fry, Simon Greenberg and Francesca Mazza, *The Secretariat's Guide to ICC Arbitration*, p. 219 (ICC Publication No. 729E, 2012).
13. Marcel Huys and Guy Keutgen, *L'Arbitrage en Droit Belge et International*, p. 579 (Bruylant, 1981); Emmanuel Gaillard and John Savage eds., *Fouchard, Gaillard and Goldman on International Commercial Arbitration*, p. 790 (Kluwer Law International, 1999).
14. The choice of a neutral law is common in cases such as shipping and freight contracts, commodity and insurance contracts because of the benefits in these subject matters that certain domestic law systems offer. Nigel Blackaby et al., *Redfern and Hunter on International Arbitration*, p. 191, mn 3.114 (6th ed., Oxford 2015); Jason Fry, Simon Greenberg and Francesca Mazza, *The Secretariat's Guide to ICC Arbitration*, p. 222 (ICC Publication No. 729E, 2012).

Principles.[15] For instance, Article 21(1) of the ICC Rules deliberately refers to "rules of law" in order "*to avoid any restrictive presumption that parties and arbitral tribunals must adopt the law of a domestic legal system, which could be inferred from use of the word 'law' alone.*"[16] The reason for this is that a combination of domestic law systems or transnational rules may better suit the nature of international transactions and help the parties who are coming from different systems of law to reach an agreement on this point.[17]

12. The drafting commission of the UNCITRAL Model Law was faced with the debate on whether it should adhere to the traditional term "law" or change to "rules of law."[18] Eventually, the commission decided on the term "rules of law" because it reflected the practice of most legal systems by recognizing the right of the parties to select different laws for different parts of the contract (referred to as *dépeçage*, in French) and to incorporate provisions of nonnational sets of rules.[19] Although the plain meaning of Article VII refers, in singular, to "law," in light of an evolutionary interpretation which takes into consideration the modern practice, the Convention should not be read to exclude the application of more than one national law to various parts of the contract.

13. While some commentators assert that the parties are free to select nonnational or supranational rules,[20] others have raised concerns as it seems the term "law" used in Article VII suggests that it "*does not allow the application of non-national sets of rules,*"[21] such as the UNIDROIT Principles.[22] One possible disadvantage of choosing a non-domestic law system over a domestic one is a lower level of certainty and predictability.[23] However, in light of the relevance that the Convention grants to party autonomy, it could be maintained that if the parties so agreed, international or supranational rules can also be chosen as the applicable law. Moreover, as it will be discussed in Section III below, the obligation of arbitrators to apply the terms of the contract and trade usages also supports this conclusion.

15. LCIA Rules, Article 24(1); ICC Rules, Article 17(1); ICDR Rules, Article 31.
16. Jason Fry, Simon Greenberg and Francesca Mazza, *The Secretariat's Guide to ICC Arbitration*, p. 222 (ICC Publication No. 729E, 2012).
17. *Ibid.*, p. 223.
18. Howard M. Holtzmann and Joseph E. Neuhaus, *A Guide to the UNCITRAL Model Law on International Commercial Arbitration: Legislative History and Commentary*, pp. 766–767 (Kluwer Law and Taxation Publishers, 1989).
19. Commission Report, A/40/17, para. 233; Second Working Group Report, A/CN.9/232, para. 162; Howard M. Holtzmann and Joseph E. Neuhaus, *A Guide to the UNCITRAL Model Law on International Commercial Arbitration: Legislative History and Commentary*, pp. 767–768 (Kluwer Law and Taxation Publishers, 1989).
20. Dominique Hascher, *European Convention on International Commercial Arbitration of 1961: Commentary*, in Vol. XXXVI, Yearbook Commercial Arbitration, 509, p. 533 (Albert Jan van den Berg ed., 2011).
21. Florian Haugeneder, *The New Austrian Arbitration Act and the European Convention on International Commercial Arbitration*, 23(4) ARBITRATION INTERNATIONAL 646, p. 658 (2007).
22. UNIDROIT Principles on International Commercial Contracts (International Institute for the Unification of Private Law, Rome 2010) ("UNIDROIT Principles").
23. Jason Fry, Simon Greenberg and Francesca Mazza, *The Secretariat's Guide to ICC Arbitration*, p. 223 (ICC Publication No. 729E, 2012).

14. In private international law, the reference to a "law" encompasses all rules of a legal system, including its case law and customs, unless otherwise agreed by the parties.[24] However, they also contain conflict of laws rules which might refer the parties to a different law system depending on the features of the contractual relationship (the *renvoi*). Article 28 of the UNCITRAL Model Law, therefore, provides that "*[a]ny designation of the law or legal system of a given State shall be construed, unless otherwise expressed, as directly referring to the substantive law of that State and* ***not to its conflict of law rules***."[25] The ECICA does not expressly exclude the conflict of laws rules of the selected law system. The parties will, therefore, be well advised to exclude the *renvoi* when drafting the choice of law clause.

[D] Mandatory Rules as Limitations to the Selection of the Applicable Law to the Merits

15. The parties' right to choose the applicable law is subject to certain limitations.[26] Many legal systems contain mandatory rules which the parties cannot derogate. Mandatory rules are usually intended to protect the core values of a particular legal system.[27] There is a margin of uncertainty about which rules qualify as mandatory rules. The distinguishing feature of mandatory rules which separates them from rules aimed at balancing the interests of the parties is the interests served by such mandatory rules: Mandatory rules serve over individual public purposes or national or economic policies. This approach is also reflected in Article 9(3) of the Rome-I Regulation which determines that mandatory rules are rules:

> the respect for which is regarded as crucial by a country for safeguarding its public interests, such as its political, social or economic organization, to such an extent that they are applicable to any situation falling within their scope, irrespective of the law otherwise applicable to the contract under this Regulation.[28]

These rules apply due to the legislative intent of the enacting State, which overrides the parties' possibility to override them by a choice of a specific legal system.

II THE CONFLICT OF LAWS RULE THAT ARBITRATORS DEEM APPLICABLE

16. If the parties fail to agree on the law applicable to the merits of the case, Article VII provides that "*the arbitrators shall apply the proper law under the rule of conflict that the arbitrators deem applicable.*" According to this provision, the arbitrators have the

24. Emmanuel Gaillard and John Savage eds., *Fouchard, Gaillard and Goldman on International Commercial Arbitration*, p. 791 (Kluwer Law International, 1999).
25. UNCITRAL Model Law, Article 28 (emphasis added).
26. Jason Fry, Simon Greenberg and Francesca Mazza, *The Secretariat's Guide to ICC Arbitration*, p. 226 (ICC Publication No. 729E, 2012).
27. *Ibid.*
28. Alfred Siwy, *Mandatory Rules in International Commercial Arbitration*, in Austrian Yearbook on International Arbitration, p. 165 (Klausegger et al. eds., 2012).

discretionary power to choose the conflict of laws rule they consider most appropriate for the case at hand, which will lead them to one, or several domestic law systems.

17. The wording of Article VII departs from some modern arbitration rules in two aspects: first, the choice of law by the arbitrators is not direct but rather an indirect one; and, second, the reasoning behind the choice shall be based on the conflict of laws rules that the arbitrators deemed applicable instead of the law they considered appropriate.

18. Similar to the scope of the parties' choice of the applicable law, the arbitrators have the possibility of resorting to the conflict of laws rule of one domestic law system, as well as to cumulative conflict of laws rules.[29]

19. Unlike other arbitration rules that grant the arbitrators a power to select directly the "laws" or the "rules of law" they consider appropriate[30] (also known from French as a *voie directe* provision),[31] the power contained in Article VII is an indirect choice of law through the selection of the appropriate conflict of laws rules. The drafting commission of the UNCITRAL Model Law discussed this difference in the form of selection of the applicable law.[32] As a conclusion, the commission held that the freedom of the parties to choose a law was wider than that of the arbitrators and, therefore, they "*adopted the more restrictive language requiring recourse to a conflict-of-law rule (which would in turn require application of the 'law' to the substance of the dispute)*."[33] Whether the indirect choice of law, in fact, has any practical advantages, such as predictability or a requirement to provide an express legal reasoning for the choice of the law applied, may be doubted in practice.

20. First, the choice of a conflict of law rule inherently implies a measure of uncertainty and, in practice, arbitrators applying a *voie directe* do not apply any legal system at random but mostly do provide reasoning for this. Indeed, " ... *the reasons invoked by arbitral tribunals when they select the governing law directly, without separate reference to conflicts rules, are often similar to the connecting factors used in such rules.*"[34]

21. Second, the rules do not only require the arbitrator to make a conflict of laws analysis but, before, to also determine the applicable conflict of laws rule. In both

29. Dominique Hascher, *European Convention on International Commercial Arbitration of 1961: Commentary*, in Vol. XXXVI, Yearbook Commercial Arbitration, 509, p. 533 (Albert Jan van den Berg ed., Kluwer Law International 2011).
30. ICC Rules, Article 21; LCIA Rules, Article 22.3; LCIA Rules, Article 31.
31. Florian Haugeneder, *The New Austrian Arbitration Act and the European Convention on International Commercial Arbitration*, 23(4) Arbitration International 646, p. 658 (2007); Stefan Kröll, *The European Convention on International Commercial Arbitration: The Tale of a Sleeping Beauty*, in Austrian Yearbook on International Arbitration, 4, p. 20 (Klausegger and others eds., Manz, 2013).
32. Howard M. Holtzmann and Joseph E. Neuhaus, *A Guide to the UNCITRAL Model Law on International Commercial Arbitration: Legislative History and Commentary*, p. 770 (Kluwer Law and Taxation Publishers, 1989).
33. *Ibid.*
34. *Ibid.*

cases, the rather rigid system of conflict of laws may not always lead to the most purposeful result and may not necessarily enhance the predictability of the decision.

22. The ECICA does not explain how the arbitrator is to determine the applicable conflict of laws rule. The ECICA states that the arbitrator shall apply those conflict of laws rules he "deems applicable." How to determine their applicability, however, may be of some relevance. While there are no hard and fast rules on determining the appropriate conflict of laws rule, various approaches to provide some guidance on the point have been suggested including the application of the conflict of laws rules of the forum or a conflict of laws rule of the legal system with the closest connection to the case.[35] The latter approach is the most stringent as the element of the closest connection is the cornerstone of most conflict of laws systems and, therefore, an obvious choice for the so-called *conflit au deuxième degré* (i.e., the choice between various conflict of laws systems).[36]

23. In practice, this different wording has not been a major issue. Indeed, "... *the reasons invoked by arbitral tribunals when they select the governing law directly, without separate reference to conflicts rules, are often similar to the connecting factors used in such rules.*"[37] In fact, the application of the test of the closest connection to determine the applicable conflict of laws rule may often have a similar effect to a *renvoi*.

III THE APPLICATION OF THE TERMS OF THE CONTRACT AND THE TRADE USAGES

[A] Application of the Terms of the Contract

24. According to Article VII, arbitrators shall take into consideration all other relevant terms of the contract when solving the dispute. The terms of the contract are a clear indicator of the parties' intention and the agreements reached after the negotiating period. In practice, in many cases arbitrators will render an award based on the terms of the contract and the facts of the case, without necessarily having to refer to the law governing the merits.[38]

35. *See* on this issue Otto Sandrock, *Welches Kollisionsrecht hat ein Internationales Schiedsgericht anzuwenden?*, 38 RIW 785, p. 791 (1992); Gerhard Kegel & Klaus Schurig, *Internationales Privatrecht*, 50 (9th ed., C.H. Beck, 2004); Jean-François Poudret & Sébastien Besson, *Comparative Law of International Arbitration*, 583ss (2nd ed.) examining the various approaches taken in practice.
36. Pierre Lalive, *Les Règles de Conflit de Lois Appliquées au Fond du Litige Par l'Arbitre International Siégeant en Suisse*, Revue De l'Arbitrage, p. 155 (1976); ICC Award 4237 YBCA 10 (1985) 52 applying the test of the closest connection.
37. Howard M. Holtzmann and Joseph E. Neuhaus, *A Guide to the UNCITRAL Model Law on International Commercial Arbitration: Legislative History and Commentary*, p. 770 (Kluwer Law and Taxation Publishers, 1989).
38. Jason Fry, Simon Greenberg and Francesca Mazza, *The Secretariat's Guide to ICC Arbitration*, p. 228 (ICC Publication No. 729E, 2012).

25. A large number of arbitration rules have followed Article VII's reference to the terms of the contract and to trade usages.[39] In some of these rules, the wording has been slightly altered to state that the tribunal shall take into account the terms of the contract "if any," instead of in "all cases."[40] This change was made *"in recognition of the growth in arbitration based on non-contractual instruments such as bilateral investment treaties or tort, where no contract exists."*[41]

[B] Application of Trade Usages

26. A trade usage can be defined as *"a custom or understanding in a given trade or industry."*[42] It has also been identified as those *"constant and repeated practices, which bear a normative force by virtue of their ubiquity and repetition."*[43] The practices of a given industry that eventually give rise to a trade usage can also be evidenced in authoritative sources such as the Uniform Customs and Practice for Documentary Credits,[44] the UNIDROIT Principles, the Incoterms,[45] and the Principles of European Contract Law.[46]

27. Article VII of the ECICA provides that arbitrators shall take into consideration trade usages together with the parties' or arbitrators' selection on the applicable law. Therefore, it is possible to argue, in this way, trade usages are implicit terms of the main contract.[47] However, there is no unanimous agreement on the scope covered by trade usages.

28. On one hand, commentators have considered that trade usages may cover a "custom specific to dealings between the disputing parties."[48] On the other hand, some tribunals have considered that these usages cannot be interpreted as a reference to what happens in the ordinary course of business of the disputing parties but shall be practiced by all the participants in the particular industry.[49]

29. Regarding the way trade usages shall be applied together with the terms of the contract or the applicable law, the arbitral tribunal in the ICC Case No. 14831, found

39. UNCITRAL Model Law, Article 28(4); ICC Rules, Article 21(2); ICDR Rules, Article 28.
40. ICC Rules, Article 21(2), as amended in 2012.
41. Jason Fry, Simon Greenberg and Francesca Mazza, *The Secretariat's Guide to ICC Arbitration*, p. 229 (ICC Publication No. 729E, 2012).
42. *Ibid.*
43. Pierre Mousseron, *Introduction terminologique: des comportements aux "bonnes pratiques"*, 92 J. Des Sociétés 12 (2011), cited in Fabien Gélinas ed., *Trade Usages and Implied Terms in the Age of Arbitration* (Oxford 2016), p. 211.
44. Uniform Customs and Practice for Commercial Documentary Credits (ICC Product No. 600LE, 2007).
45. International Commercial Terms (ICC Product No. 715E, 2010).
46. Ole Lando and Hugh Beale, *Principles of European Contract Law, Parts I and II* (prepared by the Commission on European Contract Law, 2000).
47. Jason Fry, Simon Greenberg and Francesca Mazza, *The Secretariat's Guide to ICC Arbitration*, p. 229 (ICC Publication No. 729E, 2012).
48. *Ibid.*
49. ICC Case No. 13139 (2006).

that trade usages could only be applied to matters on which the parties had not chosen applicable rules:

> Trade usages must be taken into account ... but only to supplement, not to contradict rules chosen by the parties. If the parties have chosen a national law prohibiting interest, any trade usages regarding interest would be inconsistent with the parties' own choice.[50]

30. This supplementary function is in line with the Convention's principle on the supremacy of parties' autonomy.

31. The incorporation of trade usages allows a progressive interpretation of the Convention in line with modern arbitration practice as usages have proven to evolve faster than other forms of normativity, especially domestic law.[51]

IV THE POSSIBILITY OF ARBITRATORS TO ACT AS AMIABLES COMPOSITEURS

32. Article VII(2) refers to the possibility of the arbitrators to act as *amiable compositeurs*. An arbitrator acts as *amiable compositeur* when it "*decides a case by reference to general notions of fairness and equity, rather than in accordance with a strict application of legal rules.*"[52] It provides that arbitrators shall act as *amiable compositeurs* under two conditions: (i) the parties agreed on this; and (ii) the applicable law to the arbitration allows it. Regarding the first condition, the Convention does not specify the formalities or the timing of this agreement. Taking into consideration the fundamental importance of granting the arbitrators to deliver a decision not based on legal considerations, there will hardly be any room for tacit choices.

33. The possibility to act as *amiable compositeurs* as contained in Article VII(2) of the Convention, has inspired similar provisions in modern arbitration rules, including the UNCITRAL Model Law.[53] In some, reference has been made to arbitrators acting as *amiable compositeurs* or deciding *ex aequo et bono*.[54] A distinction between these two terms has been drawn based on their understanding within domestic law systems. Arbitrators acting as *amiable compositeurs* decide the dispute "*detached from legal rules, even if they are mandatory,*" while the power to rule *ex aequo et bono* "*allows the arbitrator, ruling in law, to moderate the effects of the application of that [law].*"[55] However, this distinction remains more theoretical than practical as the core feature of

50. ICC Case No. 14831 (2009).
51. Emmanuel Bernard Jolivet, Giacomo Marchisio and Fabien Gelinas, *Trade Usages in ICC Arbitration* in Trade Usages and Implied Terms in the Age of Arbitration, p. 231 (Fabien Gelinas ed., Oxford University Press 2016).
52. YSIAC, Anya George, Schellenberg Wittmer Ltd, *The Hidden Amiable Compositeur*, p. 1 (20 April 2015 Kluwer Arbitration Blog).
53. UNCITRAL Model Law, Article 28(3).
54. LCIA Rules, Article 22(4); ICC Rules, Article 21(3); ICDR Rules, Article 31.
55. Emmanuel Gaillard and John Savage eds., *Fouchard, Gaillard and Goldman on International Commercial Arbitration*, p. 836 (Kluwer Law International 1999).

both methods is that "*the arbitrators [can] choose to have their sense of what justice requires [to] prevail over any other consideration.*"[56]

34. It is not clear whether an arbitrator, acting as an *amiable compositeur*, is obligated to take the terms of the contract and trade usages into consideration. According to the wording of Article VII, it appears that arbitrators are only obligated to consider the terms of the contract and trade usages when they are acting in accordance with paragraph 1:

> 1. The parties shall be free to determine, by agreement, the law to be applied by the arbitrators to the substance of the dispute.
> Failing any indication by the parties as to the applicable law, the arbitrators shall apply the proper law under the rule of conflict that the arbitrators deem applicable. **In both cases** the arbitrators shall take account of the terms of the contract and trade usages.
> 2. The arbitrators shall act as *amiables compositeurs* if the parties so decide and if they may do so under the law applicable to the arbitration. (emphasis added)

35. In contrast, in Article 28 of the UNCITRAL Model Law, it is more obvious that arbitrators acting as *amiable compositeurs* shall take into consideration the terms of the contract and trade usages as well:

> (...) (3) The arbitral tribunal shall decide *ex aequo et bono* or as *amiable compositeur* only if the parties have expressly authorized it to do so.
> (4) **In all cases**, the arbitral tribunal shall decide in accordance with the terms of the contract and shall take into account the usages of the trade applicable to the transaction.[57] (emphasis added)

56. *Ibid.*; YSIAC, Anya George, Schellenberg Wittmer Ltd, *The Hidden Amiable Compositeur*, p. 1 (20 April 2015, Kluwer Arbitration Blog).
57. Article 28 of the UNCITRAL Model Law.

ARTICLE VIII

Reasons for the Award

Alfred Siwy

INTRODUCTION

> *Article VIII Reasons for the Award*
>
> *The parties shall be presumed to have agreed that reasons shall be given for the award unless they*
>
> *(a) either expressly declare that reasons shall not be given; or*
> *(b) have assented to an arbitral procedure under which it is not customary to give reasons for awards, provided that in this case neither party requests before the end of the hearing, or if there has not been a hearing then before the making of the award, that reasons be given.*

1. Article VIII establishes the presumption that the parties have agreed that the award is reasoned[1] [I]. However, the presumption may be rebutted in certain cases [II].

I THE GENERAL RULE

2. As a general rule, the arbitrators must provide a reasoning for their award. The practice of reasoned awards is typical in common law systems wherein courts are required to adhere to prior decisions. However, also in civil law systems, decisions are reasoned, though the form and extent of the reasoning of a civil law judgment can differ

1. Dominique Hascher, *European Convention on International Commercial Arbitration of 1961: Commentary*, in Vol. XXXVI, YEARBOOK COMMERCIAL ARBITRATION, 509, p. 534 (Albert Jan van den Berg ed., 2011).

significantly from one country to another.[2] French decisions, for instance, are commonly very short.[3] The decisions of Dutch courts are characterized as being "straightforward, paper saving decisions."[4] In contrast, German courts often issue reasoned opinions that are remarkable for their "length and thoroughness."[5] Therefore, as reasoned decisions are common in both systems of law it is reasonable that the drafters of the ECICA considered it as a relevant requirement for an international arbitration award.

3. The ECICA does not provide any details as to the form or level of detail of the reasoning; thus, they might vary. To some extent, the lack of specification may be the result of the difficulties inherent in describing a reasoned award in the abstract.[6] Attempts to define what constitutes a reasoned award have been furnished in the context of international investment arbitration. In *MINE v. Guinea*, the Tribunal defined the requirement of a reasoned award as follows: "*the requirement that an award has to be motivated (...) is satisfied as long as the award enables one to follow how the Tribunal proceeds from Point A to Point B and eventually to its conclusion, even if it made an error of fact or law.*"[7]

4. Regarding the extent of the reasons, Sir Franklin Berman issued the following dissenting opinion which reflects the elements of the arbitrator's reasoning that should be included in the awards to comply with the requirement:

> To my mind, it is inescapable that every "crucial element" in an ICSID Tribunal's decision has to be the subject of a finding by the Tribunal; that, if the element is a factual element which is in dispute between the parties, the finding has to be the result of a proper fact-finding procedure; and that the elements and steps in this procedure must be spelled out in the Award.[8]

5. Contradictory reasons have been held to be equivalent to absence of reasons since they will not enable the reader to understand the tribunal's motives.[9]

2. S. I. Strong, *Reasoned Awards in International Commercial Arbitration*, 19 February 2016, Kluwer Arbitration Blog, available at http://arbitrationblog.kluwerarbitration.com/2016/02/19/reasoned-awards-in-international-commercial-arbitration/ (last visited 7 November 2018).
3. Jeffrey L. Friesen, *When Common Law Courts Interpret Civil Codes*, 15 Wisconsin International Law Journal 1, p. 8 (1996).
4. Erhard Blankenburg, *Patterns of Legal Culture: The Netherlands Compared to Neighboring Germany*, 46 American Journal of Comparative Law 1, p. 40 (1998).
5. *Ibid.*
6. S. I. Strong, *Reasoned Awards in International Commercial Arbitration*, 19 February 2016, Kluwer Arbitration Blog, available at http://arbitrationblog.kluwerarbitration.com/2016/02/19/reasoned-awards-in-international-commercial-arbitration/ (last visited 7 November 2018).
7. *Maritime International Nominees Establishment v. Republic of Guinea*, ICSID Case No. ARB/84/4, Decision on Annulment, 14 December 1989, paras 5.08, 5.09.
8. *Industria Nacional de Alimentos SA (Lucchetti) v. the Republic of Peru*, ICSID Case No. ARB/03/4, Dissenting Opinion of Sir Franklin Berman, 13 August 2007, para. 15.
9. Jean Rouche, Gerald H. Pointon, et al., *French Arbitration Law and Practice: A Dynamic Civil Law Approach to International Arbitration*, para. 317 (2nd ed., Kluwer Law International, 2009). In the context of investment arbitration *see Caratube International Oil Company LLP v. Republic of Kazakhstan*, Decision on the Annulment Application of Caratube International Oil Company LLP, 21 February 2014, para. 102; *Alapli Elektrik B.V. v. Republic of Turkey*, Decision on Annulment, 10 July 2014, para. 200; *El Paso Energy International Company v. The Argentine*

6. In the context of international investment arbitration, the arbitrators are not only required to address "*every question submitted to the [them], and [to] state the reasons upon which [the award] is based,*"[10] but the failure to do so is expressly listed as a ground for annulment.[11] In international commercial arbitrations, public awards are scarce and those that are available to the public are usually limited to excerpts, which do not allow other arbitrators to seek guidance from past decisions. Nevertheless, the reasons on which the award is based are relevant, *inter alia*, for the parties to understand how and why the tribunal reached its decision, particularly for the losing party.[12] Also in case of a challenge of the award, the reasons will also enhance the legitimacy of the arbitral process in the eyes of domestic courts that may be asked to enforce an award, even if there is no ability to review the merits of the award, by demonstrating the seriousness and integrity of the arbitration proceedings.[13]

7. The general rule has been followed by most national laws[14] and institutional arbitration rules which demonstrates its relevance in international arbitration. The consequences of failing to comply with the rule will disregard the agreement of the parties and give rise to the annulment of the award.[15]

II THE EXCEPTIONS

8. Article VIII provides two exceptions to the general rule. First, the parties can expressly declare that reasons are not required. Second, the parties can tacitly accept the absence of reasons by agreeing on an arbitral procedure under which it is customary not to provide a reasoning unless one party requests the arbitral tribunal to give reasons before the end of the hearing, or, in the absence of a hearing, before the making of the award.

Republic, Decision of the Ad Hoc Committee on the Application for Annulment of the Argentine Republic, 22 September 2014, para. 221; *Tidewater Investment SRL and Tidewater Caribe, C.A. v. Bolivarian Republic of Venezuela*, Decision on Annulment, 27 December 2016, para. 170.

10. ICSID Convention, Article 48(3).
11. ICSID Convention, Article 52(1)(e).
12. During the drafting of the UNCITRAL Model Law the arguments for and against the requirement of stating reasons were discussed. In favor it was sought that the requirement would improve the quality of the award whereas against it was suggested that the absence of reason would speed up the issuance of the award and would cause the award to be less subject to an annulment. Howard M. Holtzmann and Joseph E. Neuhaus, *A Guide to the UNCITRAL Model Law on International Commercial Arbitration: Legislative History and Commentary*, pp. 837–838 (Kluwer Law and Taxation Publishers, 1989).
13. S. I. Strong, *Reasoned Awards in International Commercial Arbitration*, 19 February 2016, Kluwer Arbitration Blog, available at http://arbitrationblog.kluwerarbitration.com/2016/02/19/reasoned-awards-in-international-commercial-arbitration/ (last visited 7 November 2018).
14. Netherlands Arbitration Act, 198, Article 1057, para. 4(e) of the Code of Civil Procedure; Belgian Law on Arbitration 2013, Article 1713 of the Judicial Code; German Arbitration Law, Article 1054(2) of the German Code of Civil Procedure; Spanish Arbitration Act 2003 (*Ley 60/2003*), Article 37(4). French Arbitration Law 2001, Article 1482 of the French Code of Civil Procedure.
15. Austrian Supreme Court, Judgment 28 September 2016, docket no. 18 Ocg 3/16i; Judgment of the German Supreme Court, 18 January 1990, docket no. III ZR 269/88.

9. While several institutional arbitration rules have endorsed the first exception almost in identical terms as Article VIII(a),[16] others like the ICC[17] and the Netherlands Arbitration Institute[18] Arbitration Rules do not provide for any exception. Another distinction between the rules is the agreement's form of consent. Some rules do not indicate whether the consent must be express or tacit, whereas other rules, such as the LCIA[19] and the VIAC[20] Arbitration Rules, mandate that the agreement must be in writing, which is a more similar approach to Article VIII(a).

10. The second exception refers to an arbitration procedure under which it is not customary to provide reasons for awards. Procedural rules which allow awards without reasons are becoming rare since an obligation to give reasons is now generally thought to be one of the basic requirements of the arbitral process.[21]

11. In *Efxinos v. Rawi Shipping*, an award was issued in London, in favor of Efxinos, without stating reasons. Efxinos sought enforcement before the Court of Appeal of Genova. The Court of Appeal analyzed on its own motion whether the failure to state reason violated the Italian public policy. In this connection, the Court of Appeal referred to Article 111 of the Italian Constitution which imposes the obligation to state reasons for decisions. Nevertheless, the Court noted that the ECICA's provisions were to be taken into account together with constitutional principles. After analyzing Article VIII, the Court concluded that due to Italy's acceptance of the exceptions in Article VIII, it could be submitted that an award without reasons was not contrary to the Italian public policy. Furthermore, the Court held that the parties, by agreeing to submit the dispute to English law where the English Arbitration Act of 1950 did not mandate the arbitration to provide a reasoned decision, had waived their right to a motivated decision. Therefore, the Court concluded the award did not violate Italian public policy and consequently granted its enforcement.[22]

16. ICDR International Arbitration Rules, Article 27(2) provides: "*The tribunal shall state the reasons upon which the award is based, unless the parties have agreed that no reasons need be given.*"; LCIA Arbitration Rules, Article 26.2 provides "*The Arbitral Tribunal shall make any award in writing and, unless all parties agree in writing otherwise, shall state the reasons upon which such award is based.*"; Stockholm Chamber of Commerce ("SCC") Arbitration Rules, Article 36(1) provides "*The Arbitral Tribunal shall make its award in writing, and, unless otherwise agreed by the parties, shall state the reasons upon which the award is based.*"
17. ICC Arbitration Rules, Article 31(2) provides "*The award shall state the reasons upon which it is based.*" In the context of investment arbitration *see* also ICSID Convention, Article 48(3).
18. Netherlands Arbitration Institute, Article 44 provides "*The award shall in any event contain: ... (e) the reasons for the decision given in the award.*"
19. LCIA Arbitration Rules, Article 26.2 provides "*The Arbitral Tribunal shall make any award in writing and, unless all parties agree in writing otherwise, shall state the reasons upon which such award is based.*"
20. VIAC Arbitration Rules, Article 36 provides "*Awards shall state the reasons on which they are based unless all parties have agreed in writing or in the oral hearing that the award may exclude the reasons.*"
21. Jean Rouche, Gerald H. Pointon, et al., *French Arbitration Law and Practice: A Dynamic Civil Law Approach to International Arbitration*, para. 316 (2nd ed., Kluwer Law International 2009).
22. *Efxinos Shipping Co. Ltd. v. Rawi Shipping Lines Ltd., Court of Appeal of Genova*, 2 May 1980, in Vol. VIII, Yearbook Commercial Arbitration, pp. 381–382 (Pieter Sanders ed., 1983); *Fratelli Damiano s.n.c. v. August Tropfer & Co., Italian Supreme Court*, Plenary Session, 722, 8 February 1982, in Vol. IX, Yearbook Commercial Arbitration, pp. 418–420 (Pieter Sanders ed., 1984); *X*

12. English law would not be an exception anymore, as the English Arbitration Act of 1996 does require awards to contain reasoning.[23]

13. It is often the case that when the parties settled during the arbitration procedure the award on agreed terms need not be reasoned.[24] Other cases in which a reasoning may not be required concern disputes merely about the quality or condition of goods.[25]

14. Article 36 of the VIAC Arbitration Rules provides that the general rule applies except when "*all parties have agreed (...) in the oral hearing that the award may exclude the reasons.*" Unlike Article VIII(b) of the ECICA, the VIAC Arbitration Rules do not contemplate the possibility of a procedure without a hearing.

15. Regarding the form of the request during the hearing, there is a discrepancy between the English and the French texts of Article VIII(b). Unlike the English text, the French version requires an express request in the hearing as well; it reads "*les parties ou l'une d'elles ne demandent pas* ***expressément*** *avant la fin de l'audience.*" The French text reflects that Article VIII "*purports to lay down unequivocal assumptions evidencing the parties' intent.*"[26]

16. In the absence of a hearing, which only happens in rare occasions,[27] Article VIII(b) provides that the parties can request a motivated award "before the making of the award." In most institutional international arbitration rules it is provided that the arbitrators shall "*declare the proceedings closed with respect to the matters to be decided in the award*"[28] as soon as possible after the last hearing concerning matters to be decided in an award or the filing of the last authorized submissions concerning such matters. Therefore, without a hearing, the concerning party will have to raise its request for a motivated award on or before the declaration of the closing of the procedures.

S.A. v. Y, Spanish Supreme Court, Not indicated, 14 January 1983, in Vol. XI, Yearbook Commercial Arbitration, pp. 523–524 (Albert Jan van den Berg ed., 1986).

23. English Arbitration Act of 1996, Section 52(4).
24. UNCITRAL Model Law, Article 31 provides "*The award shall state the reasons upon which it is based, unless the parties have agreed that no reasons are to be given or the award is an award on agreed terms under article 30* [i.e., an award resulting from a settlement]"; Deutsche Institution für Schiedsgerichtsbarkeit, Section 34.3 provides "*The award shall state the reasons upon which it is based, unless the parties have agreed that no reasons are to be given or the award is an award on agreed terms under section 32 sub. 2* [i.e., an award resulting from a settlement]."
25. Netherlands Arbitration Act, 198, Article 1057, para. 4(e) of the Code of Civil Procedure.
26. Dominique Hascher, *European Convention on International Commercial Arbitration of 1961: Commentary*, in Vol. XXXVI, YEARBOOK COMMERCIAL ARBITRATION, 509, p. 534 (Albert Jan van den Berg ed., 2011).
27. For instance *see* ICDR Expedite Procedures Arbitration Rules, Article E-8.
28. ICC Arbitration Rules, Article 27; Deutsche Institution für Schiedsgerichtsbarkeit, Section 31.

ARTICLE IX

Setting Aside of the Arbitral Award

Gerold Zeiler

INTRODUCTION

Article IX—Setting Aside of the Arbitral Award

(1) The setting aside in a Contracting State of an arbitral award covered by this Convention shall only constitute a ground for the refusal of recognition or enforcement in another Contracting State where such setting aside took place in a State in which or under the law of which, the award has been made and for one of the following reasons:

(a) the parties to the arbitration agreement were, under the law applicable to them, under some incapacity or the said agreement is not valid under the law to which the parties have subjected it or, failing any indication thereon, under the law of the country where the award was made; or

(b) the party requesting the setting aside of the award was not given proper notice of the appointment of the arbitrator or of the arbitration proceedings or was otherwise unable to present his case; or

(c) the award deals with a difference not contemplated by or not falling within the terms of the submission to arbitration, or it contains decisions on matters beyond the scope of the submission to arbitration, provided that, if the decisions on matters submitted to arbitration can be separated from those not so submitted, that part of the award which contains decisions on matters submitted to arbitration need not be set aside;

(d) the composition of the arbitral authority or the arbitral procedure was not in accordance with the agreement of the parties, or failing such agreement, with the provisions of Article IV of this Convention.

2. In relations between Contracting States that are also parties to the New York Convention on the Recognition and Enforcement of Foreign Arbitral Awards of 10th June 1958, paragraph 1 of this Article limits the application of Article V (1) (e) of the New York Convention solely to the cases of setting aside set out under paragraph 1 above.

1. Article IX does not aim to stipulate the applicable setting aside grounds or to regulate setting aside proceedings but addresses the effects of an annulment decision whenever, following the setting aside of an award, recognition and enforcement of the annulled award is sought. Therefore, one must not be misled by the heading of Article IX (I). The provision exclusively enumerates four grounds of annulment that may amount to the refusal of recognition and enforcement of an award (II). Article IX(2) expressly regulates the relationship with Article V(1)(d) of the NYC (III). Finally, it has to be noted that Article IX was a relevant attempt to underpin the internationality of the arbitration proceedings. Its importance can hardly be overestimated (IV).

I SCOPE OF THE PROVISION

2. Despite its heading, i.e., *"Setting aside of the Arbitral Award,"* Article IX does not stipulate the grounds for setting aside an award nor the grounds for refusing its recognition and enforcement.[1] In *X (Dutch company) v. Y (German firm)*, the Dutch company had obtained an award in its favor against the German firm, and the latter sought enforcement before the Court of First Instance of Hamburg. The Court rightly refused to apply the ECICA as the basis for analyzing the enforceability of the award as it held the ECICA does not concern the enforcement of awards.[2]

3. Neither does it concern the suspension of the enforcement proceedings pending a request for setting aside the award.[3] Nevertheless, if the suspension is related to an action to set aside an award on a ground other than those listed in Article IX, it would be reasonable to argue that neither the suspension nor the eventual setting aside would lead to nonrecognition in another Contracting State.[4]

4. Rather, the scope of Article IX limits the effects of an award which has been set aside in one Contracting State whenever thereafter its enforcement and recognition is sought in another Contracting State.[5] However, according to a commentator of the ECICA, the wording of the heading *"was formulated for an earlier draft of [Article IX] where the issue was that of making uniform amongst the Contracting States the various grounds*

1. Florian Haugeneder, *The New Austrian Arbitration Act and the European Convention on International Commercial Arbitration*, 23(4) ARBITRATION INTERNATIONAL, 646, p. 659 (2007).
2. *X (Dutch company) v. Y (German firm)*, Landgericht Hamburg, 24 April 1979, in Vol. V, Yearbook Commercial Arbitration, pp. 264–265 (Pieter Sanders ed., 1980). In contrast *see*, *X (Danish buyer) v. Y (German seller), Oberlandesgericht Köln*, 10 June 1976 in Vol. IV, Yearbook Commercial Arbitration, pp. 258–260 (Pieter Sanders ed., 1979).
3. Dominique Hascher, *European Convention on International Commercial Arbitration of 1961: Commentary*, in Vol. XXXVI, Yearbook Commercial Arbitration, 509, p. 535 (Albert Jan van den Berg ed., 2011); *see also UNI-KOD sarl v. Ouralkali*, Court of Appeal, 31 May 2001, in Vol. XXVI, Yearbook Commercial Arbitration, pp. 1136–1140 (Albert Jan van den Berg ed., 2001), and *UNI-KOD sarl v. Ouralkali*, Supreme Court, 30 March 2004, in Vol. XXX, Yearbook Commercial Arbitration, pp. 1200–1203 (Albert Jan van den Berg ed., 2005).
4. Emmanuel Gaillard and John Savage eds., *Fouchard, Gaillard and Goldman on International Commercial Arbitration*, p. 1716, mn 1000 (Kluwer Law International, 1999).
5. Gary Born, *International Commercial Arbitration*, Vol. III, p. 3173 (Kluwer, 2014); Emmanuel Gaillard and John Savage eds., *Fouchard, Gaillard and Goldman on International Commercial Arbitration*, p. 1715, mn 999 (Kluwer Law International, 1999).

for which an award may be set aside with international effects in other jurisdictions."[6] Therefore, unlike the NYC, the ECICA is not an instrument focused on the recognition and enforcement of awards,[7] its scope only tangentially reaches the enforcement stage.

5. Article IX(1) provides that its scope only encompasses awards within the protection of Article I of the ECICA. Additionally, Article IX refers to awards which were set aside "*in a State in which or under the law of which, the award has been made.*"[8] The first option is the State where the award was issued (the law of the seat)[9] whereas the second option is that of the governing law applicable to the award (the *lex arbitri*).

6. During the Special Meeting of Plenipotentiaries, the possibility of clarifying that "*the law under which the award has been made means the law governing the arbitration proceedings*" was discussed.[10] However, the proposal was rejected due to the majority's desire to follow the text of Article V of the NYC as closely as possible in view of the confusion which might otherwise arise.

7. A commentator of the ECICA noted that, by providing two options, Article IX creates the risk of contradictory decisions because the award may be set aside in the country where it was made whilst considered valid in the country under the law of which it was made.[11]

8. In this regards, the basic approach of the Model Law, and all national laws derived from it, is that the law applicable to the arbitration proceedings (the *lex arbitri*) will be the law of the seat where that arbitration takes place.[12] Therefore, generally, unless the parties agreed otherwise, both laws will coincide and no contradiction will arise.

9. Article IX only applies to cases "*for the refusal of recognition or enforcement in* ***another*** *Contracting State.*" Thus, it is inapplicable whenever the enforcement is

6. Dominique Hascher, *European Convention on International Commercial Arbitration of 1961: Commentary,* in Vol. XXXVI, Yearbook Commercial Arbitration, 509, p. 535 (Albert Jan van den Berg ed., 2011).
7. Emmanuel Gaillard and John Savage eds., *Fouchard, Gaillard and Goldman on International Commercial Arbitration,* p. 1714, mn 998 (Kluwer Law International, 1999); Dominique Hascher, *European Convention on International Commercial Arbitration of 1961: Commentary,* in Vol. XXXVI, Yearbook Commercial Arbitration, 509, p. 534 (Albert Jan van den Berg ed., 2011).
8. Article IX, para. 1 of the ECICA.
9. Article 31(3) of the UNCITRAL Model Law indicates that "*[t]he award shall be deemed to have been made at that place.*"
10. Dominique Hascher, *European Convention on International Commercial Arbitration of 1961: Commentary,* in Vol. XXXVI, Yearbook Commercial Arbitration, 509, p. 536 (Albert Jan van den Berg ed., 2011); *See also,* P. I. Benjamin, *The European Convention on International Commercial Arbitration,* 37 British Yearbook of International Law 478, p. 493 (1961), fn. 4.
11. Dominique Hascher, *European Convention on International Commercial Arbitration of 1961: Commentary,* in Vol. XXXVI, Yearbook Commercial Arbitration, 509, p. 536 (Albert Jan van den Berg ed., 2011).
12. Alastair Henderson, *Lex Arbitri, Procedural Law and the Seat of Arbitration,* 26 Singapore Academy of Law Journal 886, p. 890 (2014); Article 1(2) of the UNCITRAL Model Law.

sought in the country of origin.[13] It is also inapplicable when the setting aside proceedings took place in a non-Contracting State, as such a State falls outside the scope of the ECICA.[14]

II GROUNDS FOR ANNULMENT

10. Generally, under many domestic laws, the grounds available for refusing recognition and enforcement of an arbitral award are:

(i) the award was rendered based on an arbitration agreement that, under the applicable law, the parties lacked the capacity to make or was invalid;[15]
(ii) the parties were not given proper notice of the appointment of the arbitrator(s) or were, otherwise, unable to present its case;[16]
(iii) the award deals with an issue not falling within the scope of the arbitration clause;[17]
(iv) the composition of the arbitral tribunal or the arbitration proceedings violates the parties' agreement or the applicable law;[18]
(v) the award has not yet become binding on the parties or has been set aside or suspended by a court of the country;[19]
(vi) the subject matter of the dispute is not capable of settlement by arbitration under the applicable law;[20] and
(vii) the recognition and enforcement of the award would be contrary to public purpose.[21]

11. The first four grounds are almost identical to the grounds enumerated in Article IX, Article V(1) (a) to (d) of the NYC and Article 36(1)(a) (i) to (iv) of the UNCITRAL Model Law, except for ground (d) which in Article IX instead of referring to the law of the seat of arbitration refers to Article IV of the ECICA. The scope of the fifth ground is precisely what Article IX attempts to limit; thus, it was not included as an additional ground therein. The last two grounds, i.e., lack of arbitrability and a violation of public

13. Dominique Hascher, *European Convention on International Commercial Arbitration of 1961: Commentary*, in Vol. XXXVI, Yearbook Commercial Arbitration, 509, p. 536 (Albert Jan van den Berg ed., 2011).
14. *Stroilensky Gornoobogatitelny Combinat (Russian Federation) v. Interconstruction Project Management S.A. (Switzerland), Mabetex Project Engineering Industrieanlagenplanung und Einrichtung GmbH (Austria)*, Presidium of the Supreme Arbitration Court of the Russian Federation, 15359/03, 30 March 2004, in Vol. XXX, Yearbook Commercial Arbitration, pp. 1204-1207 (Albert Jan van den Berg ed., 2005).
15. UNCITRAL Model Law, Article 36(1)(a)(i); Article V(1)(a) of the NYC.
16. UNCITRAL Model Law, Article 36(1)(a)(ii); Article V(1)(b) of the NYC.
17. UNCITRAL Model Law, Article 36(1)(a)(iii); Article V(1)(c) of the NYC.
18. UNCITRAL Model Law, Article 36(1)(a)(iv); Article V(1)(d) of the NYC.
19. UNCITRAL Model Law, Article 36(1)(a)(v); Article V(1)(e) of the NYC.
20. UNCITRAL Model Law, Article 36(1)(b)(1); Article V(2)(a) of the NYC.
21. UNCITRAL Model Law, Article 36(1)(b)(2); Article V(2)(b) of the NYC.

policy of the country in which the award was made, were excluded in Article IX due to their close connection with domestic standards.[22]

12. During the drafting of the provision, the German delegation suggested to include an additional ground in cases of fraud. However, the proposal was rejected as it was considered the ground was already covered by the scope of Article IX(1)(d).[23]

13. Hence, under Article IX, in order to deny the enforcement and recognition of an annulled award, the award must have been set aside based exclusively on one of the following grounds.

[A] Invalidity of the Arbitration Agreement

14. The invalidity of the arbitration agreement is a ground for annulment recognized in all national systems as it conveys that consent is the cornerstone of international arbitration.[24] Under this ground, an arbitration agreement may be invalid due to (i) the parties' lack of capacity to arbitrate under the law applicable to them; and (ii) a breach of the substantive or formal provisions applicable to the arbitration agreement under the law agreed by the parties or, failing any indication in that respect, under the law of the country where the award was made. The conflict of laws rules indicated in this ground for annulment are consistent with those set forth in Article VI of the ECICA.

15. Regarding the legal capacity of the parties, the text of Article IX(1)(a) mirrors the one of Article V(1)(a) of the NYC. Notably, both instruments departed from the text of the Geneva Convention of 1927 pursuant to which the incapacity of a party was expressly dealt only in the context of improper representation in the arbitration proceedings.[25]

16. In *X (US) v. Y (Belarus)*, the parties concluded an agreement for the supply of wheels and wheel-rims, which contained an arbitration clause. The supplier was a US company and the manufacturer was a company owned by the Belarusian State. When the dispute arose the supplier commenced arbitration proceedings. The award was rendered in favor of the supplier. The supplier sought the enforcement of the award in Germany. Simultaneously, the manufacturer requested the annulment of the award in Belarus. The Supreme Court of Belarus set aside the award, *inter alia*, because the US supplier's office in Minsk was not registered under the applicable law and, therefore,

22. Stefan Kröll, *The European Convention on International Commercial Arbitration: The Tale of a Sleeping Beauty*, in Austrian Yearbook on International Arbitration, 61–74, p. 18 (Klausegger and others eds., Manz, 2013).
23. René David, *Arbitration in International Trade*, paras 405, 406 (Springer, 1985).
24. Gary Born, *International Commercial Arbitration*, Vol. III, p. 3188 (Kluwer, 2014).
25. Article 2(1)(b) of the Geneva Convention of 1927 provides: "*That the party against whom it is sought to use the award (...) being under a legal incapacity, he was not properly represented*" Convention on the Execution of Foreign Arbitral Awards, Geneva, 26 September 1927, League of Nations, *Treaty Series*, Vol. 92, p. 301; *see also* Albert Jan van den Berg, *The New York Arbitration Convention of 1958*, p. 275 (Kluwer Law International, 1981).

lacked the legal capacity when it concluded the arbitration agreement. As a consequence, the Dresden Court of Appeal refused to enforce the award. Even though the US is not a party to the ECICA, the Dresden Court of Appeal applied Article IX(1)(a) by means of an MFN clause in force between the US and Belarus.[26]

17. Regarding the law applicable to the arbitration agreement, it has been widely recognized that the invalidity of the underlying contract does not necessarily amount to the invalidity of the arbitration agreement. Therefore, an independent analysis is required.

[B] Violations of Due Process

18. Article IX(1)(b) addresses cases in which the party requesting the annulment of the award was not given proper notice of the appointment of the arbitrator(s) or was otherwise unable to present its case due to procedural malpractice.[27] The wording of Article IX(1)(b), in consonance with Article V(1)(b) of the NYC, is broader than the corresponding ground in the Geneva Convention of 1927 as the scope of the latter convention was limited to the notice of the arbitration proceedings.[28]

19. NYC's case law reveals violations of due process are one of the most popular grounds for annulment invoked by the parties. However, the invocation has rarely been successful as domestic courts are inclined to interpret this exception narrowly.[29]

20. A question that can be raised is which standards of due process shall be considered in the analysis made by the domestic court where the annulment is sought. As the objective of the ECICA is to depurate international arbitration from domestic standards, it would be reasonable to argue that international standards of due process shall apply instead of domestic standards.

21. As due process is generally considered part of public policy,[30] it may be the case that a domestic court decides to annul an award due to a violation of due process under the grounds of violation of public policy and considers unnecessary the analysis on

---

26. *Germany No. 110/E18, Supplier (US) v. State enterprise (Belarus)*, Dresden Court of Appeal, 11 Sch 18/05, 31 January 2007, in Volume XXXIII, Yearbook Commercial Arbitration, pp. 510–516 (Albert Jan van den Berg ed., 2008).
27. Dominique Hascher, *European Convention on International Commercial Arbitration of 1961: Commentary*, in Vol. XXXVI, Yearbook Commercial Arbitration, 509, p. 538 (Albert Jan van den Berg ed., 2011).
28. Article 2(1)(b) of the Geneva Convention of 1927 provides: "*That the party against whom it is sought to use the award was not given notice of the arbitration proceedings in sufficient time to enable him to present his case (...)*" Convention on the Execution of Foreign Arbitral Awards, Geneva, 26 September 1927, League of Nations, *Treaty Series*, Vol. 92, p. 301; *see also* Albert Jan van den Berg, *The New York Arbitration Convention of 1958*, p. 297 (Kluwer Law International, 1981).
29. Albert Jan van den Berg, *The New York Arbitration Convention of 1958*, p. 297 (Kluwer Law International, 1981).
30. Emmanuel Gaillard and John Savage eds., *Fouchard, Gaillard and Goldman on International Commercial Arbitration*, p. 986, mn 1697 (Kluwer Law International, 1999).

different grounds. In such a case, a question may be raised on whether the enforcement court, pursuant to Article IX, would have to uphold or refuse enforcement.

[C] Excess of Authority

22. The ground of excess of authority is closely related to the ground of the invalidity of the arbitration agreement. Both provisions ensure that the ruling of the arbitrator(s) is based on the consent of the parties generally expressed in an arbitration agreement. However, the ECICA, similar to the NYC, does not contemplate the opposite case where the arbitrator has made an incomplete award.

[D] Irregularities in the Composition of the Arbitral Tribunal or in the Arbitration Proceedings

23. The ground of procedural irregularities reflects the importance of the parties' autonomy in the organization of the arbitration proceedings, in particular in the composition of the arbitral tribunal.[31]

24. This ground departs from the text of Article V(1)(d) of the NYC and of the 1927 Geneva Convention regarding the role of the law of the seat of arbitration. Under the 1927 Geneva Convention, awards fully respecting the intentions of the parties could nevertheless be refused enforcement if the arbitrators failed to comply with the rules of the seat of arbitration. Under the 1927 Geneva Convention, the parties' autonomy was, thus, subordinated to the law of the seat of arbitration. In contrast, Article V(1)(d) of the NYC restored the primacy of parties' autonomy and treated the rules of the seat of the arbitration as applicable on a subsidiary basis.

25. The ECICA took a further step and replaced the reference to the law of the seat for the rules set forth in Article IV thereof. The omission is consistent with the ECICA's intention to free the arbitration proceedings from local standards.[32] Therefore, the enforcement court shall refuse enforcement exclusively if the arbitration proceedings were inconsistent with the parties' agreement or failing such agreement, with the rules set forth in Article IV.

III RELATIONSHIP WITH THE NYC

26. Article IX(2) expressly regulates the relationship between paragraph 1 of Article IX and Article V(1)(e) of the NYC, whenever the involved States are parties to both

31. Dominique Hascher, *European Convention on International Commercial Arbitration of 1961: Commentary*, in Vol. XXXVI, Yearbook Commercial Arbitration, 509, p. 540 (Albert Jan van den Berg ed., 2011).
32. Stefan Kröll, *The European Convention on International Commercial Arbitration: The Tale of a Sleeping Beauty*, in Austrian Yearbook on International Arbitration, 61–74, pp. 17–18 (Klausegger and others eds., Manz, 2013).

instruments.[33] It provides that paragraph 1 limits Article V(1)(e) of the NYC to the grounds listed in paragraph 1 of Article IX.

27. Although the NYC has been characterized as having a pro-enforcement bias, in the realm of the NYC the enforcement of annulled awards remains an open debate. On the one hand, the traditional view relies on Article V(1)(e) of the NYC which recognizes annulment as a ground for nonenforcement without further conditions.[34] Under the traditional view, when the court of origin annuls an award, the effect of the same is universal such that the award is not enforceable in any other jurisdiction.[35] The traditional view has been criticized by some academics, as it disrupts the internationality of the NYC by "*invit[ing] in via the back door local standards which the [NYC] tried to exclude by enumerating possible defenses.*"[36]

28. On the other hand, the opposing view relies on the permissive word "may" used in Article V(1) together with the MFN clause contained in Article VII. The opposing view endorses the idea of delocalization of the arbitration proceedings which represents a more internationalist approach and finds support in ECICA's Article IX. However, the latter view has also been criticized as it has the potential of jeopardizing the predictability and consistency of the international arbitration framework.[37]

29. The courts of the States parties to the ECICA which seem to have followed the classic view are: Germany, Hungary, and Italy. In contrast, those that are likely to enforce annulled awards are: Austria, Croatia, Denmark, Luxembourg, Poland, Spain, and Turkey.[38]

IV RELEVANCE OF THE PROVISION

30. Commentators of the ECICA consider Article IX as one of the most valuable contributions of the ECICA to the functioning and success of international arbitration, due to its attempt to restrict such local standards that could undermine the internationality of the award. The idea behind Article IX is that there is no reason to allow that the conception of public policy of the country of origin of the award may prevent the award's enforcement *erga omnes*.[39] As illustrated by P.I. Benjamin:

---

33. Dominique Hascher, *European Convention on International Commercial Arbitration of 1961: Commentary*, in Vol. XXXVI, Yearbook Commercial Arbitration, 509, p. 540 (Albert Jan van den Berg ed., 2011).
34. Albert Jan van den Berg, *Enforcement of Arbitral Awards Annulled in Russia*, 27 Journal of International Arbitration 179, p. 196 (2010).
35. Manu Thadikkaran, *Enforcement of Annulled Arbitral Awards: What Is and What Ought to Be?*, 31(5) Journal of International Arbitration, pp. 575–608 (2014).
36. Stefan Kröll, *The European Convention on International Commercial Arbitration: The Tale of a Sleeping Beauty*, in Austrian Yearbook on International Arbitration, 61–74, p. 18 (Klausegger and others eds., Manz, 2013).
37. Manu Thadikkaran, *Enforcement of Annulled Arbitral Awards: What Is and What Ought to Be?*, 31(5) Journal of International Arbitration, pp. 575–608 (Kluwer Law International 2014).
38. *Ibid.*
39. P. I. Benjamin, *The European Convention on International Commercial Arbitration*, 37 British Yearbook of International Law 478, p. 494 (1961); Emmanuel Gaillard and John Savage eds.,

> Otherwise, the situation might well arise in which an award made in State A, between nationals of State B and State C, which was to be enforced in either State B or C, could not be because it had been set aside in State A as violating public policy, and notwithstanding the fact that the award was not contrary to the public policy of either State B or C.[40]

31. In *Buyer (Austria) v. Seller (Serbia and Montenegro)*, the Seller sought enforcement of an award in Austria. However, the Buyer objected the enforcement alleging that the enforcement violated Austrian public policy. In turn, the Seller claimed that the objection of violation of public policy must be raised exclusively in set aside proceedings in the country of origin. The Court reasoned that, under the ECICA, the annulment of an award in the country of origin is not a basis for refusing enforcement and recognition. Therefore, it would be inappropriate to rule that the Buyer is required to raise the objection on public policy in setting aside proceedings in the country of origin, which would be irrelevant to the enforcement proceedings.[41] The Court stated that "*[m]aking an international arbitral award dependent on state approval in the country of origin would deprive international arbitration of its independence.*"[42]

32. In *Kajo-Erzeugnisse Essenzen GmbH (Kajo) v. DO Zdravilisce Radenska (Radenska)*, arbitration proceedings arose from a dispute relating to the breach of a contract of manufacturing and distribution of a caloric drink. The award was issued in favor of Kajo. Radenska sought annulment of the award in Slovenia while Kajo sought its enforcement in Austria.[43]

33. The Slovenian Supreme Court set aside the award on the basis that the award was contrary to the public policy of the country of origin. However, the Austrian Supreme Court found that the setting aside of an award for violating the public policy of the award's country of origin is not a ground for refusing enforcement under the ECICA.

34. The idea behind Article IX has led some courts, particularly French courts, to take no account of the setting aside of an award by the courts of the seat of the arbitration, even if the ECICA is not applicable.[44]

Fouchard, Gaillard and Goldman on International Commercial Arbitration, p. 1001, mn 1716 (Kluwer Law International, 1999); Florian Haugeneder, *The New Austrian Arbitration Act and the European Convention on International Commercial Arbitration*, 23(4) Arbitration International, 646, p. 660 (2007).

40. P. I. Benjamin, *The European Convention on International Commercial Arbitration*, 37 British Yearbook International Las 478, p. 494 (1961).

41. *Buyer (Austria) v. Seller (Serbia and Montenegro)*, Supreme Court of Austria, 30b221/04b, 26 January 2005, in Vol. XXX, Yearbook Commercial Arbitration, pp. 421–436 (Albert Jan van den Berg ed., 2005).

42. Gregor Geimer, *Internationales Zivilprozessrecht*, (5th ed. 2005), No. 3944, in *Buyer (Austria) v. Seller (Serbia and Montenegro)*, Supreme Court of Austria, 30b221/04b, 26 January 2005, in Vol. XXX, Yearbook Commercial Arbitration, pp. 421–436 (Albert Jan van den Berg ed., 2005), (Unofficial English translation).

43. *Kajo-Erzeugnisse EssenzenGmbH v. DO ZdraviliscеRadenska, ObersterGerichtshof*, 20 October 1993 and 23 February 1998 in Vol. XXIV, Yearbook Commercial Arbitration, pp. 919–927 (Albert Jan van den Berg ed., 1999).

44. Christopher Koch, *The Enforcement of Awards Annulled in Their Place of Origin*, 26(2) Journal of International Arbitration, 267–292, p. 267 (2009).

35. In the *Hilmarton* case, the French *Cour de Cassation* ruled that a Swiss arbitral award was of an international nature, i.e., that it was not attached to the Swiss legal order, and, thus, it continued to exist despite its annulment at the seat of arbitration. In the subsequent *Putrabali* case, the *Cour de Cassation* affirmed the *Hilmarton* principle and stated that an international arbitral award is an international decision grounded on a nonnational, arbitral legal order and, therefore, its annulment by a domestic court has no effect on its enforcement in another State.[45]

36. Even though the annulment of an award on the ground of public policy is excluded from the list of Article IX, this exclusion does not imply that the concept of public policy becomes irrelevant for the enforcement and recognition stage. The ECICA does not limit the power of the enforcement court to perform an independent review of public policy.[46]

37. On the other side, the parties' choice of the law (seat of arbitration) might have relied precisely on the public policy of the chosen State. The prospect of annulment at the arbitral seat may, therefore, also be seen as part of the agreement. Therefore, one may argue that by excluding public policy and local standards from the scope of Article IX(1), the principle of parties' autonomy may be undermined.

38. Furthermore, many courts have stressed that the notion of public policy is an ever-evolving concept.[47] In the context of the recognition and enforcement of international arbitral awards, many States have drawn a distinction between domestic and international public policy. It has been suggested that an award should only be set aside on public policy grounds if it is contrary to international public policy.[48]

39. In *Société Européenne d'Etudes et d'Entreprises (SEEE) v. Socialist Federal Republic of Yugoslavia and others*, the parties concluded a contract which contained an arbitration clause. When Yugoslavia refused to pay certain amounts under the Contract, SEEE resorted to arbitration. The award was issued in favor of SEEE. Following Yugoslavia's failed attempt to set aside the award in Switzerland, SEEE requested the President of the Court of First Instance of Paris for a leave of enforcement of the award.

---

45. Mike McClure, *Enforcement of Arbitral Awards That Have Been Set Aside at the Seat: The Consistently Inconsistent Approach Across Europe*, 26 June 2012 (Kluwer Arbitration Blog), available at http://arbitrationblog.kluwerarbitration.com/2012/06/26/enforcement-of-arbitral-awards-that-have-been-set-aside-at-the-seat-the-consistently-inconsistent-approach-across-europe/ (last visited 10 October 2017).
46. Dominique Hascher, *European Convention on International Commercial Arbitration of 1961: Commentary*, in Vol. XXXVI, Yearbook Commercial Arbitration, 509, p. 536 (Albert Jan van den Berg ed., 2011); Florian Haugeneder, *The New Austrian Arbitration Act and the European Convention on International Commercial Arbitration*, 23(4) Arbitration International, 646, p. 660 (2007); *see also Buyer (Austria) v. Seller (Serbia and Montenegro)*, Supreme Court of Austria, Ob221/04b, 26 January 2005, in Vol. XXX, Yearbook Commercial Arbitration, pp. 421-436 (Albert Jan van den Berg ed., 2005).
47. IBA Subcommittee on Recognition and Enforcement of Arbitral Awards, *Report on the Public Policy Exception in the New York Convention*, p. 10 (October 2015).
48. *ICCA Guide to the interpretation of the 1958 New York Convention*, p. 107 (Pieter Sanders ed., ICCA, Schiedam 2011); John K. Arthur, *Setting Aside or Non-enforcement of Arbitral Awards in International Arbitration on the Public Policy Ground—a Regional Perspective*, Australian Alternative Dispute Resolution Bulletin 115, p. 115 (December 2015).

Initially, the President granted the lift; however, eventually, the President retracted the lift as he found the arbitration proceedings were not in accordance with the parties' agreement. Thereafter, the case was remitted to the Court of Appeal of Orléans which refused enforcement on the ground that the award violated French public policy as it contained a manifest error contrary to logic and reason. However, the *Cour de Cassation* reversed the Court of Appeal's decision on the grounds that the enforcement of a foreign arbitral award in France can be refused only if it violated international public policy. According to the *Cour de Cassation*, international public policy is not violated by errors of the arbitrators even if such an error is manifest.[49]

40. Therefore, it is questionable whether the drafters of the ECICA would have excluded the ground of violation of public policy if, at the time when the ECICA was negotiated, the concept of international public policy had already crystallized.

49. *Société Européenne d'Etudes et d'Entreprises (SEEE) by its liquidator Mme. Y. Cleja v. Socialist Federal Republic of Yugoslavia, International Bank for the Reconstruction and Development (The World Bank) and others,* Court of Appeal of Orléans, 13 December of 1979 and *Cour de Cassation,* 13 October 1981, REVUE DE L'ARBITRAGE, pp. 63–68 (1983), with comment by J.-L. Delvolvé. The *Cour de Cassation* remitted the case to the Court of Appeal of Rouen which eventually granted the enforcement of the award.

Annexes

ANNEX I

Composition and Procedure of the Special Committee Referred to in Article IV of the Convention

Andrea de la Brena

INTRODUCTION

1. The appointment of the presiding or sole arbitrator was one of the most politically sensitive topics during the drafting of the ECICA due to the existing divergences between the East-West economies. Therefore, reaching an agreement on a neutral mechanism for the appointment of the presiding or sole arbitrator took more than five years of discussions that were eventually translated in the creation of the Special Committee referred to in Article IV of the ECICA.[1] The main purpose of the Special Committee is to perform the functions provided for in Article IV, including the appointment of the presiding or sole arbitrator whenever the disputing parties cannot come to an agreement or the President of the competent Chamber of Commerce does not fulfill its mandate.[2]

2. Annex I of the ECICA contains an extensive regulation on the composition and functioning of the Special Committee, which is based on a rotating system (I). The Annex also provides for the decision-making process of the Special Committee (II). The system was, nonetheless, amended a couple of years after its creation, by certain Contracting States, pursuant to the Paris Agreement (III) and the Moscow Convention

1. Ottoarndt Glossner, *The Institutional Appointment of Arbitrators: The Special Committee of the European Convention on Commercial Arbitration of Geneva, 21 April 1961*, 12(1) ARBITRATION INTERNATIONAL (1 March 1996), 95–100, p. 95 (21 November 2014).
2. *See* commentary to Article IV.

(IV). In practice, the system has impractical results and, proposals to amend the system have been raised (V).

I THE COMPOSITION OF THE SPECIAL COMMITTEE

3. Annex I provides that the Special Committee be composed of three members who will serve in this role for a period of four years.[3] One member shall be elected by the Chambers of Commerce or other institutions, designated by the Western Bloc countries. The second member shall be elected by the Chambers of Commerce or other institutions, designated by the Eastern Bloc countries.[4] Under Article X paragraph 6 of the ECICA, each Contracting State shall communicate a list of the Chambers of Commerce or other institutions in their country, which could be elected for the Special Committee, to the Secretary-General of the United Nations.[5]

4. To reach equal representation of both Blocs, the Contracting States agreed upon a rotating system for the chairman position of the Special Committee.[6] According to this system, each group of Chambers of Commerce, on an alternating basis, appoints a chairman for half the duration of the functions of the Special Committee (i.e., two years). A rotating chairmanship system was introduced to ensure an impartial functioning of the Special Committee, as the chairman who belongs to one of the groups of countries will be obliged to exercise their functions impartially, to avoid the risk of retaliation by their successor during their two-year tenure.[7] The decision on which chairman rules first is decided by the drawing of lots.[8]

5. The Chambers of Commerce or the designated institutions shall additionally elect alternates at the same time and in the same manner as they elect the chairman and other regular members, in case of the temporary inability of the regular members to act.[9]

II THE DECISION-MAKING PROCESS

6. The decision-making process of the Special Committee is also provided for in Annex I. All requests under Article IV shall be addressed to the Executive Secretary of the

3. Annex I, paras. 1 and 6.
4. Annex I, paras. 1–3.
5. Article X, para. 6 of the ECICA.
6. Alice Fremuth-Wolf, *The European Convention on International Arbitration as a Tool to Remedy Pathological Arbitration Agreements – "There's still Life in the Old Dog yet!,"* in Austrian Yearbook on International Arbitration, 61–78, 69 (Manz, 2013).
7. Lazare Kopelmanas, *La Place De La Convention Europeenne Sur L'arbitrage Commercial International Du 21 Avril 1961 dans L'évolution Du Droit International De L'arbitrage,* 7 Annuaire Français de Droit International pp. 331–354 (1961); Alice Fremuth-Wolf, *The European Convention on International Arbitration as a Tool to Remedy Pathological Arbitration Agreements – "There's Still Life in the Old Dog Yet!,"* in Austrian Yearbook on International Arbitration, 61–78, 69 (Manz, 2013).
8. Annex I, para. 7.
9. Annex I, para. 3.

Economic Commission for Europe. The Executive Secretary will thereafter send the request to the member of the Special Committee selected by the group of countries other than those represented by the chairman in turn. The member will submit its proposal to the other country-appointed member of the Special Committee for its approval. If the other country-appointed member does not uphold the proposal, the Executive Secretary shall convene a meeting in an attempt to agree on a unanimous decision. If there is a failure to reach a unanimous decision, the ruling will be adopted by the majority.[10]

III THE PARIS AGREEMENT

7. Under Article X paragraph 7 of the ECICA, the Contracting States have the right to conclude other international arbitration instruments.[11] In view of this prerogative, shortly after the conclusion of the ECICA, the Agreement Relating to Application of the European Convention on International Commercial Arbitration ("Paris Agreement") was concluded in Paris on 17 December 1962.[12]

8. The main purpose of the Paris Agreement is to exclude the influence of the Eastern Bloc in the appointment system,[13] in purely Western disputes.[14] Therefore, whenever there are arbitration proceedings involving physical or legal persons whose habitual residence or seat is located in the States who are parties to the Paris Agreement, the remedies set forth in paragraphs 2–7 are substituted by the following provision:

> [...] any difficulties arising with regard to the constitution or functioning of the arbitral tribunal shall be submitted to the decision of the **competent authority** at the request of the party instituting proceedings.

9. The agreement does not provide further explanation on the determination of the competent authority or the State to which such a competent authority should belong to. Although in most cases, domestic arbitration Acts will refer the parties to the domestic courts for judicial assistance, uncertainty still remains when determining the applicable arbitration Act and court in an international arbitration. The French text of the provision provided some clarity, referring to the "competent **judicial** authority."[15]

---

10. Annex I, paras. 8 and 9.
11. Article X, para. 7, provides the following "*[t]he provisions of the present Convention shall not affect the validity of multi-lateral or bilateral agreements concerning arbitration entered into by Contracting States.*"
12. The State parties to this agreement are Austria, Belgium, Denmark, France, Germany, Italy, Luxembourg and Republic of Moldova.
13. Ottoarndt Glossner, *The Institutional Appointment of Arbitrators: The Special Committee of the European Convention on Commercial Arbitration of Geneva, 21 April 1961*, 12(1) ARBITRATION INTERNATIONAL, pp. 95–100, p. 97 (1 March 1996).
14. P. I. Benjamin, *The European Convention on International Commercial Arbitration*, 37 BRITISH YEARBOOK INTERNATIONAL LAW 478, p. 482 (1961). Emmanuel Gaillard and John Savage eds., *Fouchard, Gaillard and Goldman on International Commercial Arbitration*, p. 526, mn 933 (Kluwer Law International, 1999).
15. Emmanuel Gaillard and John Savage eds., *Fouchard, Gaillard and Goldman on International Commercial Arbitration*, p. 144, mn 289 (Kluwer Law International, 1999) (emphasis added).

However, the uncertainty remains and might give rise to conflicts on the applicable law which is precisely what the drafters of the ECICA sought to avoid.[16]

10. In one of the publicly known cases where the Paris Agreement was invoked, the President of the *Tribunal d'arrondissement* of Luxembourg was called upon to decide on the appointment of the chairman of the arbitral tribunal, the seat of arbitration and the procedural rules.[17]

11. The applicability of the Paris Agreement was also discussed in the case *SLORA v. NV Barco.*[18] In this case, the parties concluded a first contract which contained a clause providing that "*in case of disagreement concerning the present contract, the parties may ask for the opinion of an arbitrator, who will be appointed by the President of the Commercial Court in Sarreguemines.*"[19] Thereafter, the parties concluded a second contract extending the scope of the first contract which provided that "*any dispute arising out of this contract, including its validity, which the parties cannot settle, shall be decided by arbitration in accordance with the rules of the International Chamber of Commerce of Paris.*" When the dispute arose, SLORA commenced court proceedings in Kortrijk. NV Barco objected the jurisdiction of the court based on the arbitration clause contained in the second contract and requested the court to resolve on the competent arbitral tribunal, its composition, procedure, and seat.

12. The court declined jurisdiction based on the validity of the arbitration clause in the second contract. Hence, according to the court, the Paris Agreement was not applicable because, under Article IV, paragraph 1 of the Convention, where the parties have decided to submit their disputes to a permanent arbitral institution, the rules of said institution shall rule the procedure, including the composition of the arbitral tribunal. Therefore, as the parties referred to the ICC rules and Paris as the seat, there was nothing left for the court to decide.[20]

IV THE MOSCOW CONVENTION

13. On 26 May 1972, the Eastern countries concluded the Convention on the Settlement by Arbitration of Civil Law Disputes Resulting from Relations of Economic and Scientific-Technical Cooperation (the "Moscow Convention"), under the auspices of

16. *Ibid.*, p. 527, mn 935.
17. Luxembourg No. E1, *Not indicated v. Not indicated*, President, *Tribunal d'arrondissement de Luxembourg*, E1, 7 June 1993, in Vol. XX, Yearbook Commercial Arbitration, pp. 1067–1067 (Albert Jan van den Berg ed., 1995).
18. Belgium No. E5, *Société Lorraine de Matériel Radio-électrique (SLORA) v. NV Barco Electronic, NV Barco and others*, Rechtbank van Koophandel (Commercial Court), Kortrijk, 337/91, 1 October 1993.
19. *Ibid.*
20. Belgium No. E5, *Société Lorraine de Matériel Radio-électrique (SLORA) v. NV Barco Electronic, NV Barco and others*, Rechtbank van Koophandel (Commercial Court), Kortrijk, 337/91, 1 October 1993.

the Council for Mutual Economic Assistance ("COMECON").[21] The Moscow Convention grants jurisdiction over disputes between economic organizations of its Contracting States arising in the course of economic and scientific-technical cooperation to the arbitration courts of the Chambers of Commerce of each Eastern country. When the Moscow Convention was signed there were almost no private or mixed companies in the Eastern countries; hence, the term only covered nonstock entities. The term also excluded private individuals.

14. However, the subject matter of the dispute covered by the Moscow Convention is broad enough to overlap, in certain cases, with the disputes covered by the ECICA. Therefore, if a commercial dispute arose between enterprises located in two different Eastern countries, the competent authority to decide the dispute would have been the Court of Arbitration of the Chamber of Commerce in the country of the respondent or, subject to an agreement of the parties concerned, in a third country party to the present Convention.[22] The Moscow Convention did not provide for any appointing authority in case the competent Court of Arbitration failed to fulfill its mandate. Hence, it remains doubtful whether Article IV and Annex I of the ECICA could serve as a fallback mechanism for these cases.

15. The dissolution of the COMECON and the political disintegration of the Soviet Union, Yugoslavia and the Czechoslovak Federation have raised the question on the practical relevance of the Moscow Convention. Most of the countries which were bound by the Moscow Convention had repudiated it and almost no new State has recognized it.[23] For instance, Poland repudiated the Convention in 1993 and neither the Slovak Government nor the newly organized Slovak Court of Arbitration at the Slovak Chamber of Commerce and Industry proclaimed their position on the issue of that country's succession to the Moscow Convention.[24] Therefore, the binding character and scope of application of the Moscow Convention are subject to continuous debate among commentators.[25] Most commentators have considered that the Moscow Convention is no longer in effect.[26]

21. Until 1992 the members which remain contracting parties to the Moscow Convention were Bulgaria, Cuba, Hungary, Mongolia, Poland, Romania, the successor States of Czechoslovakia and the Commonwealth of Independent States. Emmanuel Gaillard and John Savage eds., *Fouchard, Gaillard and Goldman on International Commercial Arbitration*, p. 145, mn 292, fn. 394 (Kluwer Law International, 1999).
22. Moscow Convention, Article II.
23. Nikolaus Pitkowitz, *Is There Still a Scope of Application of the European Convention on International Commercial Arbitration?*, in Austrian Yearbook on International Arbitration, 93–108, p. 97 (Klausegger and others eds., 2013).
24. Stanislaw J. Soltysinski, *Arbitation Law in States after Fundamental Changes*, in Planning Efficient Arbitration Proceedings: The Law Applicable in International Arbitration, ICCA Congress Series, Volume 7, pp. 530–541 (Albert Jan van den Berg ed., Kluwer Law International, 1996).
25. *Ibid.*
26. Emmanuel Gaillard and John Savage eds., *Fouchard, Gaillard and Goldman on International Commercial Arbitration*, p. 145, mn 293 (Kluwer Law International, 1999); Peter Schlosser, *Chronique de jurisprudence allemande*, Rev. Arb., 663, p. 665 (1995).

V THE PROPOSALS TO REVIEW THE APPOINTING AUTHORITIES

16. The mechanism provided for in Annex I and Article IV has been the subject of multiple criticisms due to its complexity and outdated *raison d'être*.[27] In practice, it has also not served any material utility. The first Special Committee was installed in 1965 and, until 1993, it was renewed every four years according to the terms of Annex I.[28] During such a period, only two applications were submitted to the Special Committee requesting its intervention.[29]

17. For the reasons stated above, in 1999, the Committee for Trade, Industry and Enterprise Development, at the request of certain Contracting States to the ECICA, approved the establishment of an Arbitration Advisory Group to the Working Party on Legal and Commercial Practice with a mandate to primarily review the usefulness of the Convention and whether any revisions would increase its usefulness.

18. During the first meeting of the Advisory Group held in February 2000, it was concluded that the ECICA remained useful, as it provided a common set of rules that are binding upon the Contracting States at an international level. However, it was also concluded that an update to Article IV, X and Annex I of the ECICA would enhance its utility in the contemporary scene.[30] The changes concerned the identity of the appointing authorities set forth therein.

19. In the revised text of Article IV, the Advisory Group eliminated the references to the President of the competent Chamber of Commerce and the Special Committee. The new text refers to the *"head of an institution appointed under the Convention by the country of the place of arbitration [...] or by the country of the respondent's habitual place of residence or seat at the time of the introduction of the request for arbitration"* and to the *"Secretary-General of the Permanent Court of Arbitration at the Hague."*[31]

20. The Advisory Group agreed that their recommendations for modifications to be made to the Convention should be included in an optional protocol with an accompanying final Act that would include explanatory material.[32] The reasoning for an optional protocol, instead of an amendment to the Convention, may be that the final clauses of the ECICA do not contemplate the possibility of amendments to its provisions.

27. Stanislaw J. Soltysinski, *Arbitation Law in States after Fundamental Changes*, in Albert Jan van den Berg (ed.), Planning Efficient Arbitration Proceedings: The Law Applicable in International Arbitration, ICCA Congress Series, Volume 7 (Kluwer Law International 1996) pp. 530–541.
28. Ottoarndt Glossner, *The Institutional Appointment of Arbitrators: The Special Committee of the European Convention on Commercial Arbitration of Geneva, 21 April 1961*, 12(1) ARBITRATION INTERNATIONAL, pp. 95–100, p. 96 (1 March 1996).
29. *Ibid.*, p. 97.
30. United Nations Economic Commission for Europe, Committee for Trade, Industry and Enterprise Development, fifth session, 13–15 June 2001, Item 17 of the provisional agenda, Revision of the 1961 European Convention on International Commercial Arbitration, TRADE/2001/16 (30 March 2001).
31. *Ibid.*
32. *Ibid.*

ANNEX II

Status of the Convention

Entry into force:	7 January 1964, in accordance with Article X(8), with the exception of paragraphs 3 to 7 of Article IV which entered into force on 18 October 1965, in accordance with paragraph 4 of the Annex to the Convention.

Registration:	7 January 1964, No. 7041

Text:	United Nations, *Treaty Series*, vol. 484, p. 349.

Note:	The Convention was prepared and opened for signature on 21 April 1961 by the Special Meeting of Plenipotentiaries for the purpose of negotiating and signing a European Convention on International Commercial Arbitration, which was convened in accordance with Resolution 7 (XV)[1] of the Economic Commission for Europe, adopted on 5 May 1960. The Special Meeting was held at the European Office of the United Nations in Geneva from 10 to 21 April 1961. For the text of the Final Act of the Special Meeting, see United Nations, *Treaty Series*, vol. 484, p. 349. The Convention has presently 31 Contracting States and 16 signatories:

Participant	Signature	Ratification, Accession (a), Succession (d)
Albania		27 Jun 2001 (a)
Austria	21 Apr 1961	6 Mar 1964
Azerbaijan		17 Jan 2005 (a)
Belarus	21 Apr 1961	14 Oct 1963
Belgium	21 Apr 1961	9 Oct 1975
Bosnia and Herzegovina [2]		1 Sep 1993 (d)
Bulgaria	21 Apr 1961	13 May 1964
Burkina Faso		26 Jan 1965 (a)
Croatia [2]		26 Jul 1993 (d)
Cuba		1 Sep 1965 (a)
Czech Republic [3]		30 Sep 1993 (d)
Denmark [4]	21 Apr 1961	22 Dec 1972
Finland	21 Dec 1961	
France	21 Apr 1961	16 Dec 1966
Germany [5, 6]	21 Apr 1961	27 Oct 1964
Hungary	21 Apr 1961	9 Oct 1963
Italy	21 Apr 1961	3 Aug 1970
Kazakhstan		20 Nov 1995 (a)
Latvia[7]		20 Mar 2003 (a)
Luxembourg		26 Mar 1982 (a)
Montenegro [8]		23 Oct 2006 (d)
Poland	21 Apr 1961	15 Sep 1964
Republic of Moldova		5 Mar 1998 (a)
Romania	21 Apr 1961	16 Aug 1963
Russian Federation	21 Apr 1961	27 Jun 1962
Serbia [2]		12 Mar 2001 (d)
Slovakia [3]		28 May 1993 (d)
Slovenia [2]		6 Jul 1992 (d)
Spain	14 Dec 1961	12 May 1975
The former Yugoslav Republic of Macedonia [2]		10 Mar 1994 (d)
Turkey	21 Apr 1961	24 Jan 1992
Ukraine	21 Apr 1961	18 Mar 1963

End Notes:

1 *Official Records of the Economic and Social Council*, Fifteenth Session, Supplement No. 3 (E/3349), p. 55

2 The former Yugoslavia had signed and ratified the Convention on 21 April 1961 and 25 September 1963, respectively. See also note 1 under "Bosnia and Herzegovina," Croatia, "former Yugoslavia,"

"Slovenia," "The Former Yugoslav Republic of Macedonia" and "Yugoslavia" in the "Historical Information" section in the front matter of this volume.

3 Czechoslovakia had signed and ratified the Convention on 21 April 1961 and 13 November 1963, respectively. See also note 1 under "Czech Republic" and note 1 under "Slovakia" in the "Historical Information" section in the front matter of this volume.

4 The instrument of ratification contained a declaration to the effect that the Convention, for the time being, would not extend to the Faeroe Islands and Greenland. In a communication received on 12 November 1975, the Government of Denmark declared that it had withdrawn the abovementioned reservation, the decision to take effect on 1 January 1976.

5 The German Democratic Republic had acceded to the Convention on 20 February 1975. See also note 2 under "Germany" in the "Historical Information" section in the front matter of this volume.

6 See note 1 under "Germany" in the "Historical Information" section in the front matter of this volume.

7 On 23 December 2013, the Government of Latvia notified the Secretary-General of the withdrawal of the following declaration under Article II (2) made upon accession:

> In accordance with article II, paragraph 2, of the European Convention on International Commercial Arbitration, the Republic of Latvia declares that Article II, paragraph 1, does not apply for state authorities and local government authorities.

8 See note 1 under "Montenegro" in the "Historical Information" section in the front matter of this volume.–

Table of Cases

I. AUSTRIA

Date	Name	Court	Parties	Related Articles	Brief Overview of the Case
20.10.1993	Austria No. 2 (3 Ob 117/93)	Supreme Court	• Claimant, X (Austria) • Respondent, Y (Slovenia)	IX	In *X (Austria) v Y (Slovenia)*, the Slovenian Supreme Court partially set aside an award under the ECICA on the basis that it was contrary to the public policy (*ordre public*) of the country of origin (*Socialist Federal Republic of Yugoslavia*). Conversely, the Austrian Supreme Court decided to enforce the award, since the violation of public policy is not a ground for setting aside an award under the ECICA. The Austrian Supreme Court indicated that the Austro-Yugoslav Agreement for the mutual recognition and enforcement of awards in commercial matters applied in conjunction with the ECICA. Therefore, enforcement should be denied only if under both agreements there is a reason to refuse enforcement. Article IX of the ECICA governs the enforcement of an award set aside in a Contracting State. The setting aside of an award shall only constitute a ground for the refusal of recognition or enforcement if such setting aside took place on one of the grounds enumerated in Article IX(1)(a)-(c). These grounds do not include violations of public policy; therefore, the Austrian Supreme Court granted the enforcement.

Date	Name	Court	Parties	Related Articles	Brief Overview of the Case
20.10.1993	Austria No. 3	Supreme Court	• Appellant, Kajo-Erzeugnisse Essenzen GmbH • Appellee, DO Zdravilisce Radenska	IX	In *Kajo-Erzeugnisse Essenzen GmbH v DO Zdravilisce Radenska*, the arbitration arose from a dispute relating to the breach of a contract of manufacturing and distribution of a caloric drink. The Slovenian Supreme Court set aside the award under the ECICA on the basis that it was contrary to the public policy of the country of origin. Conversely, the Austrian Supreme Court decided to enforce the award. The Austrian Supreme Court found that the setting aside of an award for violating the public policy of its country of origin is not a ground for refusing enforcement under the ECICA. By its second decision, dated 23 February 1998, the Austrian Supreme Court reinforced its former decision.
26.01.2005	Austria No. 4 (3Ob221/04b)	Supreme Court	• Petitioner, Buyer (Austria) • Respondent, Seller (Serbia and Montenegro)	I, V and IX	In *X (Austria) v Y* (*Serbia & Montenegro*), the arbitration arose from a dispute concerning the breach of a contract for mushrooms supply. The seller sought enforcement of the award in Austria. The buyer objected that the award violated the public policy on three grounds: (i) the award was based on a false statement, (ii) the invalidity of the arbitration agreement due to a false signature and (iii) the rate of interest used in the award.

Date	Name	Court	Parties	Related Articles	Brief Overview of the Case
					The Austrian Supreme Court held that the ECICA was applicable to the present case as both parties had their seats of business in different Contracting States. Furthermore, it indicated that the ECICA coexisted with and complemented the NYC and other bilateral applicable treaties. The Austrian Supreme Court reasoned that under the combined effects of the ECICA and the NYC, the annulment of the award on public policy grounds in the country of origin is not a ground for refusing enforcement: Art. IX European Convention aims at preventing that an arbitral award that has been set-aside in a Contracting State for violation of mandatory provisions be necessarily denied enforcement in another Contracting State, even if it does not violate that State's public policy or mandatory provisions (...). Making an international arbitral award dependent on state approval in the country of origin would deprive international arbitration of its independence. As for the violations of public policy in the State of enforcement, the Austrian Supreme Court analyzed them in a narrow basis, *i.e.*, only considering fundamental principles of the constitutional system. Regarding the invalidity of the arbitration agreement, the court posited that the buyer waived its right to raise the objection of lack of jurisdiction because under Article V of the ECICA, this objection has to be raised no later than with the submission of its statement of claim or defence relating to the substance of the dispute.

Date	Name	Court	Parties	Related Articles	Brief Overview of the Case
20.10.2004	3 Ob 73/04p	Supreme Court	• Appellant, X • Appellee, Y	--	The Appellant challenged the enforceability of an award rendered by an arbitral tribunal under the auspices of the Chamber of Commerce in Slovakia before the Austrian Supreme Court. The Appellant argued that it had already commenced court proceedings against the award before judicial authorities in Slovakia; hence the award could not be declared enforceable in another country at the same time. The Austrian Supreme Court however confirmed the rulings of the previous Austrian instances and declared the award to be enforceable. According to the Austrian Supreme Court, the grounds for refusing recognition and enforcement were not met, *inter alia* because both the ECICA and the NYC, to which Austria and Slovakia are parties, did not provide that the commencement of annulment proceedings is a ground for refusing recognition and enforcement.

Date	Name	Court	Parties	Related Articles	Brief Overview of the Case
22.07.2009	3 Ob 144/09m	Supreme Court	• Claimant (Denmark) • Respondents (Austria)	V	The dispute between the Danish Claimant and three Austrian Respondents arose out of a franchise agreement between the parties. The first and second instances, as well as the Austrian Supreme Court confirmed the enforceability of the award rendered in Copenhagen. The Austrian Supreme Court held that two multilateral conventions between Austria and Denmark were applicable: the NYC and the ECICA, which do coexist and thus do not derogate each other. According to the Danish arbitral tribunal, Respondents had to object to the lack of jurisdiction no later than with the submission of the first written pleading; however, they did so belatedly at the arbitral hearing. The Austrian Supreme Court confirmed the arbitral tribunal's rationale and stressed that a failure to object leads to cure an initially defective arbitration agreement. However, this objection still could have been examined during the enforcement proceedings, pursuant to Article V (2) ECICA, in conjunction with Austrian law.

II. BELGIUM

Date	Name	Court	Parties	Related Articles	Brief Overview of the Case
6.12.1988	Belgium No. 7 / E3	Court of Cassation of Belgium	• Claimant, Société Nationale pour la Recherche, le Transport et la Commercialisation des Hydrocarbures (Sonatrach) • Defendant, Ford, Bacon and Davis Inc.	I	In *Sonatrach v Ford*, the Court of Cassation of Belgium held that the ECICA was not applicable because Algeria was not a Contracting State. The Court of Cassation also pointed out that in the absence of a provision allowing for the retroactive application of the NYC, retroactive application is not possible.
15.11.1992	Belgium No. 4	Court of Appeal of Brussels	• Appellant, B.V. Haegens Bouw • Appellee, N.V. Theuma Deurenindustrie	VI	In *B.V. Haegens Bouw v N.V. Theuma Deurenindustrie*, the Commercial Court retained jurisdiction holding that under Belgian law the arbitration agreement was invalid. However, the Court of Appeal reversed this decision clarifying that the arbitration agreement was not governed by Belgian law and therefore it could not be held invalid: *"the arbitral clause, in the first place, is governed by the law chosen by the parties, and subsidiarily, by the law of the place of arbitration."*

Date	Name	Court	Parties	Related Articles	Brief Overview of the Case
01.10.1993	Belgium No. 5 (337/91)	Commercial Court of Kortrijk	• Claimant, Société Lorraine de Matériel Radio Électrique (SLORA) • Respondents, NV Barco Electronic *et al*	IV	In *SLORA v NV Barco Electronic et al*, the case involved two related distribution contracts, one of which contained an arbitration agreement. The parties, following Article 1 of the Agreement relating to Application of the European Convention on International Commercial Arbitration (Paris Agreement), requested the Commercial Court (as the competent authority) to determine the competent tribunal, its composition and the procedural rules to be followed. The Commercial Court found that in the arbitration agreement the parties agreed to submit the dispute to a specific permanent arbitral institution. Hence, the Court, following Article IV of the ECICA, concluded that the arbitral procedure required to be conducted according to the rules of the chosen arbitral institution.

III. CZECH REPUBLIC

Date	Name	Court	Parties	Related Articles	Brief Overview of the Case
27.05.1980	CAC Case No. Rsp. 192/78	Arbitration Court attached to the Economic Chamber of the Czech Republic	• Claimant, buyer (Austrian) • Respondent, foreign trade Company (Czechoslovak)	I and VII (1)	In *X (Austria) v Y (Czechoslovakia)*, the case concerned a long-term agreement for the delivery of wooden weekend houses, which contained an arbitration clause. The arbitration proceedings were initiated before the Arbitration Court of the Czech Republic. When indicating the applicable law, the arbitration court considered: first, that the ECICA was applicable "*as both parties had their seat in different Contracting States.*"; second, it held that Czechoslovak law applied to the dispute by mutual consent of the parties.

IV. FRANCE

Date	Name	Court	Parties	Related Articles	Brief Overview of the Case
09.10.1984	France No. 7	Court of Appeal of Paris	• Claimant, Pabalk Ticaret Ltd. Sirketi (Turkish) • Respondent, Norsolor SA (French)	I	In *Pabalk (Turkey) v. Norsolor (France)*, the dispute arose from an agency agreement which contained an arbitration clause that did not authorize the arbitrators to act as *amiable compositeurs*. The Court of Appeal of Vienna partially set aside the arbitral award because the arbitral tribunal had exceeded the limits of its authority by basing its decisions on equity. The Austrian Supreme Court reversed this decision holding that the arbitrators had not exceeded their mandate. Following this decision, enforcement was sought in France. The Court of First Instance of Paris and the Paris Court of Appeal granted the enforcement. However, the French Supreme Court reversed these two judgments. The French Supreme Court also rejected the applicability of the ECICA because when the arbitration agreement was concluded one of the parties was seated in Turkey which at that time had not ratified the Convention.

Date	Name	Court	Parties	Related Articles	Brief Overview of the Case
13.11.1984	France No. 8 / E2	Court of Appeal of Rouen	• Appellant, Société Européenne d'Etudes et d'Entreprises (SEEE) • Appellees, the former Republic of Yugoslavia; International Bank for Reconstruction and Development (the World Bank) and, the French State.	I	In *SEEE v Yugoslavia et al*, the French Supreme Court held that enforcement of a foreign arbitral award in France could be refused only if it violates international public policy, as conceived in France, which does not include an error of the arbitrators even if such error is manifest. The French Supreme Court remitted the case to the Court of Appeal of Rouen, which, by a decision dated 13 November 1984, granted enforcement of the pertaining award. Regarding the application of the ECICA, the Court of Appeal of Rouen held that: (…) it is not sufficient that it concerns an arbitration agreement, a procedure and an award based on this Convention, but it is also necessary that the subject of the dispute falls within the scope of the Convention. Furthermore, it posited that: (…) the Convention of 21 April 1961 does not deal with the requirements which the award must meet to qualify for recognition and **enforcement** in a foreign country (…) Art. IX of the Convention (…) limits the application of Art. V(1)(e) of the New York Convention solely to the cases of setting aside which it enumerates.

Date	Name	Court	Parties	Related Articles	Brief Overview of the Case
25.02.1986	France No. 11 / E3	Court of Cassation of France, Commercial Law Chamber	• Appellant, Sté Confex • Appellee, Ets. Dahan	I(2)(a)	In *Sté Confex v. Ets. Dahan*, the parties concluded an agreement for the sale of certain garments. Pursuant to this agreement it was stipulated that the Romanian seller's General Conditions containing an arbitration clause were to be applicable. Following the conclusion of this agreement, the parties agreed through two telex exchanges upon the sale of another quantity of garments, without reference to the General Conditions. The French buyer sent another letter inquiring about the possibility of modifying the size of the garments, The Romanian seller replied that the transaction was governed by the same rules than the rules governing the first agreement *i.e.*, the General Conditions. The French buyer allegedly did not react to this part of the letter. The Court of Appeal of Aix-en-Provence held that there was not a valid arbitration clause that covered the new agreement of the Parties (reached by the exchange of telexes). Consequently, Confex contended before the French Supreme Court that, under the ECICA, the arbitration agreement is not subject to any rule as to form and that it suffices that the will of the parties to submit to arbitration disputes arising out of the contract be established by any means of evidence. The Supreme Court rejected Confex's arguments. The Supreme Court held that Confex invoked the applicability of the NYC according to which recourse to arbitration

Date	Name	Court	Parties	Related Articles	Brief Overview of the Case
					requires an agreement in writing and that it did not result from its written pleadings that Confex asserted the application of the ECICA. Therefore, it concluded that, in the case at bar, the second agreement was concluded by two telexes which did not contain an arbitration clause.
04.07.1991	France No. 4	Court of Appeal of Lyon	• Appellant, SA France-Embryon • Appellee, Renato Argonauta	I(1)(a) and IV	In *Embryon v Argonauta*, the parties concluded an agreement for the establishment of a new legal entity, which contained an arbitration clause. When the dispute arose Argonauta appointed its arbitrator. Embryon failed to do the same and Argonauta requested the President of the Court of First Instance of Milan to substitute for Embryon, as provided for in Article 810 of the Italian Code of Civil Procedure. The President of the Court of First Instance appointed an arbitrator for Embryon. Failing agreement between the first two arbitrators, the President of the Turin Chamber of Commerce appointed the third arbitrator. The President of the Court of First Instance of Montbrison granted enforcement of the pertaining award. However, the Court of Appeal reversed the enforcement order, holding that the award could not be enforced in France because the arbitral tribunal had not been composed according to Article IV of the ECICA. The Court of Appeal held that the scope of the ECICA covered the dispute at hand, by providing a wide definition of international trade:

Date	Name	Court	Parties	Related Articles	Brief Overview of the Case
					The contract concluded between the parties, although aiming at activities of an agricultural nature, concerns international trade in the sense of the above-mentioned article. (…) the term 'international trade' describes all cross-border economic exchanges and does not, in any case, refer to the national definition, which is strict and technical, of commercial act or trader (*commerçant*). Any international arbitration between enterprises regarding an economic dispute should be considered as "commercial." Regarding the composition of the arbitral tribunal, the Court posited that: According to Art. IV(2), where the parties intended to submit their disputes to ad hoc arbitration, and, within thirty days of the notification of the request for arbitration to the defendant, one of the parties fails to appoint his arbitrator, the latter shall, unless otherwise provided, be appointed at the request of the other party by the President of the competent Chamber of Commerce of the country of the defaulting party's habitual place of residence or seat at the time of the introduction of the request for arbitration.

Date	Name	Court	Parties	Related Articles	Brief Overview of the Case
31.05.2001	France No. E5	Court of Appeal of Paris	• Petitioner, UNI-KOD sarl • Respondent, Ouralkali	I and IX(i)	In *UNI-KOD v Ouralkali*, the parties concluded a joint venture agreement for the establishment of an enterprise which contained an arbitration clause and simultaneously concluded another related agreement. Ouralkali commenced arbitration before the Court of International Commercial Arbitration at the Chamber of Commerce and Industry of the Russian Federation. Following the award, UNI-KOD filed an appeal against the enforcement order, alleging that there was no valid arbitration agreement between the parties and requested the Court of Appeal, based on Article IX of the ECICA, to suspend proceedings pending recourse against the award in Russia. The Court of Appeal confirmed the order for enforcement. First, it dismissed the request to suspend proceedings, holding that Article IX of the ECICA does not concern the suspension of proceedings based on a request for setting aside. It also held that the ECICA was applicable even though it was contained in a joint venture agreement because the will of the parties should be respected: Because of the autonomy of international arbitration clauses, the scope and effects of an arbitration clause are determined according to the common intention of the parties; it is unnecessary to refer to the law of a State.

Date	Name	Court	Parties	Related Articles	Brief Overview of the Case
30.03.2004	France No. E6 (539 F-P)	Court of Cassation of France, First Civil Law Chamber	• Petitioner, UNI-KOD sarl • Respondent, Ouralkali	IX	The facts of this case are related to the ones of the case France No. E5 (abovementioned). The decision rendered by the Court of Appeal of Paris was challenged before the Supreme Court. First, the Supreme Court held that the Court of Appeal did not err in disregarding the application of Russian law to the validity of the arbitration clause, since these clauses are "*severable from the main contract and their existence and validity are determined according to the common intention of the parties, not necessarily according to the law of a State*". The Supreme Court then agreed with the Court of Appeal's findings that the ECICA does not provide for the suspension of the enforcement's decision based on the existence of a request for setting aside. Hence, the Supreme Court maintained that the enforcement court "*has a discretionary power to decide whether to suspend its decision for the sake of the good administration of justice*".

V. GERMANY

Date	Name	Court	Parties	Related Articles	Brief Overview of the Case
17.03.1982	Interim Award	Arbitration Court Attached to the Chamber of Foreign Trade, Berlin	• Claimant, Yugoslav Company, Buyer • Defendant, PDR Korea Company, Seller	--	In *Yugoslav Company v PDR Korea Company,* the parties concluded a contract for the delivery of frozen arctic fish, which included the following arbitration clause: If no mutual consent is reached the arbitration of the People's Republic of China, the People's Republic of Poland and the GDR will be adopted. On the basis of this clause an arbitration was commenced before the Berlin Arbitration Court, when addressing on its jurisdiction the court held: The right of choice of a court of arbitration can be granted to one party only by agreement between both parties. Therefore we insist, that any court cannot treat his affair without agreement between both parties for choice of court. An oral hearing was organized to address the defendant's position on the jurisdiction issue, but the defendant never appeared. When analyzing the applicable law, the Arbitration Court held that "*there is no doubt that no internationally binding agreements exist between Yugoslavia and the People's Democratic Republic of Korea, which compulsorily prescribe dispute settlement by arbitration*". However, it indicated that the provisions of the ECICA could be utilized as it served as an international guideline on commercial arbitration.

Date	Name	Court	Parties	Related Articles	Brief Overview of the Case
02.12.1982	Germany No. E7	Federal Court of Justice of Germany	• Appellant, Wünsche Handelsgesellschaft • Appellee, Coop. S. Maria srl	I, IV(l) and V	In *Wünsche v Coop. S. Maria*, the parties exchanged two order confirmations regarding the sale of tomatoes. Both confirmations contained an arbitration clause. Wünsche commenced arbitration before the Hamburg Friendly Arbitration. An award was rendered in favor of Wünsche. In turn, Coop. S. Maria challenged the award arguing that it had believed the arbitration clause referred the dispute to the arbitral tribunal of the Hamburg Commodity Trade Association. The Court of First Instance rejected S. Maria's request to set aside the award. The Court of Appeal of Hamburg reversed the lower court's decision. The Supreme Court affirmed the decision of the Court of Appeal. First, the Supreme Court held that the dispute was covered by the scope of the ECICA. Second, the Supreme Court posited that the arbitration clause was valid. The parties, regardless the dispute concerning which arbitral tribunal is competent, have chosen a permanent arbitral tribunal which amounts to a valid arbitration clause under the ECICA. Third, it held that, in the case at bar, since the ECICA does not contain a specific provision on the validity of the arbitration agreement, this issue was subject to German Law. Fourth, when analyzing if the objection to the validity of the arbitration clause was raised in a timely manner, the Supreme Court noted the following:

Date	Name	Court	Parties	Related Articles	Brief Overview of the Case
					Art. V(l) of the ECICA provides that the arbitral tribunal must clarify any doubts as to the admissibility of an objection to the jurisdiction, or, in the appropriate instances, admit objections, if they are raised with delay, when the arbitral tribunal finds that the delay was justified. According to Art. V(2) of the ECICA, the arbitrator's decision on the admissibility of the objection binds the courts only after a decision has been rendered on the admission of the objection. The reasoning of the Court of Appeal would lead to the result that the arbitral tribunal, by not deciding on the admissibility of the late plea because it found the plea was ill-founded anyway, could prevent any review of the timeliness of the objection. This is not the meaning of Art. V of the ECICA.
24.09.1985	Germany No. E8	Higher Regional Court of Frankfurt am Main	• Petitioner, Polish foreign trade state enterprise • Respondent, FR German manufacturer	I and VI	In *X (Polish) v Y (German)*, the parties concluded a contract for economic and technical cooperation, which provided for ad-hoc arbitration pursuant to the Arbitration Rules of the Economic Commission for Europe. The dispute arose from the non-payment of two promissory notes related to the contract and to whether this non-payment was covered by the arbitration clause. The Higher Regional Court held: Pursuant to Art. VI(2)(a) of the Convention, a decision concerning the existence and validity of an arbitration agreement has primarily to be taken on the basis of the law to which the parties have subjected their arbitration agreement. The decision

Date	Name	Court	Parties	Related Articles	Brief Overview of the Case
					whether or not the arbitration agreement covers certain disputes falls within the scope of provisions concerning the existence and validity of the arbitration clause. The court decided that the promissory notes were covered by the arbitration clause: In principle, the reasons which motivated the parties to agree upon an arbitration clause also require that promissory note claims be shifted from the national courts that may be under consideration to an arbitral tribunal. Certainly, in respect to arbitral clauses in international trade, one of the primary reasons for the acceptance of an arbitral tribunal is the greater confidence in its neutrality and the mistrust of the parties of the national domestic courts of either contracting partner.
15.11.1995	Germany No. E11	Hanseatic Higher Regional Court of Hamburg	• Appellant, German party • Appellee, Austrian GmbH	IV and VI	In *X (German) v Y (Austria)*, the parties concluded a sales contract which contained an arbitration clause for disputes to be solved before the International Chamber of Commerce in Zurich. The Court of Appeal of Hamburg held that the arbitral clause in the contract, although ambiguous, was valid under the ECICA and therefore the dispute had to be referred to arbitration. The Court noted that:

Date	Name	Court	Parties	Related Articles	Brief Overview of the Case
					According to Article VI(2) of the [ECICA], in taking a decision concerning the existence or the validity of an arbitration agreement, the court of a Contracting State shall apply, with reference to the capacity of the parties, the law applicable to them, and with reference to other questions, the law to which the parties have subjected their arbitration agreement or, alternatively, the law of the State in which the arbitral award is to be made. When analyzing if the arbitration clause was ambiguous, the court posited that: The Court does not need to decide whether the arbitral tribunal mentioned by the parties in the arbitration clause as the Arbitral Tribunal at the International Chamber of Commerce Zurich is sufficiently determined, considering that, as claimant maintains, there exist an Arbitral Tribunal of the Chamber of Commerce of Zurich. (…) an arbitral clause is null and void where it refers the dispute to the decision of an arbitral tribunal which does not exist, or where it is not unambiguously determined or determinable to which of more arbitral tribunals the dispute is referred. However, the European Convention, which is applicable to the parties, takes priority here. The Convention provides in its Article IV(5) in conjunction with (3), on the validity of the arbitration agreement, for a procedure to determine the competent arbitral tribunal in lieu of the parties.

Date	Name	Court	Parties	Related Articles	Brief Overview of the Case
16.12.1992	Germany No. 44 / E13	Higher Regional Court of Cologne	• Appellant, Seller (Danish) • Appellee, Buyer (German)	I(2)(a)	In *X (Danish) v Y (German)*, the Danish manufacturer sent to the German buyer a confirmation of order for the sale of a labeller which referred to the manufacturer's General Conditions and to a standard contract which contained an ICC arbitration clause. However, the standard contract was not enclosed to the confirmation. The German buyer never replied in writing to said confirmation order. The Court of First Instance of Cologne refused enforcement of the award, holding that there was no valid arbitration agreement under Article II(2) of the NYC. However, the Court of Appeal of Cologne reversed the lower court's decision, holding that an arbitration agreement may be tacitly concluded under German law, which applies on the basis of the more-favorable-right provision of Article VII(1) of the NYC. When analyzing the validity of the arbitration clause, the Court held the following: Article I(2)(a) of the [ECICA], to which both Germany and Denmark are party (...), provides that arbitration agreements informally concluded can be recognised within its scope of application, where they may be informally concluded according to the law of the Contracting States.

Date	Name	Court	Parties	Related Articles	Brief Overview of the Case
23.04.1998	Germany No. E14	Federal Court of Justice of Germany	• Appellant, Buyer (German) • Appellee, Seller (Yugoslav)	VI(2)	In *X (German) v Y (Yugoslav)*, the buyer and the seller were business partners which usually concluded their contracts through a third party because the seller did not have legal capacity to conclude foreign trade contracts. The seller's representative allegedly informed the buyer that the seller could now enter into foreign trade contracts, whereupon the parties concluded the two contracts directly. A dispute arose out of one of these new contracts and arbitration was commenced. The award was rendered in favor of the buyer and the latter sought enforcement in Germany. The Court of First Instance in Bremen granted enforcement. However, the Court of Appeal in Bremen reversed this decision as it found that the seller lacked the capacity to enter into foreign trade relations. The Supreme Court upheld the decision of the Court of Appeal. The Supreme Court agreed that the seller lacked authority to conclude the contract: According to Art. VI(2) of the [ECICA] concluded between Germany and the former Socialist Federal Republic of Yugoslavia and applicable to its successor state Croatia, and according to general German conflict of laws, the legal capacity of the seller is to be ascertained according to its personal law.

Date	Name	Court	Parties	Related Articles	Brief Overview of the Case
21.05.2007	Germany No. 118/ E20 (III ZB 14/07)	Federal Court of Justice of Germany	• Appellant, Supplier (US) • Appellee, State enterprise (Belarus)	IX(1)(d)	In *X (US) v Y (Belarus)*, the parties concluded a contract for the manufacture and supply of wheels, which contained an arbitration clause. A dispute arose between the parties in respect to the non-payment of a delivery. Consequently, the US supplier commenced arbitration proceedings. An award was rendered in favor of the supplier, but it did not contain the signature of the third arbitrator as he was on holidays. The Supreme Commercial Court of Belarus set aside the award, holding that the arbitral tribunal violated the arbitration rules, since the third arbitrator did not sign the award because he disagreed with the others and that he did not participate in the decision-making process. According to the pertaining arbitration rules, in such cases the president should designate a substitute arbitrator. However, the president failed to do so. The Supreme Court concluded that as the award was rendered by only two of the three arbitrators, in violation of the arbitration rules, recognition should be refused under Article V(1)(d) NYC for an irregularity in the arbitral procedure. The Supreme Court noted that a violation of due process is also a ground under Article IX of the ECICA to refuse recognition and enforcement of the award.

Date	Name	Court	Parties	Related Articles	Brief Overview of the Case
19.01.2009	Germany No. 126 / E21 (34 Sch 04/08)	Higher Regional Court of Munich	• Claimant, Clothing manufacturer (Ukraine) • Defendant, Textiles manufacturer (Germany)	V	In *X (Ukraine) v Y (Germany)*, the parties concluded an agreement for the manufacture of clothes, which contained an arbitration clause. Later on, an additional agreement was concluded which referred to the first contract. A dispute arose between the parties on the basis of the additional contract and the Ukrainian clothing manufacturer commenced arbitration. The German textile manufacturer alleged that the arbitration agreement was invalid because the employee, who signed the original contract, was not authorized to enter into agreements on its behalf, and that his signatures on the contractual additions were forgeries. The award was rendered in favor of the claimant. The Munich Court of Appeal refused to declare the award enforceable, finding that the claimant did not provide a valid arbitration agreement. Similarly, the Court of Appeal held that the claimant did not refute the allegations of the defendant and added that the latter was not precluded from raising the objection against the existence of an arbitration agreement. The Court of Appeal held that defendant neither submitted expressly to the proceedings before the arbitral tribunal nor did it discuss the merits without raising any objection. Therefore, under the ECICA he was not precluded from raising its objection:

Date	Name	Court	Parties	Related Articles	Brief Overview of the Case
					Defendant raised its objection of the lack of jurisdiction of the arbitral tribunal because of the lack of an arbitration agreement in a timely manner under Art. V(1) [ECICA], so that [this objection] is not excluded under Art. V(2) in the context of the German proceedings for a declaration of enforceability.
27.02.2009	Germany No. 127 / E22 (34 Sch 19/08)	Higher Regional Court of Munich	• Claimant, Carrier (nationality not indicated) • Defendant, Customer (Germany)	IX	In *X v Y (Germany)*, a carrier provided transportation services to a customer. When the customer failed to pay for the services, he issued an acknowledgment of debt in favor of the carrier, which contained an arbitration clause. Consequently, the carrier commenced arbitration proceedings that eventually concluded with an award rendered on its favor. The carrier sought enforcement of the award in Germany. The Munich Court of Appeal granted the request. On the relation between the NYC and the ECICA, the Court of Appeal noted that: The [ECICA], which is in force in the Czech Republic since 1 January 1993, is primarily applicable to the recognition of the arbitral award, which was rendered in the Czech Republic. The European Convention modified the [NYC] in part (see Art. IX(2)) and prevails over it. The [ECICA] does not contain formal requirements for the declaration of enforceability of an arbitral award rendered in another Contracting State.

Date	Name	Court	Parties	Related Articles	Brief Overview of the Case
11.05.2009	Germany No. 128 / E23 (34 Sch 23/08)	Higher Regional Court of Munich	• Claimant, Creditor (nationality not indicated) • Defendant, Debtor (Germany)	IX	In *X v Y (Germany)*, the debtor made out a bill of exchange in favor of the creditor; furthermore, the parties concluded an arbitration agreement covering disputes relating to the bill. When the debtor failed to pay the complete sum, the creditor commenced arbitration proceedings. The award was rendered in favor of the creditor. The creditor sought enforcement in Germany. The Munich Court of Appeal granted the request for enforcement. On the relation between the NYC and the ECICA, the Court of Appeal noted that: The [ECICA], which is in force in the Czech Republic since 1 January 1993, is primarily applicable to the recognition of the arbitral award, which was rendered in the Czech Republic. The European Convention modified the [NYC] in part (see Art. IX(2)) and prevails over it. The [ECICA] does not contain formal requirements for the declaration of enforceability of an arbitral award rendered in another Contracting State.
22.06.2009	Germany No. 130 (34 Sch 26/08)	Higher Regional Court of Munich	• Claimant, Exclusive distributor (Spain) • Defendant, Manufacturer (Germany)	IX	In *X (Spain) v Y (Germany)*, the parties concluded an exclusive distributorship contract which contained an arbitration clause. The claimant terminated the agreement for the alleged non-compliance of the defendant and commenced arbitration proceedings. The award was rendered in favor of the claimant, but only two arbitrators signed the award. The defendant sought to set aside the award before the Madrid Court of Appeal. The court declared that the award was valid. Following this

Date	Name	Court	Parties	Related Articles	Brief Overview of the Case
					decision, the claimant sought enforcement before the Munich Court of Appeal, which granted the enforcement. On the relation between the NYC and the ECICA, the Court of Appeal noted that: The [ECICA] that applies in Spanish-German relations, modifies the [NYC] in part (see Art. IX(2)) and prevails over it. However, the more-favorable right principle [of the NYC], according to which one must fall back on a body of rules that is more favorable to recognition, also applies with regard to domestic law. The [ECICA] is silent as to the formal conditions for a declaration of enforceability in another Contracting State. To the extent that Art. IV [NYC] sets requirements for the submission of documents and translations and their characteristics (...).
18.02.2009	Germany No. E25 (11 Sch 07/08)	Higher Regional Court of Dresden	• Claimant, Principal (Czech Republic) • Defendant, Sales agent (Germany)	I and V	In *X (Czech Republic) v Y (Germany)*, the parties concluded an agreement under which the defendant became the sales agent for the claimant's radiators. The agreement also contained an arbitration clause. The claimant commenced arbitration alleging defendant's unjust enrichment. The award was rendered in favor of the claimant. The Dresden Court of Appeal declared the award enforceable. The Court of Appeal held that the arbitration clause was valid because even though it was not contained in a document signed by both parties. The agreement would be valid at any event under German law, because the parties

Date	Name	Court	Parties	Related Articles	Brief Overview of the Case
					are merchants and could therefore agree on arbitration through a contract concluded in a tacit manner. Furthermore, regarding the objection against the validity of the arbitration clause, the court held: (…) it can be left open whether Defendant is estopped from raising the objection that there was no arbitration agreement because it defended itself on the merits before the arbitral tribunal without raising this objection.
23.11.2009	Germany No. 136 (34 Sch 13/09)	Higher Regional Court of Munich	• Claimant, seller (French) • Defendant-buyer (German)	I (2)(a) and V	In *X (France) v Y (Germany)*, the seller sent to the buyer a sales confirmation of apricots through a broker. The buyer informed the seller that the apricots were defective and paid only a part of the price. Consequently, the seller commenced arbitration. The award was issued in favor of the seller, finding that the buyer failed to object the quality of the apricots within the agreed time. The seller sought a declaration of enforceability of the award in Germany. The Munich Court of Appeal refused to declare the award enforceable for lack of a valid arbitration agreement. According to the Court of Appeal, the arbitration clause in the sales confirmation sent to the broker did not meet the requirements neither of the NYC, the ECICA, nor even under the more-favorable-right provision because it was never related with the contract which contained the arbitration clause:

Date	Name	Court	Parties	Related Articles	Brief Overview of the Case
					The court noted that under the more-favorable-right provision of Art. VII(1), the formal validity of an arbitration agreement may be examined according to the less strict requirements of the [ECICA] when both parties are nationals of Member States that do not require that arbitration agreements be in writing (…) However, concluded the court, this aspect was irrelevant because Seller did not prove that the sale confirmation was sent to Buyer in connection with the conclusion of the contract The Federal Supreme Court confirmed the latter finding. The Supreme Court further held that the failure to challenge the award in the country of origin is no ground for denying enforcement under either German law or the ECICA: This Convention [ECICA] provides that the party which intends to raise a plea as to the arbitrator's jurisdiction based on the fact that the arbitration agreement was either non-existent or null and void shall do so during the arbitration proceedings, not later than the delivery of its statement relating to the substance of the dispute. Otherwise the party is prevented from raising this plea during subsequent proceedings before a state court. In the present case, Defendant argued from the beginning in the arbitration that there was no arbitration agreement, so that the objection of lack of jurisdiction was admissible under the European Convention. The court of appeal added that this Convention does not provide for preclusion where the party fails to challenge the award.

Date	Name	Court	Parties	Related Articles	Brief Overview of the Case
25.05.1970	Germany No. 7 / E1	Federal Court of Justice of Germany	• Claimant, seller (Austrian) • Respondent, buyer (German)	I (2)(a)	In *X (Austria) v Y (Germany)*, the seller commenced arbitration when the buyer refused to pay the complete price of the goods received. The arbitration was based on an arbitration clause, which was contained in the sales confirmations sent by the seller to the buyer. The buyer did not object to the terms of the sales confirmations. The award was rendered in favor of the seller. In the enforcement procedure before German courts, the buyer contended that the award could not be enforced because the arbitration agreement was not in writing. The Supreme Court held that the arbitration clause was valid under the ECICA because in Germany an arbitration agreement did not require to be in writing when both parties are merchants: (…) both the Federal Republic of Germany and Austria had acceded both to the [NYC] and to the [ECICA], both of which required that the arbitration agreement should be in writing. However, the [ECICA] adds to this requirement in its Article 1, para. 2, under a) that, "in relations between States whose laws do not require that an arbitration agreement be made in writing", any arbitration agreement concluded in the form authorized by these laws suffices. This provision of the [ECICA], being of younger date than the [NYC], prevails.

Date	Name	Court	Parties	Related Articles	Brief Overview of the Case
08.11.1971	Germany No. 8 / E2	Higher Regional Court of Düsseldorf	• Claimant, seller (Dutch) • Respondent, buyer (German)	--	In *X (Netherlands) v Y (Germany)*, the buyer bought on several occasions french-fries from the seller through an oral agreement followed by a seller's written sales confirmation containing an arbitration clause. The buyer never objected to the sales confirmation. A dispute arose regarding non-payment of the goods and the seller commenced arbitration. The award was rendered in favor of the seller. The Court of Appeal rejected the enforcement of the award because under the NYC a declaration in writing of both sides is required. Furthermore, it held that the ECICA was not applicable because The Netherlands had not ratified the ECICA.
10.06.1976	Germany No. 14	Higher Regional Court of Cologne	• Petitioner, buyer (Danish) • Respondent, seller (German)	IX	In *X (Denmark) v Y (Germany)*, on the basis of a contract concluded by the parties which contained an arbitration clause, the buyer commenced arbitration. The seller was not informed about the names of the arbitrators; only the name of the Chairman of the arbitral tribunal was communicated to him. The award was rendered in favor of the buyer and the latter sought enforcement in Germany. The Court of First Instance and the Court of Appeal denied to grant the enforcement because the fact that the seller was not informed of the names of the complete members of the arbitral tribunal amounted to a violation of due process:

Date	Name	Court	Parties	Related Articles	Brief Overview of the Case
					In international law also, great importance is attached to the disclosure of the names of arbitrators: in the [NYC] (Article V, para. 1 under b) as well as in the [ECICA] (Article IX, para. 1 under b), the lack of notification of the appointment of the arbitrators is mentioned expressly.
09.03.1978	Germany No. 17 / E4	Federal Court of Justice of Germany	• Claimant, seller (Dutch) • Respondent, buyer (German)	--	In *X (Netherlands) v Y (Germany)*, the facts of the case are related to the ones of the case Germany No. 8 / E2 (above mentioned). Following, the decision of the Court of Appeal, the buyer took recourse to the Federal Supreme Court. The Federal Supreme Court analyzed if the award made in Brussels was enforceable. The court made a brief reference to the ECICA although Netherlands was not a party: The Supreme Court considered further that, according to Article 16 of the German-Belgian Treaty, other Conventions in force between these two countries would also come into consideration. This could apply especially to the [NYC] (in force between the F.R. of Germany and Belgium since November 16, 1975) and the [ECICA] (in force between these two countries since January 7, 1976).
22.09.1978	Germany No. 20 / E5	Hanseatic Higher Regional Court of Hamburg	• Claimant, Company (Italian) • Defendant, Firm (German)	I(2)(a)	In *X (Italy) v Y (Germany)*, the parties concluded two contracts for the delivery of prunes which referred to the General Conditions of the Hamburg Commodity Exchange that, in turn, contain an arbitration clause. When the company did not deliver the prunes, the firm started arbitration in Hamburg. The company

Date	Name	Court	Parties	Related Articles	Brief Overview of the Case
					appeared before the arbitral tribunal with the sole purpose of contesting its jurisdiction alleging the broker who concluded the contracts was not authorized. The award was rendered in favor of the firm. The company sought to set aside the award before the Court of First Instance of Hamburg. The court granted the request because there was no valid arbitration agreement. However, the Court of Appeal reversed this decision. On the formal requirements of the arbitration agreement under the ECICA, the Court of Appeal held: Article I, para, 2 under a) of the [ECICA] does not constitute a mandatory requirement as to the form, which violation would render the arbitration agreement invalid in any case. Although the [ECICA] does not provide expressly for a most-favorable-right provision, it does not preclude the application of a more favorable domestic law, since the Convention's purpose is only to facilitate the recognition of arbitration agreements. The court declared that in the case at bar the requirements of Article I(2)(a) were not met because under German law an arbitration agreement between merchants need not be in writing but under Italian law such form is mandatory. However, the court did not set aside the award because it rejected the argument that the contracts were never signed by an authorized broker.

Date	Name	Court	Parties	Related Articles	Brief Overview of the Case
24.04.1979	Germany No. 21 / E6	Regional Court of Hamburg	• Claimant, Company (Dutch) • Respondent, Firm (German)	--	In *X (Netherlands) v Y (Germany)*, the case concerned the enforcement of an award in the Netherlands originated in Belgium. The Regional Court of Hamburg held that the ECICA was not applicable to the case at bar: "*The [ECICA], is also not applicable because it does not concern the enforcement of arbitral awards*".
08.10.1981	Germany No. 25 / E9	Federal Court of Justice of Germany	• Claimants, Compania Italiana di Assicurazioni (COMITAS) S.p.A. *et al* • Respondent, Schwartzmeer und Ostsee Versicherungsaktiengesellscha t (SOVAG)	--	In *COMITAS v SOVAG*, the case concerned the enforcement of a so-called *arbitrato irrituale* [informal or free arbitration]. The Supreme Court held that neither the NYC nor the ECICA applied to the recognition or to the enforcement of a *lodo irrituale*: (...) the [ECICA], and the Bilateral Treaty between F.R. Germany and Italy concerning the Recognition and Enforcement of Judicial Decisions in Civil and Commercial Matters of March 9, 1936, do not offer a possibility of declaring a *lodo irrituale* enforceable either.
12.12.2002	Germany No. 69 / E15 (4Z Sch 16/02)	Highest Regional Court of Bavaria	• Claimant, Exporter (Yugoslavia) • Defendant, Importer (Germany)	I(2)(a)	In *X (Yugoslavia) v Y (Germany)*, the parties had an import-export commercial relation. At the out-set of the negotiations, the claimant allegedly informed the defendant by phone that its General Conditions contained an arbitration clause. Three deliveries of goods were made and documented by contracts drawn up by photocopying contractual details and the

Date	Name	Court	Parties	Related Articles	Brief Overview of the Case
					claimant's signature onto a blank sheet of paper. The contracts were faxed to the defendant, which neither confirmed nor contested them in writing. A dispute arose between the parties and the exporter commenced arbitration. The award was rendered in favor of the exporter and the latter sought enforcement in Germany. The Higher Court of Bavaria denied the enforcement on the basis that the exporter did not prove the existence of a written arbitration agreement under the NYC. The court indicated that the requirements under the ECICA were also not met: The requirement that there is an arbitration agreement signed by both parties or a mutual exchange in writing cannot be set aside by applying the most-favorable-right provision (...) and the [ECICA] (...) Art. I(2)(a) of this Convention allows for oral arbitration agreements only when both legal systems involved provide for this possibility. It is not sufficient that only the law of one party or the [applicable] rules of arbitration have less stringent formal requirements.
23.09.2004	Germany No. 82 / E16 (4Z Sch 005-04)	Highest Regional Court of Bavaria	• Claimant, K Trading Company (Syria) • Defendant, Bayerischen Motoren Werke AG (Germany)	V(2)	In *K Trading Company v BMW*, the parties concluded a service agreement for BMW cars in Syria. A dispute arose between the parties when BMW terminated the agreement. The parties agreed to submit the dispute to arbitration. The award was rendered in favor of K Trading and the latter sought enforcement in Germany. BMW objected the enforcement of the award alleging the

Date	Name	Court	Parties	Related Articles	Brief Overview of the Case
					invalidity of the arbitration clause. The Higher Court of Appeal found that BMW was estopped from objecting that there was no valid arbitration agreement between the parties because BMW had participated in the arbitration without raising any objection.
30.03.2000	Germany No. 85 / E17	Higher Regional Court of Schleswig-Holstein	• Claimant, Not Indicated • Defendant, Not Indicated	V(2)	In *X v Y*, the parties concluded a sales contract as part of an on-going commercial relationship. The contract was drafted based on a standard form supplied by the claimant, which referred to General Conditions containing an arbitration clause. A dispute arose between the parties, which was submitted to arbitration. The award was rendered in favor of the claimant and the latter sought enforcement in Germany. The defendant objected to the jurisdiction of the tribunal alleging the invalidity of the arbitration clause. The Higher Regional Court in Schleswig granted enforcement because it held that the reference to the general conditions that contained an arbitration clause sufficed to meet the formal requirements of Article II(2) of the NYC. Furthermore, it did not find that the plea as to the jurisdiction was estopped pursuant to Article V(2) of the ECICA.

Date	Name	Court	Parties	Related Articles	Brief Overview of the Case
31.01.2007	Germany No. 110 / (E18 11 Sch 18/05)	Higher Regional Court of Dresden	• Claimant, Supplier (US) • Defendant, State enterprise (Belarus)	I(2)(a) and IX	In *X (US) v Y (Belarus)*, the parties concluded an agreement for the supply of wheels and wheel-rims, which contained an arbitration clause. A dispute arose between the parties regarding the payment of a delivery of goods. The award was rendered in favor of the supplier and the latter sought enforcement in Germany. In parallel, the company lodged a request to set-aside the award in Belarus. The Supreme Commercial Court of Belarus set aside the award holding that the arbitration agreement was not valid because the official who signed the contract lacked of authority to do so. In Germany, the Dresden Court of Appeal denied enforcement of the award under Article V(1)(e) of the NYC because the award had been set aside in Belarus. Furthermore, the court applied the ECICA even though United States is not a party thereto, based on the most-favored-nation principle in force between the United States and Belarus. The court reasoned that the ECICA is more favorable to enforcement and thus "*favors the free exchange of goods, which the most-favored-nation principle aims at promoting*". The court of appeal held that the Belarusian decision annulled the award at issue on two grounds listed in the ECICA: (i) the procedure followed by the arbitral tribunal was not in accordance with the agreement of the parties (the arbitral tribunal should have decided in the same composition in which it had conducted) and (ii) the invalidity of the arbitration clause (the US official had no legal capacity).

Date	Name	Court	Parties	Related Articles	Brief Overview of the Case
15.03.2006	Germany No. 117 / E19 (34 Sch 06/05)	Higher Regional Court of Munich	• Claimant, Manufacturer (Ukraine) • Defendant, Supplier, in liquidation (Germany)	IX (1) (d)	In *X (Ukraine) v Y (Germany)*, the parties concluded a contract for the manufacture of clothing, which contained an arbitration clause. A dispute arose between the parties when the supplier allegedly failed to pay certain invoices to the manufacturer and as a result arbitration proceedings were commenced. The original agreement of the parties referred to a tribunal composed by two members. However, since both parties chose the same arbitrator, the arbitral institution decided that the arbitration was to be held by a sole arbitrator. The parties did not object this decision. The award was rendered in favor of the manufacturer and the latter sought enforcement in Germany. The Munich Court of Appeal granted enforcement. The Court of Appeal held that there was no ground under Article IX(1)(d) of the ECICA to denied the enforcement: The arbitral tribunal was indeed comprised of only one arbitrator rather than two or more arbitrators, against the original agreement of the parties. In principle, a defect in the constitution of the arbitral tribunal leads to refusing recognition and enforcement. However, it is now undisputed between the parties that the representative of the defendant did not object to the composition of the tribunal.

Date	Name	Court	Parties	Related Articles	Brief Overview of the Case
21.05.2007	Germany No. 118 / E20 (III ZB 14/07)	Federal Court of Justice of Germany	• Appellant, Supplier (US) • Appellee, State enterprise (Belarus)	IX (1) (d)	In *X (US) v Y (Belarus)*, the facts of the case relate to the ones of the case Germany No. 110 (above mentioned). An appeal was lodged before the Federal Supreme Court. The Supreme Court concluded that as the award was rendered by only two of the three arbitrators, in violation of the arbitration rules agreed by the parties, recognition should be refused under Article V(1)(d) NYC and Article IX(1)(d) of the ECICA for an irregularity in the arbitral procedure.
10.05.1992	France No. E4	Higher Regional Court of Cologne	• Appellant, seller (French) • Appellee, buyer (German)	I and VI(2)	In *X (France) v Y (Germany)*, the parties concluded a distribution contract for the sale of software products, which contained an arbitration clause. When a dispute arose concerning the payment, the French party initiated court proceedings in Germany. However, the court denied jurisdiction in favor of arbitration. This latter decision was later confirmed by the Court of Appeal who held that the distribution contract felt under the scope of the ECICA: The agreement has been concluded by legal persons having their seat in different Contracting States and provides for a means for settling possible disputes arising from international trade. Regarding the types of arbitration clauses covered by the ECICA's scope, the court held:

Date	Name	Court	Parties	Related Articles	Brief Overview of the Case
					In the present case, the requirement that the agreement be in writing is met, since appellee submitted an arbitral clause undisputedly signed by both parties. The moment when appellee signed the document is, contrary to appellant's allegation, irrelevant. In fact, a subsequent agreement in writing [to the clause] suffices. According to the court, the applicable law for determining the validity was French law: Provisions of national law do not affect the arbitral clause, which we have found to be valid according to the provisions of the [ECICA]. According to Art. VI(2) of the [ECICA], French law applies to the clause, since the arbitral award is to be made in France and, further, the parties agreed that French law applied to the contract.
16.12.2010	III ZB 100/09	Federal Court of Justice	• Claimant X, Seller • Respondent Y, Buyer	V	The dispute arose out of a purchase agreement for fruits between the Parties. After the International Arbitration Chamber for Fruits and Vegetables in Paris had rendered an award in favor of the claimant, the claimant approached the German courts in order to enforce the award. Both the Higher Regional Court of Munich and the German Federal Court of Justice rejected the enforcement of the award. The German Federal Court of Justice stressed that the respondent's objection to the validity of the arbitration

Date	Name	Court	Parties	Related Articles	Brief Overview of the Case
					agreement was legitimate, since the respondent had also raised such objection before the arbitral tribunal. In this regard, the German Federal Court of Justice referred to both the NYC and the ECICA and held that there was no need for the respondent to additionally challenge the award before the competent authorities in France. It was sufficient to raise the jurisdictional objection before the arbitral tribunal.
20.03.1980	III ZR 151/79	Federal Court of Justice	• Claimant, X (Germany) • Respondent, Y (France)	---	In *X (Germany) v Y (France)*, the dispute arose out of a factoring agreement between the respondent and another company to whose financial claims the claimant had subrogated. The claimant subsequently initiated proceedings before German courts in Frankfurt against the respondent who challenged the jurisdiction of the court based on an arbitration clause. The German Federal Court of Justice, just like the previous instances, declared the arbitration clause to be effective, since it complied with the requirements set forth in the ECICA: (*i*) the parties are seated in different countries, and (*ii*) the arbitration clause rules future disputes resulting from international commercial transactions. The Court further concluded that the ECICA was applicable, and not the corresponding domestic provisions, since both Germany and France are parties to the ECICA.

Date	Name	Court	Parties	Related Articles	Brief Overview of the Case
23.04.2013	III ZB 59/12	Federal Court of Justice	• Petitioner • Respondent	IX	The subject of the dispute is the enforcement of an award which was rendered by an arbitral tribunal in Ukraine and subsequently annulled by the Ukrainian courts. Despite the annulment of the award in the country of origin, the claimant tried to enforce the award before the German courts. Both the Higher Regional Court of Munich and the German Federal Court of Justice refused the enforcement. In its ruling, the German Federal Court of Justice confirmed that the NYC as well as the ECICA were applicable to Germany and to Ukraine. It held that Article V(1)(e) of the NYC and Article IX of the ECICA provide for the same legal grounds for refusal of enforcement; however, Article IX of the ECICA narrows those grounds to the lack of jurisdiction of the arbitral tribunal, thus excluding the ground of violation of the country of origin's public policy. The German Federal Court of Justice further stated that the court of the country of enforcement has to examine whether the annulment is based on one of the four grounds stipulated by the ECICA, and not whether the court of the country of origin had correctly applied the ECICA, irrespective of the mutual recognition of foreign judgements.

VI. HAMBURG

Date	Name	Court	Parties	Related Articles	Brief Overview of the Case
07.12.1995	Award	Waren-Verein der Hamburger Börse	• Claimant, seller (Hungarian) • Respondent, buyer (German)	I (2)(a)	In *X (Hungary) v Y (Germany)*, the parties concluded a contract for the sale of sunflower seeds, which referred to the Standard Conditions of the German Grain Trade. The Hungarian seller did not sign the contract. When the seller failed to supply the sunflower seeds, the German buyer commenced arbitration. The arbitral tribunal found that they did not have jurisdiction over the dispute for lack of a valid arbitration clause because the seller did not sign the agreement: According to (...) Art. I(2)(a) [of the ECICA], an arbitration agreement is an arbitration clause in a contract or an arbitration agreement, in so far as the contract or the arbitration agreement is signed by the parties or contained in an exchange of letters, telegrams or telexes. According to the jurisprudence of the Supreme Court.
29.12.1998	Award	Hamburger Freundscha-flichen Arbitrage	• Claimant, buyer (not indicated) • Defendant, seller, (Czech)	I	In *X v Y (Czech Republic)*, the parties concluded a contract for the sale of cheese which contained an arbitration agreement. When the dispute arose, the Czech seller did not appear in the arbitration. The arbitrators derived their jurisdiction from the arbitration agreement, the ECICA, among other instruments.

Date	Name	Court	Parties	Related Articles	Brief Overview of the Case
18.07.1986	Award (WVHB Case No. 1/1986)	Waren-Verein der Hamburger Börse	• Claimant, buyer (German) • Defendant, seller (Greek)	I	In *X (Germany) v Y (Greece)*, the parties concluded an agreement based on a standard contract provided by the buyer. By a telex, the Greek seller confirmed that the contract had been concluded in accordance with the "terms" of the standard form which contained an arbitration clause. The arbitrators found that they have jurisdiction over the dispute, as the arbitration clause was valid under the NYC. Regarding the material scope of the ECICA, the arbitrators noted: Unlike the [ECICA], the New York Convention regulates in a direct manner only recognition and enforcement of arbitral awards rendered abroad.

VII. ITALY

Date	Name	Court	Parties	Related Articles	Brief Overview of the Case
15.10.1992	Italy No. E16 (11261)	Supreme Court of Cassation of Italy	• Petitioner, Agrò di Reolfi Piera & C sn • Respondent, Ro Koproduct oour Produktiva	I (2)(a)	In *Agrò di Reolfi v Ro Koproduct*, the parties concluded two contracts for the purchase of potatoes which contained an arbitration clause. When the dispute arose, Agrò lodged an action before the Court of First Instance of Turin. Ro Koproduct objected the jurisdiction of the court because of the arbitration clause contained in the contracts. The Court of First Instance found that it had jurisdiction only over the dispute arising under the first contract. Both the Court of Appeal and the Supreme Court confirmed the Court of First Instance's decision. Regarding the formal requirements of the arbitration clause under the ECICA, the Supreme Court held: The so-called Geneva Convention provides in its Article I(2)(a) that the arbitral clause may be stipulated also by telegram or "communication by teleprinter" (...) Thus, we hold that the decision [of the Court of Appeal] on this issue is correct and that the arbitral clause in favor of foreign arbitrators, contained in a contract concluded by telex between an Italian and a foreign party after the entry into force of the [ECICA] is valid and operative.

Date	Name	Court	Parties	Related Articles	Brief Overview of the Case
13.10.2000	Italy No. E17	Supreme Court of Cassation of Italy	• Petitioner, Il Nuovo Castoro • Respondent, Ministry of Foreign Affairs	--	In *INC v Italian MFA*, the parties concluded a contract regarding the excavation of water wells in the context of a development aid project. When the dispute arose, arbitration proceedings were commenced, leading to an award in favor of INC. The Italian MFA attempted to set aside the award before the Court of Appeal in Rome. However, INC argued that the award was international and hence it could not be set aside in Italy. The Court of Appeal held that under Italian law an award was deemed international if a predominant part of the contractual obligations are performed abroad. In this case, the excavation of the wells was not considered a predominant part of the whole project. The Supreme Court reversed this decision based on the definition of "international" provided for in the ECICA as a source of inspiration: With the aim of promoting international trade, the European Convention binds its Member States to recognize international commercial arbitrations concerning the import and export of goods, where part of the contractual obligations is performed in different countries, independent of where the goods are delivered or the contractual price is paid (…).

Date	Name	Court	Parties	Related Articles	Brief Overview of the Case
04.12.2007	Italy No. E19	Ordinary Court of Turin	• Plaintiff, G & C, S.p.A. (Italy) • Defendant, Gersan Elektrik Tic. ve San. A.Ş. (Turkey)	I and IV	In *G & C (Italy) v Gersan Elektrik (Turkey)*, the parties concluded a license agreement which contained an arbitration clause for disputes to be solved by a panel of three arbitrators "*appointed according to the Rules of the International Arbitration of Arbitration*". A dispute arose between the parties and G & C lodged an action before the Court of First Instance in Turin. Gersan, in turn, objected jurisdiction due to the existence of a valid arbitration clause. Consequently, the Court of First Instance agreed with the Gersan's objection and declined jurisdiction. The Court of First Instance held that the ECICA was applicable to the case because Italy and Turkey were Contracting States. The court also maintained that the ECICA's provisions allow remedying any failure by the parties to determine the procedural rules applicable to the arbitration by laying down rules to be followed in the absence of a choice by the parties. In particular, the Convention provides for rules concerning the appointment of the arbitrators and the organization of the arbitration. Furthermore, the court noted that the reference to the "Rules of the International Arbitration of Arbitration" in the arbitration clause should be understood to be a reference to the ICC Rules.

Date	Name	Court	Parties	Related Articles	Brief Overview of the Case
08.08.190	Italy No. 114 / E15	Supreme Court of Cassation of Italy	• Petitioner, Vento & C snc • Respondent, E. D. & F. Man (Coffee) Limited	IX	In *Vento v E.D. & F.*, the parties concluded two contracts for the sale of coffee which contained an arbitration clause. When the dispute arose between the parties, arbitration was commenced before the Arbitration Committee of the Dutch Coffee Trade Association. The award was rendered in favor of E.D. & F. and the latter sought enforcement in Italy. The Italian Supreme Court confirmed the decision of the Court of Appeal of Rome granting the enforcement of the award. The Supreme Court noted that the NYC and the ECICA regulate the enforcement of international awards and therefore domestic courts are not allowed to review the merits of the arbitration: (…) national exequatur is regulated solely by these Conventions. Both Conventions provide for a review of the merits in certain, specifically indicated cases, but exclude the review of the totality of the issues decided in the award for which recognition or enforcement is sought in a Contracting State. Hence, exceptions which can be raised during the arbitral proceedings cannot be raised during the exequatur proceedings. Also, the Court of Appeal correctly held that the issues concerning the merits and the procedure of the arbitration had to be decided by the arbitrators.

Date	Name	Court	Parties	Related Articles	Brief Overview of the Case
21.05.1976	Italy No. 16 / E2	Court of Appeal of Venice	• Claimant, S.A. Pando Compania Naviera • Defendant, S.a.S. Filmo	I	In *Pando v Filmo*, the parties concluded a charter-party concerning the transportation of fertilizers which contained an arbitration clause for disputes to be solved by three arbitrators. A dispute regarding Filmo's alleged non-payment of its contractual obligations arose between the parties and Pando commenced arbitration. Since Filmo failed to appoint an arbitrator, the arbitration was held by a sole arbitrator appointed by Pando. The award was rendered in favor of Pando and the latter sought enforcement in Italy. Filmo objected to the enforcement of the award on the basis that the appointment of the arbitral tribunal was made in breach of the will of the parties and Article IV of the ECICA. The court rejected Pando's objection, it held that the ECICA was not applicable in the present case since one of the parties was seated in Panama.
22.10.1976	Italy No. 18 / E3	Court of Appeal of Florence	• Claimant, S.A. Tradax Export • Defendant, S.p.a. Carapelli	IX	In *Tradrax v Carapelli*, Tradax sold to Campelli certain amount of soya beans. When Carapelli refused to take delivery of the soya, Tradax initiated arbitration based on the arbitral clause contained in the contract before the Grain and Feed Trade Association. The award was rendered in favor of Tradax and the latter sought enforcement in Italy. Filmo objected to the enforcement *inter alia* on the following basis: (i) the NYC was not applicable since Panama was not a party thereto; (ii) the ECICA superseded

Date	Name	Court	Parties	Related Articles	Brief Overview of the Case
					the NYC; (iii) the award was not covered by the NYC as it arose from an *arbitrato rituale* and (iv) the award was contrary to public order as it did not contain reasons. Regarding the first point, the court indicated that the NYC does not require both parties to be nationals of Contracting States. Second, regarding the relation between the NYC and the ECICA, the court held: The [ECICA] does not supersede the [NYC] as the former integrates partially the latter without abrogating it. The [ECICA] limits itself to indicating, which are the grounds for setting aside (Article IX of the [ECICA]), and by doing so it elaborates the general provision of Article V, para. 1 under e of the [ECICA]. On the third point, the court held that the majority of the doctrine considers awards resulting from *arbitrato rituale* to be covered by the NYC. Finally, as to the fourth point, the court posited that neither the NYC nor the ECICA require that the award necessarily contain reasons. The court concluded that the lack of reasoning was not contrary to the public order. The court referred to the ECICA even though one party was seated in Panama, which is not a Contracting State to the ECICA.

Date	Name	Court	Parties	Related Articles	Brief Overview of the Case
18.05.1978	Italy No. 35 / E4 (2392)	Supreme Court of Cassation of Italy, Plenary Session	• Claimant, Società Atlas General Timbers S.p.a. • Respondent, Agenzia Concordia Line S.p.a.	I (2)(a)	In *Atlas v Concordia*, Atlas bought certain amount of wood to a company, Bombay Trading, the bill of lading, issued by the agent of the carrier (New India Marittima Agencies Private Ltd.) and endorsed by Bombay Trading, contained an arbitration clause. The shipping agent was Concordia. At the arrival to the pertaining port, the wood appeared to have been damaged. Atlas lodged an action against Concordia before the Court of First Instance of Genoa. Concordia objected the jurisdiction of the court because the bill of lading contained an arbitration clause. The Court of First Instance accepted Concordia's jurisdictional objection since it held that the arbitration clause contained in the bill of lading was binding upon the parties. However, the Supreme Court reversed this decision and held that the Italian court did have jurisdiction over the case. Regarding the formal requirements of the arbitration clause, the Supreme Court held: grammatically the word 'signed', like the word 'contained', refers, besides to the submission, to the arbitral clause contained in the contract, and not to the contract itself. Under this interpretation the arbitral clause would be invalid because the clause, contained in a printed model contract, was not signed. However, such a strict and literal interpretation is not in conformity with the reality of international trade for which a separate signature for the arbitral clause would be a too heavy burden.

Date	Name	Court	Parties	Related Articles	Brief Overview of the Case
					In contrast, the court maintained that a more liberal definition can be found in the Article I of the ECICA which defines an arbitration agreement as "*either an arbitral clause in a contract or an arbitration agreement, the contract or arbitration agreement being signed by the parties, or contained in an exchange of letters, telegrams, or in a communication by teleprinters*". However, at the end the Supreme Court found, *inter alia*, that the signatures of the bill of lading were not valid and therefore, the parties were not bound by the arbitration clause.
02.05.1980	Italy No. 51 / E5	Court of Appeal of Genoa	• Claimant, Efxinos Shipping Co. Ltd. • Respondent, Rawi Shipping Lines Ltd.	VIII	In *Efxinos v Rawi*, the parties agreed upon a charter-party for the shipment of certain products, which contained an arbitration clause. When Rawi failed to pay, Efxinos commenced arbitration. The award, which did not contain reasons, was rendered in favor of Efxinos and the latter sought enforcement in Italy. Rawi objected the enforcement of the award because it did not contain reason and therefore it was contrary to Italian public policy. The Court of Appeal of Genova rejected Rawi's objection on this point and granted enforcement: The Court deduced two conclusions from the acceptance by Italy of Article VIII of the [ECICA]. In the first place, it appears to be no longer contrary to Italian public policy to recognize a foreign award which does not contain reasons, provided that

Date	Name	Court	Parties	Related Articles	Brief Overview of the Case
					the parties have agreed in advance that reasons shall not be given. In the second place, an award without reasons no longer gives rise to a Constitutional question and a question of public policy if the award is rendered in an arbitral procedure under which it is not customary to give reasons for awards. The Court concluded that the English award without reasons did not offend Italian public policy.
08.06.1981	Italy No. 54 / E6	Court of Appeal of Ancona	• Claimant, H. & H. Hackenberg G.m.b.H. • Respondent, Nino Pizza	I	In *Hackenberg v Nino Pizza*, the parties concluded two contracts for the purchase and delivery of wood which contained an arbitration clause. When the dispute arose between the parties, Hackenberg commenced arbitration. The award was rendered in favor of Hackenberg and the latter sought enforcement in Italy. The Court of Appeal of Ancona granted the enforcement of the award on the basis of the NYC and the ECICA. The court noted that the requirements of the ECICA were present and therefore the provisions of the ECICA were applicable.
08.02.1982	Italy No. 57 / E7 722	Supreme Court of Cassation of Italy, Plenary Session	• Appellant, Fratelli Damiano s.n.c. • Appellee, August Tropfer & Co.	I and VIII (b)	In *Damiano v Tropfer*, the parties concluded a contract for the purchase and delivery of sugar, which contained an arbitration clause. When the dispute arose, the Tropfer commenced arbitration. The award was rendered in favor of Tropfer and the latter sought enforcement in Italy. Based on Article VIII of the

Date	Name	Court	Parties	Related Articles	Brief Overview of the Case
					ECICA, Damiano objected to the enforcement, *inter alia*, stating that the award did not contain reasons even though Damiano had specifically requested for a reasoned award during the arbitral proceedings. The Court of Appeal held that the ECICA was not applicable because, "*whilst Italy and F.R. Germany adhered to this Convention, the award was made in the United Kingdom, a country that does not adhere to the Convention.*" However, the Italian Supreme Court reversed this decision and held that the ECICA was applicable in the case: (…) both parties in the case at issue pertain to States (*i.e.*, Italy and F.R. Germany) which adhere to the [ECICA], regulating transnational "mercantile" (*mercantile*) arbitration (called by others "international commercial (*commerciale*) arbitration"). By signing and ratifying this Convention, both States incorporate the Convention into their respective legal systems, thereby making it *diritto comune* (*ius communis*). By providing for an arbitration clause that refers the resolution of future disputes to the permanent Arbitration Board of the Sugar Association of London, the contracting parties implicitly refer to the provisions of the [ECICA] that are incorporated in the legislative body of the ratifying State. Furthermore, the Supreme Court added that for the application of the ECICA the nationality of the parties was irrelevant:

Date	Name	Court	Parties	Related Articles	Brief Overview of the Case
					It should be added that for the purpose of deciding whether the [ECICA] is applicable to the arbitral matter at issue, the nationality of the arbitrator, *i.e.*, whether or not he belongs to a State which has ratified the Convention, is irrelevant. The Supreme Court also pointed out that novelty of the ECICA in the field of international commercial arbitration: The [ECICA] is different because it departs from the old State-minded logic. This Convention makes use of the experience of mercantile arbitration and, in using a modern approach, denies the principle of a double connection of the arbitration, i.e., with the State a quo [i.e., where the arbitration takes or took place] and the State where recognition is sought. It does not even require a presupposition of the arbitral decision's effectiveness in the State where the arbitration took place or the law of which has been chosen. It further regulates arbitration by providing for, subject to the parties' agreement, new, special organs, including their duties. Finally, the Supreme Court found that the award without reasons violated Article VIII(b) of the ECICA, as Damiano expressly requested a reasoned award during the arbitration hearing.

Date	Name	Court	Parties	Related Articles	Brief Overview of the Case
02.07.1982	Italy No. 71 / E8	Court of Appeal of Trieste	• Claimant, Jassica S.A. • Defendant, Ditta Polojaz	I	In *Jassica v Polojaz*, the parties concluded a contract for the sale of coffee, which referred to the "Conditions of the European Coffee Contract" containing an arbitration clause. When Polojaz failed to perform according to the contract, Jassica commenced arbitration. The award was rendered in favor of Jassica and the latter sought enforcement in Italy. The Court of Appeal refused enforcement because no written arbitration agreement was submitted when the enforcement was requested. The court found that the ECICA was not applicable to the case without providing further reasons.
23.05.1983	Italy No. 75 / E9	Ordinary Court of Bassano del Grappa	• Claimant, Ditta R.I.L. s.n.c. • Defendant, Ditta Metalexport	--	In *Ditta v Metalexport*, the parties concluded a contract for the purchase of a furnace for the hardening of aluminium pipes which contained an arbitration clause. When the dispute arose Ditta lodged an action before the Court of First Instance. However, the court denied jurisdiction because of the existence of an arbitration clause in the contract: According to Art. 37 of the Italian Code of Civil Procedure, the question of the jurisdiction of the court must be considered *ex officio* by the court, notwithstanding the provisions of the [ECICA] on which R.I.L. relies.

Date	Name	Court	Parties	Related Articles	Brief Overview of the Case
16.03.1984	Italy No. 82 / E12	Court of Appeal of Milan	• Petitioner, Arenco-BMD Maschinenfabrik GmbH • Respondent, Societá Ceramica Italiana Pozzi Richard Ginori S.p.A.	IX	In *Arenco v Pozzi,* Arenco sold to Pozzi certain machinery. The transaction eventually led to a dispute, which the parties decided to submit to arbitration. The award was rendered in favor of Arenco and the latter sought enforcement in Italy. Pozzi objected the enforcement alleging that it was incompatible to refer to the NYC and the ECICA simultaneously for the enforcement of the award. However, the Court of Appeal dismissed Pozzi's objection, holding that the application of both conventions could be done in parallel.
10.01.1984	Italy No. 84 / E11 (174)	Supreme Court of Cassation of Italy, Plenary Session	• Petitioner, Holtz & Willemsen GmbH • Respondent, P., D. and L. Farchioni	I (2)(a)	In *Holtz v Farchioni*, Farchioni sent to Holtz four supply requests for soya-seed oil which contained an arbitration clause. Holtz did not object to the supply request and sent back its own sales confirmations, which, in turn, referred disputes to German courts. When the dispute arose, Farchioni lodged an action before the Court of First Instance of Spoleto. Holtz objected to the jurisdiction of the court based on the arbitration clause. The Italian Supreme Court found that the arbitration clause did not comply with the formal requirements neither of the NYC nor the ECICA: [Holtz] could not invoke the provisions of Art. I(2)(a) of the [ECICA] and, implicitly, the provisions of the [NYC], since the arbitration clause at hand was not an agreement in writing within the meaning of Article II of the [NYC].

Date	Name	Court	Parties	Related Articles	Brief Overview of the Case
					However, it held that the Court of First Instance did not have jurisdiction because German court were the competent courts to rule over the case.
22.04.1985	Italy No. 91 / E13	Magistrate's Court of Verona	• Claimant, Pama Industrie S.p.A. • Defendants, Shultz Steel Company and Banca Nazionale del Lavoro	VI (4)	In *Pama v Shultz*, the parties concluded a contract for the purchase of certain machinery which contained an arbitration clause. When the dispute arose, Pamma commenced arbitration and lodged an action before the Pretore of Verona, seeking a suspension of payment by Schultz until an arbitral award was rendered. The Pretore held that according to Article VI(4) of the ECICA, the granting of interim measures by a domestic court is not incompatible with arbitration and should not be regarded as a submission of the case's substance to domestic courts. However, the Pretore did not grant the requested interim measures as Pama's request did not meet all necessary conditions under Italian law for interim measures.
16.10.1985	Italy No. 94 / E14 5071	Supreme Court of Cassation of Italy	• Petitioner, SpA Cifuindus • Plaintiff, OFAG – Ofenbau und Feuerungstechnik AG	VI	In *Cifuindus v OFAG*, the parties concluded an agreement for *inter alia* the supply of electro-mechanic ceramic parts which contained an arbitration clause. When the dispute arose between the parties, OFAG applied for an injunction against Cifuindus before the President of the Court of First Instance of Milan. Cifuindus counterclaimed the injunction and in the subsequent stage objected to the jurisdiction of the Italian courts based on the arbitration clause.

Date	Name	Court	Parties	Related Articles	Brief Overview of the Case
					The court rejected Cifuindus's objection, holding that Cifuindus should have raised the preliminary question of jurisdiction in its reply to the injunction. The Supreme Court also rejected the objections raised by Cifuindus, holding that under Article VI of the ECICA its right to object precluded when it filed the counterclaim in the injunction phase: In the case at issue, Cifuindus did not object to the lack of jurisdiction, on the grounds of a foreign arbitration clause, when replying to the injunction: he has defended itself on the merits of the case and has filed a counterclaim...On the other hand, the [ECICA] provides in Art. VI that a plea based on an arbitration agreement must be raised before or at the moment the defence on the merits is submitted, depending on whether the law of the competent court considers the objection of lack of jurisdiction a question of procedure or substance. Since Italian law considers this objection to be of a procedural nature, Cifuindus' objection was indeed precluded since Cifuindus had submitted its defence on the merits without [first[1]] raising the point of lack of jurisdiction.

1. The translation provided in the Kluwer summary does not contain the word 'prior' which appears in the original Italian version of the decision.

Date	Name	Court	Parties	Related Articles	Brief Overview of the Case
28.10.1983	Italy No. 99 / E10	Court of Appeal of Bari	• Claimant, H. & H. Hackenberg • Defendant, Ventrella Guido Francesco e Figli snc	I (2)(a)	In *Hackenberg v Ventrella*, the parties concluded two contracts for the purchase of pine-wood which contained an arbitration clause. When the dispute arose, Hackenberg commenced arbitration. Ventrella did not appear in the proceedings. The award was rendered in favor of Hackenberg and the latter sought enforcement in Italy. The Court of Appeal of Bari granted enforcement only for the part relating to the first contract between the parties because it found that there was no valid arbitration agreement in the second contract: [The ECICA], which provide[*sic*] that an arbitration clause be contained in an exchange of letters, telegrams or telexes, do not derogate from the requirement of authenticity (...) the said requirement can be derogated from only "between States whose laws do not require that an arbitration agreement be made in writing" and the arbitration agreement may be concluded "in the form authorized by these laws.
10.03.2000	Italy No. 157 / E18 (58/SU)	Supreme Court of Cassation of Italy, Plenary Session	• Petitioner, Krauss Maffei Verfahrenstechnik GmbH et al. • Respondent, Bristol Myers Squibb	I (2)(a)	In *Krauss v Bristol*, Krauss sent a sales offer to Bristol concerning the purchase of drying equipment. Bristol accepted the offer through a sales confirmation. In the offer, Kraus held to submit the disputes arising from the transaction to arbitration. Bristol's sales

Date	Name	Court	Parties	Related Articles	Brief Overview of the Case
					confirmation did not refer to this clause. When the dispute arose between the parties, Bristol lodged an action before the Latina Court of First Instance. Krauss objected to the jurisdiction of the court based on the arbitration agreement. The Italian Supreme Court held that the parties did not conclude a valid arbitration agreement because "*the parties must sign the arbitral clause and (...) their univocal intention to refer the dispute to arbitrators must appear unambiguously*". The Supreme Court held that "*an arbitral clause in the seller's offer, which is not mentioned in the buyer's confirmation, is invalid*". The Court noted that in case of doubt preference should be given to the jurisdiction of the domestic courts.

VIII. LUXEMBOURG

Date	Name	Court	Parties	Related Articles	Brief Overview of the Case
07.06.1993	Luxembourg No. E1	District Court of Luxembourg	• Not Indicated	IV	In *X v Y*, the President of the District Court of Luxembourg was called upon to appoint an arbitrator applying the Agreement Relating to Application of the European Convention (Paris Agreement).

IX. MONACO

Date	Name	Court	Parties	Related Articles	Brief Overview of the Case
27.11.1986	Monaco No. 1 / E1	Court of First Instance of Monaco	• Appellant, Sea Trading Monaco • Appellee, Nemo SpA	I	In *Sea v Nemo*, the parties concluded a distributorship contract which contained an arbitration clause. When the dispute arose between the parties, Sea lodged an action before the Court of First Instance in Monaco. The Court of First Instance and the Court of Appeal referred the parties to arbitration in view of the arbitration clause contained in the contract. Regarding the application of the ECICA, the Court of Appeal held: It is indeed accepted as confirmed by "*lex mercatoria*" and by the [ECICA] that the prohibition to refer disputes to arbitration on the basis of provisions analogous to those in the above [domestic law restrictions] mentioned articles cannot apply to a private international law contract concluded for the needs and under the usages of international commerce

X. POLAND

Date	Name	Court	Parties	Related Articles	Brief Overview of the Case
15.12.1978	Award	International Court of Arbitration for Marine and Inland Navigation	• Claimant, ship-owner (German) • Defendant, consignee (Swedish)	I (2)(a)	In *X (Germany) v Y (Sweden)*, the parties concluded a charter-party for transporting ammonium nitrate from Poland to Sweden which contained an arbitration clause. The captain of the ship signed a bill of lading regarding the ammonium that referred to the charter-party. When the ship arrived to Sweden, the German ship-owner requested the Swedish consignee to pay demurrage costs. When the dispute arose between the parties, the ship-owner commenced arbitration. The consignee objected to the competence of the Arbitration Court because the bill of lading did not refer explicitly to the charter-party. The Arbitration Court rejected the consignee's objection, holding that the bill of lading did refer to the charter-party and was signed by the consignee. Furthermore, the court held that the formal requirement of international commercial arbitration had adapted to the needs of international trade and referred to the ECICA in this context: The [ECICA] goes even further, holding valid an arbitration agreement done in accordance with the law of countries which do not require a written form. In this context it should be added that Swedish law does not provide for a special form for arbitration agreement.

XI. RUSSIA

Date	Name	Court	Parties	Related Articles	Brief Overview of the Case
1985	Award (MAC Case No. 38)	Maritime Arbitration Commission at the Chamber of Commerce and Industry of the Russian Federation	• Claimant, Danube Steamship Company (Soviet) • Defendant, Firm, charterer (German)	VII	In *Danube Steamship Company (Russia) v Y (Germany)*, the parties concluded a contract which contained an arbitration clause under the auspices of the Maritime Arbitration Commission. When the dispute arose between the parties, Streamship commenced arbitration. However, the defendant objected jurisdiction alleging that such a dispute settlement mechanism had been imposed on it by Streamship. The commission rejected the jurisdictional objections, holding that the arbitration clause was binding for both parties because the defendant never produced evidence indicating that it was imposed on it against its will. Since there was no indication on the applicable law in the arbitration clause, the commission, according to Article VII of the ECICA, deemed appropriate to refer to the conflict rules of Article 14 of the USSR Merchant Shipping Code.
30.03.2004	Russian Federation No. E1 (15359/03)	Presidium of the Supreme Commercial [Arbitrazh] Court of the Russian Federation	• Petitioner, Stroilensky Gorno-obogatitelny Combinat (Russian Federation)	I and IX	In *Stroilensky v Mabetex*, the parties concluded a contract which contained an arbitration clause. The contract, later on, was assigned to Interconstruction. When the dispute arose between the parties, arbitration proceedings were commenced and eventually an award was rendered in favor of Mabetex and

Date	Name	Court	Parties	Related Articles	Brief Overview of the Case
			• Respondents, Interconstruction Project Management S.A. (Switzerland) and Mabetex Project Engineering Industrieanlagenplanung und Einrichtung GmbH (Austria)		Interconstruction. Stroilensky lodged an action to set aside the award before the *Arbitrazh* Court. This latter court granted the setting aside request. However, the Russian Supreme Court reversed the decision. Regarding the scope of the ECICA to multiparty proceedings where one of the parties is not a Contracting State, the Supreme Court held: both parties had their seat in Contracting States to the ECICA. Sweden, however, was not a Contracting State. Art. IX of the ECICA did not apply to the setting aside of arbitral awards made in non-Contracting States. The setting aside of the award in question was regulated by the Swedish Arbitration Act and had to be challenged in Sweden.
25.07.2007	Russian Federation No. 24 / E3 (A 05-4274/2007)	Federal Commercial [Arbitrazh] Court of the Northwestern District	• Appellant, Collective Fishing Farm Krasnoye Znamya (Russian Federation) • Appellee, White Arctic Marine Resources Ltd. (Norway)	IX	In *Collective Farm v White Arctic*, an award was rendered in favor of White Arctic. Collective Farm sought to set aside the award before the *Arbitrazh* Court. However, the court and subsequently the Federal *Arbitrazh* Court denied the set aside application on the basis that the conditions for annulling an award before Russian courts were not met.

Date	Name	Court	Parties	Related Articles	Brief Overview of the Case
					According to the court: two conditions are necessary for the Russian courts to have jurisdiction to annul a foreign arbitral award: (1) the award must have been made in a Contracting State of the [ECICA] and (2) Russian substantive law must have been applied. In the case at bar, the second condition was not met *i.e.* that Russian law was the applicable law to the case. Therefore, the court concluded that it was irrelevant whether Norway indeed was not a party to the European Convention because Russian courts were not competent to annul the award.
20.07.2011	Russian Federation No. 33 (Case No. A27-781/ 2011)	Commercial [Arbitrazh] Court of the Kemerovo District	• Petitioner, Ciments Français • Respondent, Holding Company Sibirskiy Cement OJSC	IX	In *Ciments v Sibirskiy*, the parties concluded a share sale and purchase agreement which contained an arbitration clause. When the dispute arose between the parties Ciments commenced arbitration and, in turn, Sibirskiy filed a counterclaim. A partial award was rendered in favor of Ciments. Sibirskiy applied to the Turkish courts to have the award set aside. The Court of First Instance for the Kadiköy District granted the application and annulled the award on the basis that the award had not been rendered within the prescribed time limit. In parallel, Ciments sought the recognition of the award in Russia. Sibirskiy objected the enforcement alleging the award violated Turkish public policy. However, the Kemerovskaya *Arbitrazh* Court granted enforcement of the award. The court noted that "*that violation of the public policy of the country of rendition is not a ground listed in the [ECICA]*". Therefore, according to the court "*the violation of the public policy of the state of rendition is irrelevant at the enforcement stage*".

XII. SPAIN

Date	Name	Court	Parties	Related Articles	Brief Overview of the Case
27.02.1991	Spain No. 28	Supreme Court of Spain, First Civil Law Chamber	• Claimant, Nobulk Cargo Services Ltd. • Defendant, Compañía Española de Laminación SA	I and V	In *Nobulk v CEL*, an award was rendered in favor of Nobulk, the latter sought enforcement in Spain. CEL objected the enforcement alleging there was no valid arbitration agreement between the parties. However, the Spanish Supreme Court granted the enforcement on the basis that CEL's objections were precluded under the ECICA. Regarding the relation between the ECICA and the NYC, the Supreme Court held: (…) the [ECICA] concerns the applicable law and the jurisdiction of judicial authorities and arbitrators, whereas the [NYC] concerns the recognition and enforcement of arbitral awards. In this sense, although their chronology is different, the logical-juridical order of interpretation and application dictates that the [ECICA] be considered first, as it defines the applicable law, the capacity of the parties, the requirements for the subject matter, the efficacy and validity of the arbitration agreements, considered both per se and as part of a contract, and the means against arbitration, as a basis for the objection of lack of jurisdiction or the inefficacy and validity of the arbitral clause and the award (…).the discussion on the [ECICA] has logical and juridical priority,

Date	Name	Court	Parties	Related Articles	Brief Overview of the Case
					since the coming into existence of the arbitration, the jurisdiction and the (continued) validity of the award depend on it. On the contrary, the [NYC] assumes the undisputed existence of the award. As things are, and from this logical-juridical point of view, defendant's objection to the recognition is not possible. When analyzing CEL's objection on jurisdiction, the Supreme Court found that according to Article IV of the ECICA, these objections should have been raised during the arbitration proceedings: Article V(1) provides that the plea of lack of jurisdiction of the arbitrator because there is no arbitration clause shall be made when filing submissions in the arbitration; (...) Thus, that would have been the moment to [raise such plea]; not now, when this is impossible.
22.01.1991	Spain No. E11	Provincial Court of Barcelona	• Appellant, Domingo Torm Colóm • Defendant-Appellant, Saltor SA (Andorra) • Claimant-Appellee, Mecánicas y Automatismos SA	VI	In *Domingo, Saltor v Mecánicas Automatismos*, Saltor and Mecánicas concluded a contract for the sale and installation of certain machinery which contained an arbitration clause. Mecánicas lodged an action against Saltor, Domingo, Saltor's owner and manager ("defendants"), before the Court of First Instance of Sabadell. The defendants alleged the court did not have jurisdiction because of the arbitration clause contained in the contract and commenced arbitration proceedings. However, the court upheld jurisdiction. The Barcelona Court of Appeal affirmed the lower court's decision, holding that, under the Arbitration Law of 1953, an arbitral clause in a contract is a mere agreement to conclude

Date	Name	Court	Parties	Related Articles	Brief Overview of the Case
					a definitive arbitration agreement once a dispute has arisen, and that therefore it does not suffice to exclude the jurisdiction of the Spanish courts. Furthermore, regarding *lis pendens* between arbitration and court proceedings, the Barcelona Court of Appeal noted the following: (…) once a party has introduced a claim before a Spanish court, the other party, which has initiated arbitral proceedings on the same matter or dispute, must await the decision of the court (Art.VI(3) of the [ECICA] a *contrario sensu*).
11.06.2007	Spain No. 65 / E23 (584/06)	Court of First instance and Examination of Rubí	• Claimant, Pavan s.r.l.(Italy) • Defendant, Leng d'Or, SA (Spain)	IX	In *Pavan v Leng*, the parties concluded a contract concerning four production lines for manufacturing snack pellets which contained an arbitration clause. When the dispute arose between the parties, Pavan commenced arbitration proceedings. The award was rendered in favor of Pavan and the latter sought enforcement in Spain. In turn, Leng sought to have the award set-aside in France. The Court of First Instance of Rubí granted enforcement based on the NYC and the ECICA. Leng objected the enforcement on the grounds *inter alia* that a set-aside proceeding was pending in France. However, the court rejected Leng's objections. Regarding the relation between the ECICA and the NYC, the court held that "*Art. V(1)(e) [NYC] will only apply [in accordance with] Art. IX(1) [ECICA]*".

Date	Name	Court	Parties	Related Articles	Brief Overview of the Case
					The court distinguished the consequences arising from an annulled award, on the one hand, and a pending set-aside proceeding, on the other hand: A systematical interpretation of the [NYC] and the [ECICA] also excludes that "binding award" means an award that has not been impugned through an action aiming at annulling it [*recurso rescisorio*], such as an action for setting aside (as argued by defendant). If we examine the regime established by these treaties, we must distinguish between two distinct situations: (1) the arbitral award has been annulled in the country of origin; (2) the arbitral award awaits a decision in an action for setting aside – which is the case here. On the first scenario – annulled award – the court held that, under the ECICA, denial on the enforcement is only possible if the annulment was granted on a ground provided for in Article IX(1): (...) in the system of the [ECICA] the annulment of the award in the State of origin does not lead necessarily to a refusal to recognize and enforce it in another State, unless the award was annulled on a ground provided for in Art. IX(1) [ECICA](...) Conversely, an award that was annulled because, for instance, it resolved a dispute that was non-arbitrable in the State of origin or was contrary to the public policy of the State of origin must be homologated. On the second scenario – pending annulment proceedings – the court held that denial of enforcement is not automatic:

Date	Name	Court	Parties	Related Articles	Brief Overview of the Case
					it is clear and undiscussed in doctrine and jurisprudence that the fact that an annulment action is pending is not a sufficient ground to automatically deny recognition and enforcement of an arbitral award; rather, this mechanism – a 'power' under the Convention – can be used by the court at its discretion, if it deems it appropriate.
01.04.2009	Spain No. 66 / E24 (163/2009 (Section 10)	Court of Appeal of Madrid	• Plaintiff, Cadena de Tiendas Venezolanas SA – Cativen (Venezuela) • Defendants, GMR Asesores SL (Spain) and Inmomercado, CA (Venezuela)	IV	In *Cativen v GMR and Inmomercado*, an award was rendered in favor of Cativen and the latter sought enforcement in Spain before the Court of First Instance no. 2 of Pozuelo de Alarcón. This court declined jurisdiction holding that the competent tribunal was the Court of First Instance of Madrid. However, on appeal the Madrid Court of Appeal found that the competent court was indeed the Court in Pozuelo. On the historical background of the ECICA and its contributions to international commercial arbitration, the Court of Appeal held: The [ECICA], which is very limited in its scope of application and whose provisions are not always clear, came into being with the concrete purpose of facilitating arbitration between Western and Eastern European enterprises during the Cold War. Its acceptance has been very limited: barely about twenty States, some of which non-European (such as Cuba and Burkina Faso), have ratified it; countries of great importance in international commerce (such as the United Kingdom and the Scandinavian States) are not among the signatories. Apart from filling some gaps in

Date	Name	Court	Parties	Related Articles	Brief Overview of the Case
					the [NYC], the basic contribution of the [ECICA] is the following: the parties may agree on a simple and generic clause in which they state their intention to submit to arbitration, knowing that all other procedural details necessary for the validity of the award (e.g., manner of constitution of the arbitral tribunal, phases of the proceeding etc.) are automatically regulated under the [ECICA].
29.04.2009	Spain No. 68 / E25 (86/2009 (Section 15))	Provincial Court of Barcelona	• Appellant, Licensing Projects SL (Spain) • Appellee, Pirelli & C. SpA (Italy)	VI	In *LP v Pirelli*, the parties concluded a license agreement for the marketing of shoes which contained an arbitration clause. When the dispute arose between the parties, Pirelli commenced arbitration proceedings. The tribunal rendered a partial award upholding jurisdiction. In parallel, LP lodged an action before the Commercial Court no. 5 of Barcelona, alleging unfair competition and breach of contract and seeking damages. However, the Commercial Court and the Barcelona Court of Appeal found they lacked jurisdiction because of the existence of a valid arbitration agreement. Regarding the applicable law to determine the validity of an arbitration agreement, the Court of Appeal noted that [the ECICA] provides that, absent a choice by the parties, the law of the country in which the award is to be made applies; here, France. There was no evidence that the arbitration agreement was invalid under French law. Furthermore, the court maintained that "*neither the [NYC] nor the [ECICA] provide for a limitation of the efficacy of arbitration agreements in case of bankruptcy*".

Date	Name	Court	Parties	Related Articles	Brief Overview of the Case
08.10.1981	Spain No. 2 / E1 (ATS 457/1981)	Supreme Court of Spain, First Civil Law Chamber	• Claimant, X • Respondent, Y	I	In *X v Y*, an award was rendered in favor of X, the latter sought enforcement in Spain. The Spanish Supreme Court granted the request for enforcement. Regarding the types of arbitration covered by the ECICA, the Supreme Court noted: [the ECICA] refers to 'arbitration' as meaning not only the settlement by arbitrators appointed for each case (ad hoc arbitration), but also by permanent arbitral tribunals (...) This Convention gives the parties very broad powers regarding the organization of the arbitral procedure, by permitting them (in case a permanent institution, which has to act according to a specific procedure, is not involved), to appoint freely the arbitrators, to indicate their number, to determine the place of arbitration, and to lay down the procedure to be followed.
24.03.1982	Spain No. 3 / E2	Supreme Court of Spain, First Civil Law Chamber	• Claimant, Cominco France S. A. • Respondent, Soquiber S. L.	IX	In *Cominco v Soquiber*, the parties concluded three contracts for the purchase of bismuth metal which contained an arbitration agreement. When the dispute arose between the parties, Cominco commenced arbitration proceedings. Soquiber did not participate in the arbitration. The award was rendered in favor of Cominco and the latter sought enforcement in Spain. The Spanish Supreme Court granted the enforcement. Soquiber objected that the enforcement of the award should be denied because it was the result of a proceeding in which it did not participate. However, the Supreme Court rejected this objection on the following grounds:

Date	Name	Court	Parties	Related Articles	Brief Overview of the Case
					Art. V, para. 1 under b, of the New York Convention provides "(...) that the party against whom the award is invoked was not given proper notice of the appointment of the arbitrator or of the arbitration proceedings". The same ground for refusal can be found in the [ECICA] (Art. IX, para. 1 under b) (...) Notwithstanding the foregoing, the burden of proof of this ground of refusal for lack of notice is placed on the party against whom the award in question is rendered and who invokes it. (...) the award shows that notice of commencement of the proceedings and the summons for the hearing in Geneva was given to Soquiber S. L.
14.01.1983	Spain No. 6 / E3	Supreme Court of Spain, First Civil Law Chamber	• Claimant, X (Panamanian) • Respondent, Y (Spanish)	Preamble, I, V and VIII	In *X (Panama) v Y (Spain)*, the parties concluded a contract which contained the following arbitration clause: "*[a]ll disputes relating to the execution of the contract shall be submitted to arbitration London or any other place to be agreed upon by the parties*". When the dispute arose between the parties, X commenced arbitration proceedings. The award was rendered in favor of X and the latter sought enforcement in Spain. The Spanish Supreme Court granted the enforcement. First, Y objected the enforcement *inter alia* because the parties had not agreed on the place of arbitration. The Supreme Court rejected this argument holding that, under Article V of the ECICA, Y was precluded from raising this objection at the enforcement stage.

Date	Name	Court	Parties	Related Articles	Brief Overview of the Case
					Second, Y opposed to the enforcement of the award on the grounds that the award lacked reasons. The Supreme Court rejected this objection because, under Article VIII of the ECICA, Y could not prove that an award without reasons violated the public order of the place where it was rendered. Finally, Y objected to the application of the ECICA because Panama is not a Contracting State. The Supreme Court noted that according to the ECICA's preamble, the convention is a complement of the NYC and does not require the condition of reciprocity.
22.12.1983	Spain No. 11 / E5	Supreme Court of Spain, First Civil Law Chamber	• Petitioner, Fletamentos Maritimos S.A. • Respondent, Star Dispatch Shipping	I(2)(a)	In *Fletamentos v Star*, Fletamentos concluded a contract with a U.S. firm Magelán, by which Fletamentos had to purchase certain goods on behalf of a buyer to be determined later on. The contract contained an arbitration clause. Subsequently, Star was named as the buyer of the goods. When the dispute arose between the parties, Fletamentos commenced arbitration proceedings. The award was rendered in favor of Fletamentos and the latter sought enforcement in Spain. The Spanish Supreme Court granted the enforcement. The Supreme Court held that the validity of the arbitration clause should be ascertained according to Article II(2) of the NYC and Article I(2) of the ECICA, which have superseded the more demanding requirements of the Spanish domestic law.

Date	Name	Court	Parties	Related Articles	Brief Overview of the Case
30.01.1986	Spain No. 12 / E6	Supreme Court of Spain, First Civil Law Chamber	• Claimant, X • Respondent, Y	I(2)(a)	In *X v Y*, the parties had a commercial relation concerning the supply of shipments of fruits. Their transactions were documented by sales and standard confirmations, which referred to certain conditions containing an arbitration clause. When the dispute arose between the parties, X commenced arbitration proceedings. The award was rendered in favor of X and the latter sought enforcement in Spain. The Spanish Supreme Court granted the enforcement. Regarding the formal requirements of the arbitration agreement, the Supreme Court held that according to Art. II, the signing of the arbitration clause is not necessary when an agreement is "contained in an exchange of letters or telegrams," or in "communications by teleprinter" as provided in Art. 1(2)(a) of the ECICA.
13.07.1982	Spain No. 14 / E7	Supreme Court of Spain, First Civil Law Chamber	• Claimant, Billerud Uddeholm Aktiebolag • Respondent, R. Cervigón Guerra	IV(1)	In *Billerud v Guerra*, Billerud sought the enforcement of an award rendered in its favor before the Spanish Supreme Court. The Supreme Court was unable to make personal service on the Guerra and at last the matter was handed over to the Attorney General's office for his opinion. The Attorney General filed an opinion in favor of the enforcement and consequently the Supreme Court granted the request for enforcement. Regarding the will of the parties as the driving force of the arbitration proceedings, the Supreme Court noted: [The ECICA] confers ample possibilities to the parties to submit the dispute to an arbitral institution under the rules

Date	Name	Court	Parties	Related Articles	Brief Overview of the Case
					of which the arbitration will be conducted, to freely name the arbitrators, to determine their number, to determine the place of the arbitration and to fix the procedural rules to be observed (Article IV(1)).
07.10.1986	Spain No. 21 / E8 (STS 5279/1986)	Supreme Court of Spain, First Civil Law Chamber	• Claimant, T.H. • Respondent, Juan Antonio Dominguez	IX(1)(b)	In *TH v Juan Antonio Dominguez*, TH sought the enforcement of an award rendered in its favor before the Spanish Supreme Court. Mr Dominguez, having passed away, was represented by his son who opposed the enforcement. The Spanish Supreme Court denied the enforcement. The Supreme Court noted that according to the record of the arbitration proceedings, Mr Dominguez passed away before being notified of the request for arbitration. Since the proceedings were not conducted against his heirs; the Supreme Court concluded that the party against whom the arbitrator's decision was invoked was not duly notified of the arbitration proceedings. Therefore, the court concluded that according to Article IX(1)(b) of the ECICA, enforcement should be refused if one of the parties was not duly notified about the commencement of the arbitration proceedings or did not have the opportunity to present its case.
14.07.1998	Spain No. 30bis / E13	Supreme Court of Spain, First Civil Law Chamber	• Petitioner, Thyssen Haniel Logistic International GmbH • Respondent, Barna Consignataria SL	I(2)(a)	In *Thyssen v Barna*, the parties concluded a charter party. When the dispute arose between the parties, Thyssen commenced arbitration proceedings. The award was rendered in favor of Thyssen and the latter sought enforcement in Spain. The Spanish Supreme Court granted the enforcement.

Date	Name	Court	Parties	Related Articles	Brief Overview of the Case
					Barna objected to the enforcement alleging that there was no arbitration agreement between the parties. The Supreme Court rejected Barna's objection holding that "*the exchange of telexes between the parties showed their common intention to submit their differences to arbitration.*" The telexes exchanged between the parties made reference to the conditions provided in a former charter party, which contained an arbitration clause. Thyssen made some changes to the terms of the former charter party but never expressed its intention to modify the arbitration clause. Barna agreed with the changes made by Thyssen and replied: "*Thank you for your telex no. 660; the charterers agree, thus we have a contract with no open issues*". Based on these telexes, the Supreme Court held: These communications clearly show the common intention of the parties to submit disputes which could arise under their charter party to arbitration. Among their [contractual] conditions is an arbitral clause such as the arbitral clause in the charter party previously agreed between them, which was the basis on which the charter party at issue was negotiated [...] Hence, we must conclude that Thyssen has met the requirement of Art. IV together with Art. II and with Art. 1(2) (a) of the [ECICA].

Date	Name	Court	Parties	Related Articles	Brief Overview of the Case
06.10.1998	Spain No. 31 / E14	Supreme Court of Spain, First Civil Law Chamber	• Petitioner, Delta Cereales España SL • Respondent, Barredo Hermanos SA	I(2)(a)	In *Delta v Barredo*, the parties concluded a sales contract through Bertran Trading, a broker, which referred to the application of a standard contract's provisions including an arbitration agreement. Delta sent to Barredo two copies of the contract, one of which was to be signed and returned. Barredo kept both copies. When the dispute arose between the parties, Delta commenced arbitration proceedings. The award was rendered in favor of Delta and the latter sought enforcement in Spain. The Spanish Supreme Court denied enforcement. According to its findings, there was no arbitration agreement in writing between the parties as Barredo had not expressed in any way its intention to be bound by the arbitral clause in the standard contract: (…) we cannot hold that Delta supplied the document(s) containing the arbitral agreement according to the formal requirements in Art. II(2) [in agreement with the provisions of the ECICA]. There is no signature or declaration by Barredo, expressing its intention to submit to arbitration.

Date	Name	Court	Parties	Related Articles	Brief Overview of the Case
20.02.2001	Spain No. 32 / E15	Supreme Court of Spain, First Civil Law Chamber	• Claimant, Consmaremma Consorzio tra produttori agricoli Società Cooperativa a responsabilità limitata • Defendant, Hermanos Escot Madrid, SA	I(2)(a)	In *Consmaremma v Escot*, Consmaremma purchased certain goods from Escot through a broker under a sales confirmation which contained an arbitration clause. Escot did not sign the sales confirmation. Later on, the parties concluded a complementary agreement to the sales confirmation, which was signed by both parties. When the dispute arose between the parties, Consmaremma commenced arbitration proceedings. The award was rendered in favor of Consmaremma and the latter sought enforcement in Spain. The Spanish Supreme Court granted enforcement. Regarding the formal requirements of the arbitration agreement under the NYC and the ECICA, the Supreme Court held: Clearly, this [sales confirmation] does not by itself meet the requirement of Art. IV(1) (b) of the New York Convention together with Art. II, as interpreted by this Court. It does not show the parties' common intention to submit disputes concerning their contract's validity and contents to arbitrators (...) However, we cannot ignore that a reference is made in the Facts of the award at issue to a later agreement in writing between the parties (...) to fully implement the original contract, Therefore, the Supreme Court concluded that the formal requirements were met and granted the enforcement.

Date	Name	Court	Parties	Related Articles	Brief Overview of the Case
16.04.1996	Spain No. 33 / E16 (3868/1992)	Supreme Court of Spain, First Civil Law Chamber	• Claimant, Actival Internacional SA • Defendant, Conservas El Pilar SA	I(2)(a)	In *Actival v El Pilar*, Actival purchased certain goods from El Pilar through a broker under a sales confirmation which contained an arbitration clause. El Pilar did not sign the sales confirmation. When the dispute arose between the parties, el Pilar commenced arbitration proceedings. The award was rendered in favor of Actival and the latter sought enforcement in Spain. In parallel, el Pilar sought to set aside the award in France. The Spanish Supreme Court denied enforcement. According to the Supreme Court there was no valid arbitration agreement between the parties since El Pilar did not sign the sales confirmation: (…) the letter of confirmation does not meet the requirements set for arbitration agreements by the [NYC] (Art. II(2), which requires that the arbitration clause be at least signed by the parties or contained in an exchange of letters or telegrams) and by the [ECICA] (Art. I(2)(a), with identical requirements).
05.05.1998	Spain No. 35 / E18	Supreme Court of Spain, First Civil Law Chamber	• Claimant, ETS Louis Zanatta • Defendant, Pillanet	I(2)(a)	In *Zanatta v Pillanet*, Zanatta sent a sales confirmation containing an arbitration clause to Pillanet. Pillanet did not sign the confirmation but issued certain international waybills referring to the sales confirmation. When the dispute arose between the parties, Zanatta commenced arbitration proceedings. The award was rendered in favor of Zanatta and the latter sought enforcement in Spain. The Spanish Supreme Court granted enforcement.

Date	Name	Court	Parties	Related Articles	Brief Overview of the Case
					Regarding the formal requirements of the arbitration agreement under the NYC and the ECICA, the Supreme Court held: Although the confirmation attached to the request [for arbitration], which contains the arbitration clause, is not signed by the buyer, which is the party presently opposing enforcement, the party requesting enforcement supplies photocopies of two international waybills (...) reading at no. 5: "Attached documents: Olifat c/0324101". This number coincides with the number of the sales confirmation containing the arbitration clause. This suffices to allow us to hold that the arbitration clause was incorporated in the contract and became part of it. Hence, the applicant complied with the formal requirements.
23.07.2001	Spain No. 44 / E20	Supreme Court of Spain, First Civil Law Chamber	• Petitioner, Kern Electrónica, S.A. (Spain) • Respondent, Goldstar Company Limited (Korea)	VI	In *Kern v Goldstar*, the parties concluded an exclusive distributorship contract which contained an arbitration agreement. When the dispute arose between the parties, Kern lodged an action before the Court of First Instance no.6 of L'Hospitalet de Llobregat. The Court of First Instance declined jurisdiction in light of the arbitration clause contained in the contract. The Court of Appeal and the Supreme Court affirmed the first instance's decision. Despite Goldstar was seated in Korea, the Supreme Court made reference to the ECICA's provisions:

Date	Name	Court	Parties	Related Articles	Brief Overview of the Case
					The same is true of the [ECICA], whose Art. [IV(1)](b) applies here because the parties have provided that their disputes be submitted to an ad hoc arbitral procedure. This Convention also provides that the defendant make a plea as to jurisdiction before the court seized either before or at the same time as the presentation of his substantive defence (Art.VI(1)).This is the case here. [The ECICA] also provides that in respect of the capacity of the parties the national courts of the Contracting States shall apply the law applicable to them. In respect of other questions, however, they shall apply "the law to which the parties have subjected their arbitration agreement; (b) failing any indication thereon (...) the law of the country in which the award is to be made". Only failing such indications, where the country [of rendition] cannot be determined, the rules of conflict of the court seized of the dispute shall apply (Art. VI(2)).
08.10.2002	Spain No. 54 / E21	Supreme Court of Spain, First Civil Law Chamber	• Claimants, Scandlines, AB (Sweden) and Scandlines Danmark A/S (Denmark) • Defendant, Ferrys del Mediterráneo, S.L. (Spain)	I	In *Scandlines v Ferrys*, the parties concluded a charter party which contained an arbitration clause. When the dispute arose between the parties, Ferrys commenced arbitration proceedings. The award was rendered in favor of the claimants and the latter sought enforcement in Spain. The Spanish Supreme Court granted enforcement. Although, the Supreme Court denied the application of the ECICA in the case, since neither Sweden nor Denmark are Contracting States.

Date	Name	Court	Parties	Related Articles	Brief Overview of the Case
17.05.2007	Spain No. 63 / E22 (558/2007)	Supreme Court of Spain, First Civil Law Chamber	• Appellant, Cerámicas Casao, S.A. (Spain) • Appellee, I.A.G. Impianti Automazione Gestione srl (Italy)	VI	In *Casao v Impianti*, the parties concluded a contract which contained an arbitration clause. When the dispute arose between the parties, Impianti lodged an action before the Court of First Instance in Voghera, Italy. Impianti objected to the jurisdiction based on the arbitration clause contained in the contract. However, the court rejected Impianti's objection because under Italian law an arbitration agreement concluded prior to the bankruptcy declaration of one of the parties cannot be invoked against said party after the bankruptcy declaration. The court rendered a decision in favor of Impianti and the latter sought enforcement of the court decision in Spain. The Spanish Supreme Court affirmed the Court of First Instance's decision. Regarding the applicable law to determine the validity of the arbitration clause, the Supreme Court held: (…) the validity and efficacy of the arbitration agreement, due to its autonomy, must be examined under Art. VI(2) [ECICA](…) which provide that when the parties do not indicate the law applicable to the arbitration clause or submission agreement, the law of the country where the award shall be made applies.

Date	Name	Court	Parties	Related Articles	Brief Overview of the Case
12.06.1991	Spain No. E9	Provincial Court of Cádiz	• Appellant, Bahia Industrial, S.A. • Appellee, Eintacar Eimar, S.A.	VI(4)	In *Bahia v Eintacar*, arbitration proceedings were commenced between the parties. Eintacar requested interim measures in Spain and the Court of First Instance of Cádiz granted the request. The Court of Appeal of Cádiz affirmed the lower court's decision based on the provisions of the ECICA, which allow for the taking of interim measures in support of arbitration: [According to the text Article VI(4) of the ECICA] we may conclude that it is possible for a Spanish judge to adopt interim measures in support of arbitration, even though the arbitral proceedings are taking place in a different country.

XIII. INTERNATIONAL ARBITRATION INSTITUTIONS

Date	Name	Court	Parties	Related Articles	Brief Overview of the Case
18.11.1983	Interim Award	Ad-Hoc	• Claimants, Dipl. Ing. Erick Benteler KG and Helmut Benteler KG • Respondents, Belgian State and S.A. ABC	I and II	In *Benteler v Belgium and ABC*, the parties concluded a contract which contained an arbitration clause. When the dispute arose between the parties, Benteler commenced arbitration proceedings. Belgium objected to the competence of the arbitrators, arguing that Belgian law prohibits the State from agreeing to arbitration. Furthermore, Belgium objected that the matter was not commercial within the meaning of Belgian domestic law and therefore was not governed by the ECICA. In turn, Benteler invoked Article II of the ECICA to prove that Belgium was authorized to conclude arbitration agreements and also alleged that domestic law could not be invoked to evade the compliance of an international obligation. The arbitral tribunal rejected Belgium's objections. First, it held that "*the contract, which could broadly be characterized as a joint venture agreement, was indisputably within the meaning of 'international commerce' as that term was used in the Convention*". Second, the tribunal found that Belgium had indeed the legal capacity to enter into a private law contract containing an arbitration clause in respect of such a dispute.

Date	Name	Court	Parties	Related Articles	Brief Overview of the Case
1990	Award (ICC Case No. 6379)	International Court of Arbitration of the International Chamber of Commerce	• Claimant, X principal • Defendant, Y distributor	VI	In *X v Y*, the parties concluded a distribution contract which contained an arbitration clause. When X gave to Y a three-month notice of termination of the contract, Y objected that mandatory Belgian law provisions require a notice of at least 36 months and compensation. In turn, X commenced arbitration proceedings. Regarding the applicable law to the contract, the sole arbitrator found that the parties agreed to apply Italian law and therefore Belgian law was not applicable: The [ECICA], which has become part of the Italian legal system and which prevails over internal provisions, allows the parties to agree on the law applicable to their contract. It provides that the validity of the arbitral clause must be ascertained according to the law chosen by the parties (Article 6(2)), *i.e.*, in the present case, according to Italian law. The [ECICA] makes no exception for foreign provisions of mandatory application.
18.08.1987	Award (ICC Case No. 5485)	International Court of Arbitration of the International Chamber of Commerce	• Claimant, Company (Bermudian) • Defendant, Company (Spanish)	V(3) and VI(2)(a)	In *X v Y*, the parties concluded a "basic agreement" for the establishment of a Spanish joint venture which contained an arbitration clause. When the dispute arose between the parties, X commenced arbitration proceedings. Y objected the jurisdiction of the arbitral tribunal on the grounds that the arbitration clause was not valid under Spanish law. The arbitral tribunal found that the object of the dispute was an international transaction and hence under Article V(3) of the ECICA it has the authority to rule on its own jurisdiction.

Date	Name	Court	Parties	Related Articles	Brief Overview of the Case
					According to the arbitral tribunal, Article VI(2)(a) of the ECICA allows the parties to agree on a different body of laws to govern the arbitration clause and the other provisions of the contract. Therefore, the tribunal concluded that, in the case at bar, the arbitral clause was not subject to Spanish law and therefore it was valid under the applicable international instruments.
1992	Award (ICC Case No. 6850)	International Court of Arbitration of the International Chamber of Commerce	• Claimant, Manufacturer Y S.A. • Defendant, Distributor X GmbH	VI	In *X v Y*, the parties concluded a distribution agreement which contained an arbitration clause. The contract was signed on behalf of X by two of its agents, as X did not have legal personality because it had not yet been registered in the Commercial Register. When the dispute arose between the parties, X commenced arbitration proceedings. Y objected the jurisdiction of the sole arbitrator on the grounds of lack of validity of the arbitration clause. When discussing the validity of the arbitration clause, the arbitral tribunal found that under the ECICA the capacity of the parties should be analyzed under the law applicable to them: Although the Contract is governed by the provisions of French law, as provided for in [the arbitral clause], in the present case we may not ignore the provisions of German law, as the arbitral clause was concluded by officers of a German company. All the more so as Article VI(2) of the [ECICA] provides: "In taking a

Date	Name	Court	Parties	Related Articles	Brief Overview of the Case
					decision concerning the existence or the validity of an arbitration agreement, courts of Contracting States shall examine the validity of such agreement with reference to the capacity of the parties, under the law applicable to them"... The parties' authority of free choice of law is confirmed as an internationally valid principle by Article 7 of the [ECICA]. The parties are to be enabled to subject their legal relations to the law they choose, and to exclude the national law which would otherwise apply.
1994	Award (ICC Case No. 7047)	International Court of Arbitration of the International Chamber of Commerce	• Claimant, Consultant • Defendants, State agency and State owned bank	VII	In *X v Y*, the parties concluded a contract for the advisory and assistance of military products and services which contained an arbitration clause. When the dispute arose between the parties, X commenced arbitration proceedings. Y objected the validity of the arbitration clause. Regarding the applicable law to the agreement, the arbitral tribunal held: Both parties desired that Swiss law should be applied to the Agreement in case of a legal dispute. The defendants' state of origin, the State of Z, has joined the [ECICA]. Pursuant to Art. 7 of the Convention the parties are free to determine by agreement the law to be applied by the arbitrators to the substance of the dispute. Therefore internal law of the State of Z did not hinder the defendants to subject the Agreement to Swiss law (...).

Date	Name	Court	Parties	Related Articles	Brief Overview of the Case
1993	Partial Award (ICC Case No. 7920)	International Court of Arbitration of the International Chamber of Commerce	• Claimant, Distributor (Spanish) • Defendant, Manufacturer	IV	In *X (Spain) v Y*, the parties concluded a distribution contract which contained an arbitration clause referring to the International Chamber of Commerce of Geneva. When the dispute arose between the parties, X commenced arbitration proceedings. The sole arbitrator rendered a partial award whereby it held that, even though the arbitral clause was ambiguous, ICC arbitration in Geneva could be translated as the parties' unambiguous intention to have their disputes settled by international arbitration in Geneva: While it is true that there is no International Chamber of Commerce of Geneva; it is also well-known that the denomination "International Chamber of Commerce" identifies the organization having its seat in Paris (...). Also, for example, the index of arbitral institutions prepared by the European Commission of the United Nations lists 127 arbitral institutions in the world, with only one having the name "International Chamber of Commerce"; also, the Annex to the [ECICA] refers to the International Chamber of Commerce without further qualification and detail.

Date	Name	Court	Parties	Related Articles	Brief Overview of the Case
1997	Award (ICC Case No. 8817)	International Court of Arbitration of the International Chamber of Commerce	• Claimant, Agent • Defendant, Principal	VII	In *X v Y*, the parties concluded a distribution contract which contained an arbitration clause. When the dispute arose between the parties, X commenced arbitration proceedings. Regarding the applicable law to the contract, the arbitral tribunal held: (…) since this is a distributorship contract, the applicable law must be determined according to Art. VII of the [ECICA] and to Art. 4.2 of the Rome Convention of 1980 on the Law Applicable to Contractual Obligations.

Index

www.ingramcontent.com/pod-product-compliance
Ingram Content Group UK Ltd.
Pitfield, Milton Keynes, MK11 3LW, UK
UKHW020803290926
15470UKWH00003B/933

9 789041 185907